The Price Waterhouse Personal Tax Strategy

1998 EDITION

Canadian Cataloguing in Publication Data

The National Library of Canada has catalogued this publication as follows:

Personal tax strategy (Canadian ed.)
  Personal tax strategy

Annual.
ISSN 1189-0169
ISBN 0-385-25666-3

1. Income tax — Canada — Popular works.
I. Price Waterhouse (Firm).   II. Title: The Price
Waterhouse personal tax strategy

HJ4661.P463   343.7105'1'05   C91-032798-X

Cover design by Avril Orloff
Cover illustration by Mike Custode
Text design by David Montle
Information graphics concept and design by Price Waterhouse
Printed and bound in the USA

Published in Canada by
Doubleday Canada Limited
105 Bond Street
Toronto, Ontario
M5B 1Y3

Personal Tax Strategy is intended to provide information that is accurate,
comprehensible and useful. This book, however, is not a substitute for legal
or accounting advice, which should be obtained from competent professionals
before important tax planning decisions are made. Please see the section
"Beyond this book" on page 7 for further information.

The Price Waterhouse Personal Tax Strategy

1998 EDITION

Doubleday Canada Limited

Personal Tax Calendar

This Personal Tax Calendar shows key **tax deadlines**, indicating the day of the month for 1998. (Some dates change slightly from year to year.) The calendar also raises **planning reminders** that may need consideration.

To avoid missing deadlines or valuable planning opportunities, **check this calendar periodically**. You may want to add your own tax-related dates and planning reminders.

iv

January

Deadlines
- 15 Fourth U.S. estimated tax payment for prior year
- 30 Interest on employee and family loans (p. 25)
- 31 Inform employer of personal use of car

Planning reminders
- Contribute to RRSP – for last year and this year? (p. 42)
- Superficial loss? (p. 119)
- Use Home Buyers' Plan (p. 236)

February

Deadlines
- 14 Reimburse employer for personal automobile expenses

Planning reminders
- Expecting a tax refund? File early. (p. 210)
- Slips and receipts to assemble?
- Review and update your will? (p. 241)
- Use Home Buyers' Plan (p. 236)

May

Deadlines

Planning reminders
- Contribute to RRSP? (p. 42)
- Superficial loss? (p. 119)
- 183 days in Canada this year? (p. 62)
- Review and update your will? (p. 241)
- QSSP strategy formulated? (p. 140)

June

Deadlines
- 15 Second tax instalment (p. 80)
- 15 Tax return due for individuals reporting business income
- 15 Second U.S. tax instalment
- 15 U.S. tax returns, or 2-month extension request due (U.S. citizens living in Canada and non-resident aliens not subject to withholding)
- 30 Bonus from own corporation? (p. 93)
- 30 Non-resident rental property returns (p. 135)
- 30 Non-resident special payment returns (e.g., alimony, pension) (p. 135)

Planning reminders
- Purchase qualifying home? (p. 236)

September

Deadlines
- 15 Third tax instalment (p. 80)
- 15 Third U.S. estimated tax payment
- 30 Acquire home if Home Buyers' Plan withdrawal made in 1997 (p. 236)

Planning reminders
- Superficial loss? (p. 119)
- Contributing to charities or political parties? (p.189 and 194)
- CNIL problems to eliminate? (p.115)

October

Deadlines
- 15 U.S. Individual tax returns – last day for filing if you obtained a 2-month extension from August 15

Planning reminders
- Contribute to RRSP? (p. 42)
- Affected by changes in recent budgets? (p. 9)
- Moving soon? (p. 33)
- 183 days in Canada this year? (p. 62)
- CNIL problems to eliminate? (p.115 and 234)

The symbols beside each deadline or planning question indicate the relevant jurisdiction.

🍁 Canada   ⚜ Québec only   ★ U.S.   ⬤ International

March

Deadlines
🍁 1   RRSP contribution in respect of prior year (p. 42)
🍁 15   First tax instalment (p. 80)
🍁 30   Trust returns and preferred beneficiary elections (p. 245)

Planning reminders
🍁 Expecting a tax refund? File early. (p. 210)
🍁 Slips and receipts to assemble?
🍁 Superficial loss? (p. 119)
🍁 Affected by changes in recent budgets? (p. 9)

April

Deadlines
★ 15   U.S. tax return or 4-month extension request due, or file for extension for non-resident aliens (subject to withholding)
★ 15   First U.S. estimated tax payment
★ 15   U.S. Trust and Partnership Returns or 3-month extension request due
🍁 30   File tax return (p. 216)
🍁 30   Taxes due for individuals reporting business income

Planning reminders
🍁 Purchase qualifying home? (p. 236)

July

Deadlines
★ 15   U.S. Trust and Partnership returns – filing deadline if automatic 3-month extension obtained.

Planning reminders
🍁 Superficial loss? (p. 119)
🍁 Claiming enhanced capital gains exemption? (p. 95 and 112)
🍁 Moving soon? (p. 33)
🍁 Objecting to a notice of (re)assessment? (p. 220)

August

Deadlines
★ 15   U.S. Individual tax returns – last day for filing if you obtained a 4-month extension or last 2-month extension request due

Planning reminders
🍁 Review and update your will? (p. 241)
🍁 Contribute to RRSP? (p. 42)
🍁 Purchase qualifying home? (p. 236)

November

Deadlines
🍁 1   Canada Savings Bonds

Planning reminders
🍁 Superficial loss? (p. 119)
🍁 Claiming enhanced capital gains exemption? (p. 95 and 112)
🍁 CNIL problems to eliminate? (p. 115 and p. 234)
⚜ Any QSSP transactions required? (p. 140)

December

Deadlines
🍁 15   Fourth tax instalment (p. 80)
🍁 31   Expenses to claim (p. 87)
🍁 31   RPP contributions (p. 40)
🍁 31   RRSP conversion at age 69 (p. 146)
🍁 31   Car operating benefit election (p. 51)

Planning reminders
🍁 Contributing to charities or political parties? (p. 189 and 194)
🍁 CNIL problems to eliminate? (p. 115 and p. 234)
⚜ QSSP strategy complete? (p. 140)
★ Make fourth estimated state tax payment to allow it to be deducted when the federal U.S. return is filed.

Contents

A detailed table of contents appears at the beginning of each chapter.

Introduction

Using this book – special features

This book has several features to make personal tax planning easier. It has a chapter especially for you if you are:

- an employee;
- an owner/manager;
- separated or divorced;
- an investor;
- retired;
- a taxpayer with U.S. connections.

Issues that could affect all taxpayers are covered in sections on:

- 1997 highlights;
- calculating your taxes;
- looking ahead.
- significant cases;
- filing returns and paying your taxes;

This year's **tax highlights** and recent significant **court cases** are set out on pages 9 to 21.

Each chapter has a **distinctive graphic icon**, which appears at the top of each right-hand page of the chapter. The chapters begin with "What's new" – one or more highlights of recent tax-related changes.

Throughout the book, **international** aspects are marked by a stylized globe (like the one in the margin here). Numerous tax tips highlight valuable tax-saving techniques.

A **detailed table of contents at the beginning of each chapter** helps you find topics that interest you. An **index** is also provided.

Québec taxpayers have to deal with not only the federal system but a different provincial tax regime. At the end of each chapter, a special **Québec section** sets out tax matters that are significantly different in that province. Each Québec section is marked by a fleur-de-lis in the margin and at the top of the right-hand page.

Key tax numbers are collected in **appendices**. Graphs and tables present information in an easily digestible form throughout the text and in the appendices. The **Personal Tax Flowchart** on pages 183 and 196 gives you the "big picture," revealing the components and structure of your income tax calculation.

Tax involves numerous abbreviations such as AMT and CNIL. A **glossary** (page 279) decodes them.

You'll find the **Personal Tax Calendar** before the table of contents of this book. Referring to your Personal Tax Calendar several times throughout the year will remind you of tax planning opportunities as well as important deadlines.

1 Developing Your Personal Tax Strategy

Developing Your Personal Tax Strategy

Your personal tax strategy is important. This introductory chapter outlines steps you should consider to begin your tax planning, and explains the features of this book that can help you.

Why develop a personal tax strategy?

Investing time in your personal tax strategy can help you minimize your taxes, both short-term and long-term. You may be able to cut your tax bill by:

• reducing the amount payable this year; and

• deferring payment until a later year.

Cash flow management is part of a good personal tax strategy. The success of your tax plan, whether it is basic or complex, may be undermined if you do not give enough consideration to cash flow issues.

Make sure that you refer to Chapter 9, **Filing Returns and Paying Your Taxes** (page 209). You may find that you can save some money, or at least improve cash flow, by applying some of the simple tactics described in that chapter, both at tax time and throughout the year. For example, managing your instalment payments or reducing the tax withheld from your paycheque may leave you with more discretionary income with which to implement some of your tax strategies – or just to save or spend.

It is probably a good idea to review the **Significant cases: an overview** section (page 12) that follows **1997 Highlights**. You may be able to take a favourable filing position on an issue decided on by the courts that is similar to one you are dealing with yourself. Alternatively, you may find that you have to adjust a prior year's return if a decision on which you based a particular filing position has subsequently been reversed. Before taking any action on jurisprudence that you believe may be relevant in your own situation, consider discussing your conclusions with your professional advisor.

This book will show you the many advantages of tax planning. Now may be a good time to get started.

Getting the most out of this book

You can use this book to:

- reduce your tax bill by identifying tax planning opportunities to implement yourself or with professional advice;

- understand the process of preparing your income tax return, whether you do it yourself or have it done for you; and

- save time and money by answering many of your questions and focusing your attention.

Beginning your tax planning

To begin your tax planning:

- Review your 1996 returns and assessments to help you recall the sources of your income and the deductions you have claimed.

- Note extraordinary transactions, events or amounts for later consideration and possible special action.

- Review the section **Significant cases: an overview** on page 12. You may find that a recent court decision affects your own tax situation.

- Estimate your 1997 taxable income by calculating your income and deductions, using your 1996 return and this book as guides (see Chapter 8, **Calculating Your Taxes**, page 179).

- Check your liability for tax instalments. If your tax deductions at source do not cover most of your total tax liability, you may be required to make quarterly instalments. If you are required to make tax instalments, Revenue Canada or Revenue Québec should already have sent you notices for each of your four 1997 instalments. You may pay your instalments according to this system, or you may use the method you have used in the past. As long as you base your instalments on the Revenue Canada or Revenue Québec notices and pay your instalments on time, you won't be charged interest and penalties, even if your payments fall short of your total tax liability for the year. If you missed any instalment payments that were required during the year, you can minimize charges by making a catch-up payment now. (See page 215.)

- On the Personal Tax Calendar (page iv), mark any dates and planning points that apply to you. On your own calendar or appointment book, mark a few reminders to review the Personal Tax Calendar. Use *Personal Tax Strategy* to identify planning techniques and to help you assess tax saving opportunities.

- Balance the cash flow requirements of possible deferral techniques against the potential for reduced tax.

- If you disagree with the reassessment for 1996 or a prior year, dispute it by discussing it with Revenue Canada or Revenue Québec and perhaps by filing a Notice of Objection (see pages 220 and 227). A disagreement can invalidate the amounts for your quarterly instalments specified in Revenue Canada or Revenue Québec notices.

After completing your analysis, consider discussing your conclusions with a professional advisor.

Start now

To get the most out of *Personal Tax Strategy*, don't wait until your tax return is almost due before looking through it for tax planning opportunities – start now. Use whatever approach works best for you: for example, flip through the pages, scan the table of contents, use the index, or start with the Personal Tax Calendar on page iv. Then zero in on material that applies to you.

Use *Personal Tax Strategy* throughout the year

Personal Tax Strategy is a planning tool, so you may want to refer to it several times throughout the year. That's why we suggest marking a few dates in your own calendar or appointment book. On those dates, a glance at the Personal Tax Calendar will remind you of important tax-related deadlines and planning opportunities.

At tax time

When the time comes to prepare your tax return, *Personal Tax Strategy* will help you understand how the various entries are related and why they are calculated the way they are. *Personal Tax Strategy* complements the tax guides that the taxation authorities provide, which help you with the details of filling out your return.

Beyond this book

This book is no substitute for competent professional advice. Tax planning is a complex process that must be tailored to your circumstances. Accordingly, the comments and advice in this book are not intended to be a definitive analysis of the law, but rather to guide you in understanding some of the ways to minimize your tax burden.

Throughout *Personal Tax Strategy* you will encounter references to the 1997 federal and provincial budget proposals, as well as to other draft legislation and technical amendments. How should you deal with rules that are still just proposals or drafts? Usually, you should assume that these measures will become law, whether they give or take away your opportunity to do something.

If you are thinking about implementing a complex tax plan, or when significant amounts are involved, you should consult your professional advisor before proceeding.

Effective dates for implementation are provided for particular changes or proposals.

This book is based on:

- legislation enacted up to the end of June 1997;

- draft legislation released up to June 30, 1997;

- Department of Finance Press Releases announced up to June 30, 1997;

- proposals in provincial budgets or information releases up to June 30, 1997 (all provinces had presented their 1997-98 budgets when *Personal Tax Strategy* was written); and

- the new draft Protocol to amend the Canada-U.S. Tax Convention.

Post-publication changes in the interpretation of the law or in the Department of National Revenue's administrative policy could affect the information in this book.
Additional information on any of the matters discussed in *Personal Tax Strategy* is available from any Price Waterhouse office in Canada. See pages 280-1 for addresses.

1997 Highlights

To assess your overall personal tax position, you should review the changes that come into effect each year and understand how they could alter your tax planning. The tax changes highlighted below will help you see how you may be affected.

A number of personal tax changes introduced in the 1997 federal budget will affect your personal tax planning.

Proposals to broaden the tax relief for students and the individuals who support them might be of interest. In particular, the education tax credit is to be increased in 1997, with a further increase to take effect in 1998. A new measure will allow for the carry forward of unused tuition fee and education tax credits.

In the area of savings for education, the annual limit for contributions to RESPs is scheduled to increase. Measures designed to handle RESP income when named beneficiaries do not go on to pursue post-secondary education have also been announced.

Tax assistance for retirement savings does not go untouched. The budget proposes to introduce a pension adjustment reversal (PAR) that will restore lost RRSP contribution room for individuals who leave RPPs or DPSPs before retirement.

A number of measures to increase assistance to persons with disabilities have been proposed, including: a broadening of the list of expenses eligible for the medical expense tax credit; elimination of the $5,000 limit on the attendant care deduction; and the introduction of a refundable medical expense supplement for workers.

Finally, the budget continues the trend set in the last few budgets to enhance tax assistance for charitable giving. The annual net income limit for claims for charitable donations will increase to 75%. The income inclusion rate on capital gains arising from eligible donations of certain securities will be halved to 37.5% from 75%. Further, the budget proposes to increase the net income limit by 25% of any CCA recapture arising from donations of depreciable assets.

Although many of the provinces left personal income tax rates virtually untouched in their 1997-98 budgets, there were a number

10   of changes. New Brunswick's personal income tax rates will drop significantly within a little over two years. For 1997, the rate drops from 64% of basic federal tax to 62.5%. Prince Edward Island proposes to reduce the threshold at which the provincial high income surtax comes into effect from P.E.I. tax payable in excess of $12,500 to provincial tax payable in excess of $5,200. Personal income taxes in Nova Scotia will decrease 3.4% effective July 1, 1997. Ontario continues to implement the personal income tax changes introduced in last year's budget, but announced a further decrease in the provincial tax rate to 48% of basic federal tax for 1997, rather than the first announced 49%. In addition, for 1997, surtax rates are higher, and thresholds at which the surtaxes come into effect are lower than those announced in the 1996 budget. Finally, Quebec announced major tax reform for individuals that will come into effect January 1, 1998. The proposals include, among other things: a reduction in the number of tax brackets from five to three; the elimination of the 5% and 10% surtaxes and the 2% income tax reduction; an increase in the non-refundable tax credit rate to 23% from 20%; and an option for spouses to file joint returns.

The appendices at the end of this book (page 251) provide more detail on income tax rates.

	Tax changes	Implications for you
Higher tax bills	The federal tax brackets and personal and other tax credits are much the same in 1997 as they were in 1996. (See Appendices)	If your income increased by at least the rate of inflation, you will face a small "hidden" tax hike. Federal tax brackets and credits increase from one year to the next, but only to the extent that the increase in the Consumer Price Index exceeds 3%. Because inflation has been less than 3%, tax brackets and many credits have remained unchanged since 1992.

	Tax changes	Implications for you
Higher tax bills (continued)	The $100,000 lifetime capital gains exemption has been eliminated. (See page 112)	Capital gains will generally be subject to an income inclusion rate of 75%. The $400,000 enhanced capital gains exemption is still available, however, for capital gains arising on the disposition of shares of a QSBC or of a qualified family farm operation.

	Tax changes	Implications for you
Lower tax bills	The 1997 federal budget proposes further changes to tax incentives for charitable donations. (See page 189)	The annual limit on charitable donations will increase to 75% from 50% of net income. To encourage "gifts in kind," capital gains arising from the donation of certain appreciated capital property will be subject to an income inclusion rate of 37.5%, rather than the usual 75%. Further, the net income limit will be increased by 25% of any CCA recapture arising from donations of depreciable capital property.
	The 1997 federal budget proposes to enhance tax assistance for education and training through changes to the tuition fee and education tax credit mechanism. (See page 186)	Students and supporting individuals will benefit from: proposed increases to the tuition fee and education tax credit; broadening of fees eligible for the tuition credit; and an indefinite carryforward of unused amounts on which the tuition fee and education credit is based.
	The 1997 federal budget contains several measures aimed at providing increased tax assistance to persons with disabilities. (See pages 184 and 188)	The list of expenses eligible for the medical expenses tax credit is to be broadened. The $5,000 ceiling on attendant care expenses incurred to allow an individual with a severe and prolonged mental or physical impairment to work will be removed. As well, a refundable tax credit will be available to low-income working Canadians with higher than average medical bills.

Tax changes	Implications for you
Retirement savings The 1997 federal budget proposes to reintroduce the pension adjustment reversal ("PAR") to increase the fairness of the pension system. (See page 39)	The PAR will restore lost RRSP contribution room for individuals who leave RPPs or DPSPs before retirement (because of job changes early in a career, for example).
Canada–U.S. Tax Treaty A draft Protocol to the Canada-U.S. Tax Treaty was signed early in 1997. (See page 168)	The draft Protocol proposes new measures that will change the rules for capital gains on company shares whose value is attributable to real estate. The Protocol will amend yet again the rules dealing with the taxation of social security benefits.
Other topics In response to investor concerns and to rising tuition fees, the 1997 federal budget proposes changes to the treatment of registered education savings plans ("RESPs"). (See page 232)	The annual limit on contributions to an RESP will increase to $4,000 from $2,000 per beneficiary. Further, contributors will be able to receive RESP income directly under certain conditions if named beneficiaries do not pursue post-secondary education.
Individuals who own foreign property or who are beneficiaries of non-resident trusts may have to comply with new foreign reporting rules. (See page 231)	You may have to file forms separate from your income tax returns if you own or have an interest in foreign property with a total cost of more than $100,000Cdn. Reporting will also be required if you receive funds or property from, or become indebted to, a non-resident trust in which you have or will have absolute or conditional rights as a beneficiary. Penalties for non-compliance with the new reporting requirements could be significant.

Significant cases: an overview

An in-depth discussion of the jurisprudence dealing with income tax issues over the last year or so is beyond the scope of *Personal Tax*

Strategy. However, some court decisions relate specifically to the material in this book. A brief overview of several important decisions
follows.

If you intend to take a filing position based on any of these decisions, discuss your plans with your professional advisor first. Your
situation may not be parallel to the case you have in mind, or the
decision you consider favourable may have been reversed on appeal.

Reasonable expectation of profit

Dan Brown v. Her Majesty the Queen, 97 DTC 5195 (FCA)
The taxpayer had been involved in racing snowmobiles and automobiles for several years. He had a full-time job and started to race
as a hobby, personally financing his racing interest. He became successful and received a sponsorship commitment. He claimed that the
losses he incurred prior to receiving sponsorship were for the purpose of earning income. The Tax Court of Canada found that
notwithstanding his subsequent success, there was little expectation
of profit and that the losses were related to recreational pursuits, not
business ventures. In the judge's view, "the subjective hopes of commercial success of this applicant, made no doubt in good faith, are
of themselves insufficient to confer upon this venture a reasonable
expectation of profit." The taxpayer applied to the Federal Court of
Appeal for a judicial review. The Court denied the application,
finding that the Tax Court had not erred in its conclusions.

Possible implications for you: To successfully substantiate a deduction for
business losses, there must be a bona fide business venture and there
must be a reasonable expectation of profit. Although based primarily
on the facts and circumstances of a particular situation, a determination of whether an activity has a reasonable expectation of profit is
measured by a number of factors, including: the conduct of the
individual involved; the nature of the activity; the performance of

14

the activity over a period of time; the status, capacity, experience and interest of the person involved; the time spent on the activity; and the extent of efforts made to realize revenues from it.

Directors' liability

Neil Soper v. Her Majesty the Queen, 97 DTC 5407 (FCA)
When a taxpayer joined a corporate board, he was aware that the company was experiencing financial difficulties. He never discussed with any of the company's employees or fellow board members whether there were any problems with the various tax remittances. The Tax Court of Canada found the taxpayer liable as a director of the company for unremitted source deductions, rejecting his due diligence defence. When he found the company to be in serious financial difficulty, he was under a positive duty to act and failed to do so. The Federal Court of Appeal rejected the taxpayer's appeal of the lower court's decision, and concluded that the standard of care is a hybrid "objective subjective standard", i.e., it is partly objective (the standard of a reasonable person) and partly subjective in that the reasonable person is judged on the basis of his or her particular knowledge and experience. The Court found it insufficient for a director who failed to act reasonably and prudently to simply assert that he or she did his or her best. At the same time, however, the Court rejected any notion that directors should consider undertaking "positive steps" such as going to the comptroller's office to inquire directly about withholdings and remittances unless there is cause for suspicion.

Robert E. Kyte v. Her Majesty the Queen, 97 DTC 5022 (FCA)
The taxpayer was assessed for the unpaid tax and interest of the corporation of which he was a director. He argued that the assessment was not valid because the certificate registered in the Federal Court by the Minister of National Revenue contained an error as to the amount of tax in question. The court upheld the decision of the lower

court that the assessment against the director should not be vacated because of any irregularity or error contained in the certificate.

Possible implications for you: The decision to accept a position as a director of a corporation should not be made lightly. Directors of corporations may be jointly and severally liable (i.e., as a group and as individuals) together with the corporation, for amounts the corporation has failed to withhold and remit to the Receiver General, as well as for related interest and penalties. Liability extends to income tax, employment insurance premiums and Canada Pension Plan contributions.

No explicit guidelines deal with how much a director must do to meet the level or degree of care, diligence and skill necessary to absolve an individual of personal liability. Further, ignorance of the law is not a defence. To protect yourself, ensure that the corporate system of withholding and remitting source deductions is well established and works properly. If you have any doubts about the integrity of the corporation of which you are a director, consider tendering a formal resignation to the corporation itself as well as to the appropriate federal or provincial corporate registry office.

Employment income and expenses

Louis Guay v. Her Majesty the Queen, 97 DTC 5267 (FCA)
The taxpayer worked for the Department of External Affairs and International Trade. He was regularly transferred and had to be prepared to leave Canada at any time for varying periods. To allow his children to continue their education under the French system of education while in Canada and to simplify transfers to other countries, the taxpayer enrolled his children in a private French school. The taxpayer was reimbursed for his children's school tuition fees.

The Court overturned the decision of the lower court, finding that the reimbursement amount was not of a personal nature and that it did not have to be included in the taxpayer's income from employment. The Court concluded that the government's reimbursement of the tuition fees in no way enriched him. He ended up in the same situation as if he had not been required by the nature of his employment to send his children to the private school, i.e., he was in the same economic situation as any Canadian taxpayer whose children attend an educational institution free of charge in Canada.

Sandra E. Gernhart v. Her Majesty the Queen, 96 DTC 1672 (TCC)
The taxpayer was an employee of a U.S. corporation and worked in a group of international service personnel. She accepted a position at one of the company's plants in Canada. The new position carried no increase in grade or level of employment, nor any increase in base salary. The taxpayer worked in Canada for approximately two and one-half years before returning to the U.S.

The corporation's tax equalization policy provided that the amount of income tax during an out-of-country assignment would approximate what would have been paid had an employee remained in his or her home country. Accordingly, if the tax rate in the new country were higher than in the U.S., the employee would receive the same after-tax amount as would have been received in the U.S.

The Tax Court of Canada agreed with the Minister of Revenue's inclusion in employment income of the amount of the equalization payments received by the taxpayer. The Court rejected the taxpayer's argument that the payment was a reimbursement and not a taxable benefit. The Court found that a benefit was received because there is a direct addition to the wealth of an employee when an employer discharges an income tax burden that would otherwise fall on the employee. Further, the Court distinguished the case from other decisions where employees were called upon by their employers to move and the payments were reimbursements associated with the cost of the move. In this case, the Court found that the payments were made pursuant to the taxpayer's overall ongoing compensation package and were designed to induce her to serve outside the U.S.

The taxpayer has appealed the decision to the Federal Court of Appeal.

Karen L. Turner-Lienaux v. Her Majesty the Queen, 97 DTC 5294 (FCA)
The taxpayer participated in a competition for a job promotion within the provincial government. When she did not succeed in obtaining the promotion, she brought suit against her employer. The case went to the provincial Supreme Court and the taxpayer lost. She deducted the legal fees incurred in the actions on the basis they were incurred to collect salaries or wages.

The Court upheld the decision of the Tax Court of Canada that found that the legal fees were not incurred to collect money she was owed. Rather, they were incurred to obtain a declaration that she was entitled to the promotion and therefore a higher salary.

Alan M. Schwartz v. Her Majesty the Queen, 96 DTC 6103 (SCC)
The taxpayer had accepted an offer of employment from a company. He was to receive an annual salary of $250,000 plus stock options. Both parties agreed that he would begin work once a current assignment was completed. A few months later, although the taxpayer had not yet started working for the company, he was informed that his services would not be required and he was offered $75,000 in exchange for a full and final release. The taxpayer refused and following negotiations, settled for $360,000 in damages plus $40,000.

The Tax Court of Canada allocated the bulk of the settlement for embarrassment, anxiety and inconvenience and held that the taxpayer did not receive any income from, or as a result of, the employment agreement. The Federal Court of Appeal overturned the lower court's decision and allocated the bulk of the damages as being for loss of salary.

The Crown argued that the damages were taxable as income from an unenumerated source, i.e., that the employment agreement was a source of income; or, alternatively, that it was a retiring allowance. The Supreme Court rejected the argument that it was income from

18

an unenumerated source and held that the requirement that one must be in the service of another person to be characterized as an employee excludes any notion of prospective or intended employment and, therefore, the amount could not be a retiring allowance. The Supreme Court restored the Tax Court's holding.

Possible implications for you: The breadth of topics that have been dealt with by the courts emphasizes that the taxation of employment income, normally considered to be straightforward, may be anything but.

The inclusion of equalization payments in income is yet another example in a growing list of payments or reimbursements from an employer that are outside normal remuneration. Normally, benefits provided to you or members of your family that are enjoyed as a consequence of employment are taxable in your hands. But there are exceptions. Careful planning may mean the difference between taxable and non-taxable benefits.

Awards for damages to compensate for pain and suffering and mental distress may be non-taxable receipts, depending on the facts and circumstances of the particular case.

Before proceeding with any legal action against your employer, consider the nature of the suit, to what extent you are willing to pursue your action, the costs involved and the deductibility, if any, of the costs you incur.

Interest deductibility

John M. Tennant v. Her Majesty the Queen, 96 DTC 6121 (SCC)
The issue before the Supreme Court was whether interest can be deducted by a taxpayer on a loan to purchase shares when the shares have been subsequently disposed of in a tax-free rollover in exchange for shares with a substantially reduced fair market value. The Court held that the full amount of the interest was deductible. To deduct interest payments, the taxpayer must establish a link between the

current eligible use property, the proceeds of disposition of the original eligible use property and the money that was borrowed to acquire the latter. The Court found that this link existed; both the original and replacement shares on the rollover were directly traceable to the loan as the taxpayer reinvested all the proceeds of disposition. The basis for an interest expense deduction is not the value of the replacement property but the amount of the original loan.

Possible implications for you: Tax practitioners and the courts have opined at length on the deductibility of interest when funds have been borrowed to acquire property used for business or investment purposes and the property has subsequently been disposed of and replaced. The decision of the Supreme Court confirms that for the integrity of the interest deduction to be maintained, replacement property must be traced to original property and to the funds borrowed (and the obligation to pay the interest, of course) and, in the process, it must be ensured that the entire amount of the loan can be accounted for. The value of the replacement asset is not the basis for the interest deduction. Refer to page 110 for a discussion of how interest may continue to be deductible even if the source of the income from business or property is no longer held.

Income splitting

Her Majesty the Queen v. Melville Neuman, 96 DTC 6464 (FCA)
The taxpayer incorporated a company as a tax planning vehicle with the specific purpose of splitting income with his spouse. The issue was whether a dividend received by the taxpayer's spouse on non-voting preferred shares in the corporation was properly attributed to the taxpayer as income. The Crown contended that the amount of the dividend was a payment or transfer of property made (to his spouse) pursuant to the taxpayer's direction or with his concurrence.

Both the Tax Court of Canada and the Federal Court Trial Division held that the dividend was not includable in the taxpayer's income on the basis of a Supreme Court of Canada decision that established that, as a general rule, the measures dealing with indirect payments do not apply to dividends. The Federal Court of Appeal in this case, however, found sufficient evidence in the minutes of shareholders' meetings and board of directors' meetings to prove that the dividend was declared to the taxpayer's spouse with his concurrence. The spouse immediately lent the amount of the dividend back to the declaring company, providing further evidence that the dividend payment was tax-motivated.

Possible implications for you: Although a number of income splitting techniques are sanctioned by the tax authorities (for example, spousal RRSP contributions), attempts to indulge in more complicated strategies should be pursued with great care and advice from your professional tax advisor.

Misrepresentation

John G. Nesbitt v. Her Majesty the Queen, 96 DTC 6588 (FCA)
The taxpayer incorrectly reported a capital gain on his 1981 income tax return. The working papers supporting the calculation of the gain contained sufficient information for the tax authorities to discover the error and correct the capital gain. The taxpayer's return was reassessed outside the statutory period on the basis that there was a misrepresentation. The Federal Court of Appeal upheld the decision of a lower court that the reassessment was correct. The Court agreed that a misrepresentation occurs if there is an incorrect statement on the return when the statement is material to the purposes of the return and any future reassessment. It remains a misrepresentation even if the Minister could or does, by a careful analysis of the supporting documents, find the error on the return.

Possible implications for you: Taxpayers are responsible for their tax returns, in particular for ensuring that they are true, correct and complete. Although one might interpret "misrepresentation" to mean neglect, carelessness or wilful default, it may also refer to any representation that is false in substance and in fact at the material time. Accordingly, ensure that you carefully review your returns prior to filing. This may be especially important when they are prepared by someone else.

2 Employees

Employees

What's new?

- The Pension Adjustment Reversal (PAR) is to be reintroduced (proposed).

- $5,000 ceiling on attendant care expenses is to be eliminated (proposed).

For most employees, salary is the main component of income. Employment benefits are often a major component too. The T4 slip that your employer gives you provides the tax information you need. Some recent court cases that relate to employment income and expenses are outlined on page 15.

The tax consequences of salary are straightforward. Salary is generally taxed when it is received. However, if your salary is deferred and one of the main reasons is to postpone payment of tax, special rules impose tax on the amount deferred.

In addition to being an employee, you may also be a director, either of the corporation for which you work or of another corporation. If you are a director and are earning directors' fees, those fees are also employment income and must be included in your tax return. Directors' fees are "earned income" for the purposes of determining how much you can contribute to your own or a spousal RRSP. Refer to page 225 as well for a discussion concerning directors' liability.

Taxable benefits and employment deductions can be more complex than salary. Company cars are a major topic on their own, and are dealt with on page 50. Other taxable benefits, non-taxable benefits and employment deductions (including pension, RRSP and DPSP contributions) are covered first in this chapter.

Taxable benefits

You must include in your income from employment the value of any taxable benefits you received during the year as a result of employment.

The most important taxable benefits are employee loans, stock options and company cars. Frequent flyer points also deserve some attention.

Employee loans

Generally, if your employer makes a loan to you or to a member of your family and charges little or no interest, you receive a taxable benefit. The benefit is computed as the interest on the loan at a pre-scribed rate, less any interest you actually paid within the year or 30 days after year-end. The table shows the 1997 prescribed rates for these loans. Rates are subject to adjustment every quarter to reflect market interest rates.

		Prescribed rate for deemed interest on employee and shareholder loans*
Quarter of 1997	1st	4%
	2nd	3%
	3rd	4%
	4th	

* For prescribed rates for overdue taxes, penalties, refunds etc. see the table on page 81.

If you use the loan proceeds for investment purposes, the loan may be essentially tax-free because the benefit is offset by an equal interest expense deduction.

The taxable benefit on a loan to acquire a home that you will occu-py, or to refinance a mortgage on your current home, is calculated using the lesser of the prescribed interest rate in effect at the time the loan was made or renewed, and the current prescribed rate. These loans are considered to be renewed every five years.

The five-year renewal rule allows you to have the best of both worlds if you benefit from a loan from your employer to purchase a home. For example, assume you received a low interest or interest-free loan from your employer in a year when the prescribed rate was 5%. A year passes and the rate has increased to 9%. Your employment benefit is calculated using the 5% rate, even though the prescribed rate has increased significantly. If the prescribed rate had dropped, however, the benefit would have been calculated using the lower rate. If you can negotiate a housing loan from your employer as part of your compensation package, this rule can result in a very attractive benefit.

✔ Tax Tip 1

If you started work at a new job (in Canada) that involved moving (within Canada) to a home at least 40 kilometres closer to your new work location, the interest benefit on the first $25,000 of a home relocation loan will be tax-free. This exemption is available for the first five years of the loan. You must still report the full amount of the interest benefit. The special deduction for interest on a home relocation loan must be claimed as a separate item on your tax return.

✔ Tax Tip 2

If you change employers within five years of receiving a home relocation loan and your new employer gives you a loan to repay your former employer, the replacement loan is considered to be the same as the original loan. As long as the replacement loan is no bigger than the original loan, you will be entitled to the special deduction as though the original loan were still in place.

Stock options

Stock options that you get from your employer are taxed differently depending on whether the corporation is a Canadian-controlled private corporation (CCPC). In either case, you face no immediate income tax consequences when you receive an employee stock option.

If your employer is not a CCPC, when you exercise an option you are deemed to have received income from employment equal to the difference between the fair market value of the stock when the option is exercised and the total amount you paid to acquire the option and the shares themselves. You may deduct one-quarter of this deemed benefit from your taxable income, (as long as the options are qualifying stock options granted after February 15, 1984). Consequently, just three-quarters of the benefit received on the exercise of these options will be taxable as employment income.

A stock option is a "qualifying option" if the exercise price for the related shares is not less than their fair market value when the option is granted, the employee deals at arm's length with the corporation and the shares under the option arrangement are common shares meeting specific criteria.

The exercise price criterion is applied without reference to fluctuations in the value of a foreign currency relative to the Canadian dollar during the period between the acquisition of the option and the time the share is acquired. Accordingly, if the stock options are denominated in a foreign currency, the deduction will not be denied by reason only of a foreign exchange fluctuation.

On a subsequent sale of the shares, three-quarters of any gain accruing after the exercise date is treated as a taxable capital gain.

Stock options granted to employees of CCPCs are not subject to tax until the employees dispose of shares. When you dispose of shares in a CCPC, the amount treated as employment income is the difference between the fair market value of the shares at the time the option was exercised and the total amount you paid to acquire the options and the shares themselves. One-quarter of this amount is deductible in arriving at taxable income, provided you have held the shares for at least two years. As with options in non-CCPCs, three-quarters of any gain on the sale of the shares accruing after the exercise date is treated as a taxable capital gain.

You will generally be subject to tax on taxable capital gains realized on the disposition of shares that you acquired when you exercised stock options.

Although the $100,000 lifetime capital gains exemption has been eliminated, gains on sales of stock in a qualifying small business corporation (QSBC) acquired by exercising options are still eligible for the enhanced $400,000 capital gains exemption. (When the expression "enhanced capital gains exemption" is used in this book, the amount of the exemption will be taken to be $400,000. This assumes that the general lifetime capital gains exemption has already been claimed. For individuals who never used their $100,000 capital gains exemption in respect of other property, the enhanced exemption will be $500,000.)

When unexercised options under an employee stock option plan are held on the date of death of a taxpayer, an employment benefit will have to be included in the taxpayer's final income tax return. The employment benefit is equal to the difference between the fair market value of the options immediately before the employee's death and the amount paid by the employee to acquire the options.

✔ Tax Tip 3

In general, decisions to invest or sell should be based on economic factors, with tax considerations secondary. However, in some cases clear tax advantages should be taken into account. For example, your shares of a CCPC acquired as a result of exercising a stock option prior to May 23, 1985 should be sold before selling your other securities. There will be no taxable benefit and the full gain is a capital gain. Although the $100,000 lifetime capital gains exemption has been eliminated, gains realized on the disposition of QSBC shares remain eligible for the enhanced capital gains exemption.

✔ Tax Tip 4

If you borrow to finance the purchase of shares when exercising stock options, the interest expense on the loan is tax-deductible. The interest expense will, however, be added to your cumulative net investment losses (see page 115).

Frequent flyer points

If you accumulate frequent flyer credits while travelling on business trips paid for by your employer and then use the points for yourself or your family for personal air travel, Revenue Canada requires you to determine and include in your income the fair market value of any benefits enjoyed. If your employer did not control the program, it is your responsibility to calculate and report the benefit.

Taxable benefits and the GST

Salaries, wages, commissions and other remuneration paid to employees are not subject to the Goods and Services Tax (GST). In contrast, fringe benefits or perks may be. Some of the more common perks that are included in your income as taxable benefits and that are subject to GST are:

- the benefit from personal use of your employer's automobile;

- short-term board and lodging (less than one month);

- subsidized meals that do constitute a taxable benefit;

- the cost of tools, certain gifts and frequent flyer programs;

- tuition fees for GST-taxable courses;

- non-cash incentives such as prizes, awards and holiday trips that are GST-taxable in the marketplace and that are provided as benefits to employees; and

- a reimbursement of travelling expenses of a spouse who accompanies an employee on a business trip.

GST will not apply to prizes or awards given to employees in the form of cash or a cheque.

Employers who are not registered for GST generally do not have to remit the GST on employee benefits. However, the GST element of taxable employee benefits must still be included in an employee's income for income tax purposes.

Non-taxable benefits

Many employees receive compensation in forms other than those discussed already. These non-cash benefits are known as fringe benefits or perquisites ("perks" for short). Here are some examples of the dwindling number that are received tax-free:

- employer contributions to registered pension and deferred profit sharing plans (within limits);
- reimbursement of moving expenses;
- employee counselling services (including tobacco, drug or alcohol counselling, stress management counselling and job placement and retirement counselling) provided by or paid for by the employer;
- tuition fees for courses taken for the employer's benefit;
- employee discounts (within limits);
- subsidized meals, if the employee is required to pay a reasonable charge;
- distinctive uniforms and special clothing (including safety footwear);
- use of employer's recreational facilities (except board and lodging at a vacation property such as a summer hotel or hunting lodge);
- social or athletic club memberships, but only if the membership is advantageous to the employer;
- reimbursement of a loss on the sale of a home due to an employment transfer;
- reasonable allowances for taxi fares, "para-transport" and parking provided to employees who are eligible for the disability tax credit by reason of a severe and prolonged impairment of mobility or sight; and

- allowances for attendant care required to enable an employee who qualifies for the disability tax credit to perform employment duties.

Employee relocation reimbursements

A job transfer could require you to move from one city to another within the same province, or across the country. Depending on the location and timing of a move, an employee could incur significant additional costs to acquire a home comparable to the one left behind. As part of an employment package, many employers compensate employees for higher housing prices in the new work location.

A number of court decisions have dealt with payments of various types to employees in partial reimbursement of increased costs in new locations.

Essentially, a distinction was made between relocation payments that compensate employees for increased housing costs in a new location and for losses suffered on the sale of a previous home. The cases affirm the taxability of payments for relocating to more expensive locations and the exemption from tax of relocation payments that reimburse an employee for actual losses incurred on a sale.

Recent case law has significantly narrowed the scope for providing employees with tax-free relocation payments. Indeed, a payment must meet all of the following criteria to be considered a non-taxable benefit:

- the payment must reimburse actual expenses or losses that are a direct consequence of a change in the employee's place of residence due to a change in work site;

- the payment must result in no economic benefit to the employee;

- the payment must reimburse an actual, quantifiable loss or expense, and not be merely an allowance or reimbursement of a general economic loss; and

- the payment must be made to reimburse an expense incurred in respect of, in the course of, or by virtue of the taxpayer's employment.

Other than home loss reimbursements and mortgage interest differential payments, the government has not acknowledged the tax-free status of any other type of relocation payment. Each arrangement must be evaluated on its own merits. Further, the jurisprudence does not provide support for excluding from an employee's income, employer relocation payments directed at defraying higher costs at a new work location, such as amounts paid as housing subsidies, cost-of-living differentials and reimbursements of excess tax costs.

You might like to read some of the higher-level court decisions that dealt with employee relocation payments and that are the basis of the foregoing criteria, or bring them to the attention of your professional advisor. Here are some of the more important case citations: *Cyril John Ransom v. Minister of National Revenue,* 67 DTC 5235 (Ex.Ct.); *Her Majesty the Queen v. Vincent Lao,* 93 DTC 5251 (FCTD); *Attorney General of Canada v. Roland M. MacDonald,* 94 DTC 6262 (FCA); *Her Majesty the Queen v. William R. Phillips,* 94 DTC 6177 (FCA); *Her Majesty the Queen v. Eugene Joseph Blanchard,* 95 DTC 5479 (FCA); *Attorney General of Canada v. Enrique Hoefele et al; David Krull v. Attorney General of Canada,* 95 DTC 5602 (FCA).

✔ Tax Tip 5

If, as a result of a job transfer, you received a relocation payment in a prior year that is not statute-barred and you excluded the amount from income, you should reconsider the circumstances to determine whether the exclusion is still justified.

✔ Tax Tip 6

If you will be relocating soon, consider suggesting that your employer review, and possibly restructure, the company's relocation program to ensure the most effective tax treatment. For example, payments for defraying higher costs at a new work location appear to be taxable (e.g., subsidies or allowances for the incremental interest cost of assuming a new mortgage with both a higher interest rate and a higher principal amount). Reimbursements made to offset a difference in interest rates for the remaining term of a mortgage when an employee incurs a higher interest rate on a mortgage resulting from an employer-initiated move may not be taxable.

Employment deductions

The Income Tax Act is not generous in permitting deductions in the computation of employment income. Only a handful of expenses are deductible. Some of those with more general application are discussed below.

Moving expenses

Eligible moving expenses incurred in connection with beginning employment or full-time post-secondary education at a new location in Canada are deductible if your new residence is at least 40 kilometres closer to your new work or school location and if the expenses are not reimbursed by your employer. Eligible expenses are deductible only from income earned at the new location. Amounts not deducted in one year may be carried forward to the next year.

Prior to a recent Federal Court of Appeal decision, the courts had never before considered the issue of how the 40 kilometre distance is measured. Revenue Canada has always applied a straight line measurement, basically an "as the crow flies" test. The Federal Court of Appeal agreed with the taxpayer that this method bears no relation to how an employee actually travels to work and found that the appropriate test to meet the 40 kilometre criterion is the shortest normal route available to the travelling public.

Eligible moving expenses include travelling costs for you and your family, including a reasonable amount for meals and lodging; moving and storage costs for your household effects; the costs of cancelling a lease or selling the old home; and legal costs of purchasing a new home.

A reimbursement of reasonable moving costs by your employer is not a taxable benefit. On the other hand, you cannot deduct costs that the employer reimburses.

Taxes imposed on the transfer or registration of title to a new residence are eligible moving expenses (as long as you are selling your old one). However, changes to the rules clarify that the GST related to the purchase of a new residence is not included in the definition of taxes eligible for deduction.

✔ Tax Tip 7

Provincial tax is based on your province of residence on December 31. If you would face a higher tax liability as a result of a move to another jurisdiction, consider postponing your move until after the year-end. On the other hand, consider accelerating the move if you are moving to a province with a lower tax rate.

Legal expenses

You may deduct legal costs paid to collect salary or wages from your employer or former employer. Legal expenses paid to collect or establish a right to a retiring allowance or pension benefit are deductible (within a seven-year carryforward period) in computing income for the year in which the allowance or benefit is received. The deduction is limited to the amount of retiring allowance or pension benefits you received, less any portion that has been transferred to an RPP or RRSP.

✔ Tax Tip 8

If you incurred legal costs to collect pension income in the last three years, consider asking Revenue Canada to reassess your return for the period in question. Your tax refund could be substantial.

Child care expenses

Working parents may deduct the cost of child care within specific limits. In most cases, the deduction must be claimed by the spouse who has the lower income.

The age limit for children for whom the child care expense deduction may be claimed is 16 years.

The child care expense deduction is generally available to help offset the cost of child care that you incur to enable you to earn income. If you are working and your spouse is a full-time student, you may claim a deduction while your spouse is studying. Single parents who are studying full-time may claim the child care expense deduction against all types of income. This also applies to two-parent families when both parents are attending school full-time at the same time.

A parent's attendance in high school is also recognized for purposes of the child care expense deduction. Full-time attendance at school is defined as enrolment in a program lasting for at least three consecutive weeks and that requires at least ten hours per week on courses or work in the program. Child care expenses are limited to $150 per child under seven and $90 for older eligible children, multiplied by the number of weeks that the parent is in full-time attendance at school.

The maximum child care deduction depends on the child's age and any infirmity, as the table shows.

The maximum deduction is $5,000 for each child who is less than seven years old at the end of the year or who has a severe or prolonged mental or physical impairment for which a Disability Credit

Certificate has been submitted. The maximum deduction is $3,000 for each child who is less than 17 years old at the end of the year or who is not eligible for the $5,000 deduction but has a mental or physical infirmity and is dependent.

Child care expense: maximum deductions

			Child's age (at December 31)		
			17 or more	7 to 16	Under 7
	No Infirmity				
Mental or physical infirmity	**Infirmity does not qualify** for the $5,000 maximum deduction	**Child not dependent** on taxpayer or taxpayer's spouse	None		
		Child is dependent on taxpayer or taxpayer's spouse	$3,000		
	Severe and prolonged impairment, for which a Disability Credit Certificate has been submitted		$5,000		

Eligible costs include day-care or babysitting, boarding school and camp expenses. Medical expenses, tuition, clothing or transportation expenses are not eligible for this deduction.

✔ Tax Tip 9

For child care payments to be deductible in respect of the current year, they must be made by December 31. If you make January's payment in December, however, you are not permitted to deduct the amount until the following year.

Attendant care deduction

An individual with a severe and prolonged mental or physical impairment may deduct attendant care expenses that are necessary to allow the individual to work. The current deduction is limited to the lesser of two-thirds of earned income and $5,000. The 1997 federal budget proposes to eliminate the $5,000 ceiling and to allow workers with disabilities to deduct the cost of attendant care expenses up to two-thirds of earned income.

Contributions to RPPs, RRSPs, DPSPs

Employees often accumulate funds to provide future retirement benefits through tax deductible contributions to a registered pension plan (RPP), a registered retirement savings plan (RRSP), a deferred profit sharing plan (DPSP) or some combination of these plans.

In the federal government's annual modify-the-retirement-savings-tax-rules effort, the 1997 federal budget proposes only moderate tinkering. The pension adjustment reversal (PAR) is a concept that was introduced with pension reform in 1989. The PAR rules were never enacted. Instead, the government announced its intention to review the PAR in the 1995 budget. The 1997 budget re-introduces the PAR to the system for tax-assisted retirement savings. Refer to page 39 for details about the PAR.

Dollar limits for contributions to RRSPs, RPPs and DPSPs will remain frozen until at least 2003. Refer to each section below – RPPs, RRSPs and DPSPs – for additional details.

The rules that govern tax assistance for saving in pension and retirement savings plans are intended to ensure that individuals are treated equally, whether they save through RPPs, RRSPs or DPSPs.

Although the rules are fairly straightforward if you save for your retirement solely through RRSPs, they can be complicated if you are a member of an RPP or a DPSP. The pension adjustment (see following) determines what portion, if any, of the maximum RRSP contribution is replaced by benefits accrued under an RPP or a DPSP. The maximum amount you can contribute to your RRSP must then be reduced accordingly.

• Pension Adjustment (PA)

Simply put, your pension adjustment (PA) measures the benefits accrued to you as a member of a pension plan. The maximum you will be allowed to contribute to an RRSP is reduced by your PA.

The following table shows how the PA calculation depends on the type of pension plan:

The PA (pension adjustment) calculation

	Type of plan		
	DPSP	**RPP**	**No pension**
	Money purchase	**Defined benefit**	
PA	Total employee and employer contributions in the year (generally)	Complex calculation intended to measure value of benefits accrued in the year	None

In a money purchase plan, the pension you receive depends on the investment earnings of the pension fund. In a defined benefit plan, pension payments are independent of the fund's earnings, depending instead on a formula that usually involves a percentage of your average earnings and your period of pensionable employment.

Your employer is responsible for determining your PA. Your T4 slip for 1996 employment earnings will tell the amount of your PA. You will have to reduce your RRSP limit by the prior year's PA. Revenue Canada will also advise you of your 1997 RRSP deduction limit on your 1996 Notice of Assessment or late in 1997.

If you are a member of a foreign pension plan, you may still have a PA. For example, if you are a resident in Canada, but work primarily outside Canada, you may be required to calculate your own PA-like amount with respect to any foreign plan to which you belong. In other circumstances, it will be your employer's responsibility to calculate and report your PA. PA calculations can be complex. If you are concerned about whether your PA has been calculated and reported correctly, consider having your tax advisor discuss the matter with your employer.

If you are a member of a foreign pension plan, you may have had to reduce your RRSP deduction room by certain prescribed amounts. Generally, however, you would still have about $1,000 worth of RRSP room available to you. This RRSP room has been eliminated for high-income earners during those years in which the RRSP limit is less than $15,500, i.e., until the year 2005.

To complicate matters further, a "past service pension adjustment" (PSPA) may result if, for example, your pension plan is retroactively upgraded to provide better benefits or if you transfer benefits to a new plan and purchase additional past service benefits. If you have a PSPA, the amount that you may contribute to your RRSP will require adjustment. Once again, the onus is on your employer to provide you with the necessary information regarding these intricate rules.

RRSP contribution limits may be reduced by your PA and PSPA

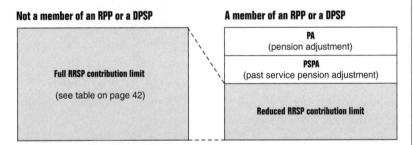

• Return of the Pension Adjustment Reversal

A guiding principle of the pension system is that RRSP contribution room is foregone based on participation in employer-sponsored arrangements. RRSP contribution room is reduced by Pension Adjustments (PA) and Past Service Pension Adjustments (PSPA), if any. (Both of these concepts are discussed in the preceding section.) The Pension Adjustment Reversal (PAR) was originally intended to restore RRSP contribution room if benefits proved to be of a lower value than prior PAs and PSPAs indicated. To reduce the complexity of the pension system, however, the rules relating to PARs were never passed. The 1997 federal budget proposes to reintroduce the PAR to increase the fairness of the system.

The PAR will be measured when, after 1996, an individual ceases to have any entitlement to benefits under a deferred profit sharing plan or a registered pension plan. Accordingly, no PAR can be created if a pension is taken instead of a lump sum payment or transfer to an RRSP or RPP. The PAR will equal the excess, if any, of the PAs and PSPAs reported as a result of participation in a plan over the payments received or transferred from the plan with respect to service after 1989. The PAR will then be added to an individual's RRSP contribution room in the year of termination. In keeping with the objective of remaining revenue neutral, the cost of the PAR subsystem will be offset by a change in the calculation of PAs for defined benefit provisions of an RPP. Currently, the calculation contains a $1,000 offset that reduces an RPP member's PA and increases RRSP deduction room. For pension credits calculated for 1997 and future years, the $1,000 offset will be reduced to $600, i.e., RRSP contribution room will be reduced by $400.

Transitional rules apply for 1997. Accordingly, any PAR arising in 1997 will affect only PSPAs and RRSP contribution room in 1998. Further, the PSPA rules will be modified to ensure integration with the new PAR system.

• Registered pension plans (RPPs) – money purchase

The contribution limit for money purchase RPPs will remain frozen at $13,500 until the end of 2002. The limit will increase to $14,500 for 2003, and to $15,500 in 2004. The limit will be indexed to the average industrial wage in Canada beginning in 2005.

If you belong to a money purchase RPP, you may make a tax-deductible contribution to your plan in 1997 equal to 18% of your 1997 employment income, to a maximum of $13,500, minus the contribution your employer makes to your plan. (See the table on page 42). You reach the $13,500 maximum when your employment earnings are $75,000.

• Registered pension plans (RPPs) – defined benefit

Generally, the amount you may contribute to a defined benefit RPP and deduct for tax purposes is not limited, as long as the contributions are in respect of current service and are required under the provisions of the plan. However, the government caps the amount of pension an individual may receive. The provisions of your RPP will ensure that these restrictions are met by limiting how much you and your employer can contribute. Maximum contributions relate to the maximum benefit that can be accrued, which in turn is based on a maximum annual pension allowed in the first year of retirement. That maximum pension equals your years of pensionable service, multiplied by the lesser of:

- 2% of the average of the best three consecutive years of salary; and
- $1,722 (this limit is frozen through 2004; it will be indexed to the average industrial wage beginning in 2005).

As the graph below shows, the $1,722 cap corresponds to an average of $86,111 for the best three consecutive years of salary, $1,722 being 2% of $86,111.

Maximum pension (per year of pensionable service)

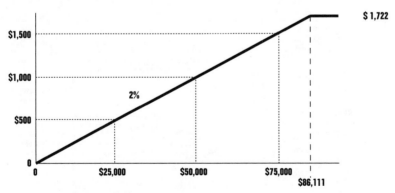

Average of three best consecutive years of salary

42 **• Registered retirement savings plans (RRSPs)**

An RRSP is a tax-deferred investment vehicle that allows you to invest money now, with a view to using the accumulated funds as retirement income commencing not later than the end of the year in which you turn 69 (formerly, age 71; see the discussion below for the new rules). Your contributions are tax-deductible within specified limits. If you borrow money to make an RRSP contribution, the interest payments are not tax-deductible.

The annual RRSP dollar limit for tax-deductible contributions is frozen at $13,500 until the end of 2003. The limit will increase to $14,500 for 2004 and to $15,500 for 2005. The limits will be indexed to the average industrial wage in Canada beginning in 2006.

As the table below shows, your RRSP contributions for 1997 cannot exceed 18% of your earned income for the previous year, up to a dollar limit of $13,500 (which corresponds to $75,000 of

Retirement savings contribution limits

		RRSP (Limits to be reduced by the PA and PSPA for members of RPPs or DPSPs)	DPSP (Employer's contributions only)		RPP	
					Money purchase (Limits apply to total employer and employee contributions)	Defined benefit
Fixed dollar limit*	1996	$13,500 (if income > $75,000*)	$6,750 (if income > $37,500*)		$13,500 (if income > $75,000*)	No direct limit (Contributions governed by actuarial principles and specific rules.)
	1997					
	1998					
	1999					
	2000					
	2001					
	2002					
	2003		$7,250 (if income > $40,278*)		$14,500 (if income > $80,556*)	
	2004	$14,500 (if income > $80,556*)	$7,750 (if income > $43,056*)		$15,500 (if income > $86,111*)	
	2005	$15,500 (if income > $86,111*)	Indexed			
	2006					
Income-based limit (all years)		18% of previous year's earned income	18% of employment income			

* Below the given level of income, the 18% income-based limit applies rather than the fixed dollar amount.

earned income, $13,500 being 18% of $75,000). If you are a member of an RPP or a DPSP, these limits are reduced by your:

- pension adjustment (PA) for the previous year, described on page 38; and

- past service pension adjustment (PSPA), described on page 39.

To be deductible in a particular year, your RRSP contributions must be made before the end of the year or in the first 60 days of the following year. You may carry forward unused RRSP room indefinitely. The objective of the carryforward rule is to allow you to use accumulated unused RRSP room in years when you are in a better position to save.

Remember that earned income does not include any type of periodic retirement or pension payment or benefit, including retiring allowances, death benefits and amounts received from an RRSP. In addition to your regular RRSP contribution, you may be able to transfer a portion of a retiring allowance to your RRSP. Although tax-free rollovers to RRSPs are being phased out, you may continue to transfer up to $2,000 per year of service before 1996, plus $1,500 per year of service before 1989 during which you were not a member of an RPP or DPSP.

The age at which you must arrange to mature your RRSP has been reduced to 69 from age 71. This applies for maturing RPPs, RRSP and DPSPs. You are not permitted to contribute to retirement plans or accrue pension benefits after the end of the year in which you turn 69. You will have to begin receiving retirement income out of your plans, or roll them into an RRIF, by the end of that year.

If you have RRSP deduction room after age 69, you may contribute to a spousal RRSP up until the end of the year in which your spouse turns 69.

The reduction in the age limit does not apply to you if you were 70 or more at the end of 1996. You will still be able to mature your plan by the end of the year in which you turn 71. If you turned 69 in 1996, you will be required to accelerate maturity by one year, i.e., your plan will have to be matured by the end of 1997, the year in which you turn 70.

If you were under 69 at the end of 1996, the date by which you must arrange to mature your plans will be accelerated by two years.

You may transfer lump sum amounts from a defined benefit RPP to an RRIF after you reach 72. You may transfer an amount equal to the annual pension given up under your RPP, multiplied by a factor corresponding to your age.

• Self-directed RRSPs

Funds in your RRSP may be invested in a number of ways. If you choose to establish your RRSP at a financial institution such as a bank, trust company or life insurance company, you will probably have a deposit account with investments such as term deposits or Guaranteed Investment Certificates (GICs).

Holders of outstanding Compound Interest Canada Savings Bonds (C-Bonds, Series 43 to 51), may transfer their bonds into their RRSPs without having to open a self-directed plan.

A new Canada RRSP bond was launched in early 1997. The bond offers guaranteed annual interest rates for ten years and annual compound interest on the anniversary of issue. The bond will be available for purchase in November of each year for a limited time, possibly until the RRSP deadline date for making tax deductible contributions. Purchasers may cash-in or transfer-out each year on the anniversary date. There are no fees and the bond may be purchased and held by your RRSP or a self-directed plan.

You may also choose to have a self-directed RRSP. This option is somewhat riskier and takes more time and effort on your part than a simple deposit account. Ordinarily, you will set up a self-directed RRSP through a financial institution or your broker.

There are restrictions on the types of investments your RRSP may hold. Some of the more popular qualified investments include: cash, shares or bonds of corporations listed on Canadian stock exchanges,

T-Bills, GICs, government bonds, mutual funds and certain small business shares. Further, up to 20% of your portfolio may be invested in foreign assets. If the total cost amount of the foreign property held exceeds the 20% limitation, the excess will generally be subject to a significant penalty tax.

Shares and debt issued by a Canadian corporation are not considered foreign property if the Canadian corporation has a substantial presence in Canada. Subject to the substantial Canadian presence exemption, shares and debt issued by a Canadian corporation will be foreign property if the shares issued by the corporation derive their value primarily from any foreign property – not merely portfolio investments in foreign property.

• Spousal RRSP contributions

Contributions to your spouse's RRSP based on your contribution limit are deductible from your income. These contributions, however, reduce the amount you can contribute to your own plan for the year.

Contributing to your spouse's RRSP allows your spouse to use the pension income credit eventually (see page 149 in Chapter 5, **Retired Persons**). Further, receipts from a spousal RRSP may help equalize the amount of retirement income you both receive, and may place you in a lower tax bracket.

If you have RRSP deduction room after age 69 (refer to the new rules in the general RRSP discussed above), you will be able to continue to contribute to a spousal RRSP until the end of the year in which your spouse turns 69.

✔ Tax Tip 10

Don't get trapped by a timing rule associated with withdrawals from a spousal RRSP. If you withdraw amounts from a spousal RRSP, you, rather than your spouse, will have to include the withdrawals in your income to the extent that you paid the tax-deductible premiums into the spousal plan in the year or in the immediately preceding two taxation years. Many people make the mistake of thinking of RRSP contributions as having been made in the year they are deductible, rather than in the year they were actually made. For example, a contribution made in February 1997 and deducted on your 1996 tax return will be included in your income and taxed on your return if the amounts are withdrawn before 2000, i.e., within two years of the time when the contribution was made.

• Over-contributions to an RRSP

As discussed on page 42, if you contribute to an RRSP, you need to be concerned with the maximum amount of RRSP contributions that you may deduct for tax purposes for a particular year. You also need to ensure that you do not incur a penalty tax because you have over-contributed to your RRSP. An allowance of $2,000 is intended as a protective cushion against inadvertent or unavoidable over-contributions. (Prior to 1996, the over-contribution allowance was $8,000.) Transitional rules permit existing excess contributions to be retained until they can be drawn down and deducted against new RRSP room, rather than forcing them to be withdrawn. If you had an over-contribution greater than $2,000 on February 27, 1995, you must apply the contributions against your unused RRSP room. There is no transitional amount for individuals who had not attained 18 years of age before 1995.

The rules dealing with group RRSPs ensure that, within limits, non-discretionary contributions can be made to a group RRSP on the basis of current year earnings, without triggering the penalty tax.

Further, a past service pension adjustment (PSPA) will not cause RRSP contributions to become subject to the penalty tax in the year in which the PSPA arises. PSPAs, however, reduce the unused RRSP deduction room that is carried forward and are therefore taken into account for penalty tax purposes in subsequent years.

The penalty is 1% per month of your "cumulative excess

amount" (the amount of the over-contribution above $2,000) at the end of the month. The $2,000 over-contribution threshold is not available if you are under the age of 19.

If you over-contribute (perhaps because of lower-than-expected earned income), you may end up paying double tax, i.e., you don't get a deduction for tax purposes for the excess amount and you will pay tax on the amount when it is eventually withdrawn as retirement income. You can, however, avoid paying double tax: when you receive your Notice of Assessment for the year in which the excess arose, you may withdraw that excess amount tax-free, in:

- the year of the over-contribution;

- the year you receive the assessment; or

- the year immediately following either of those years.

If the over-contribution is intentional, you lose the ability to make a tax-free withdrawal.

Even though you have this opportunity to withdraw the excess amount tax-free, you will still be liable for the penalty tax if the over-contribution exceeds $2,000. If your over-contribution was due to a reasonable error, you can ask Revenue Canada to waive the penalty tax.

• Deferred profit sharing plans (DPSPs)

A deferred profit sharing plan (DPSP) can be used in lieu of an RPP. A DPSP is an arrangement under which an employer makes tax-deductible contributions to a trustee — based, for example, on a percentage of annual profits. (Employee contributions, although no longer allowed, were permitted prior to 1991.) The trustee holds and invests the contributions for the benefit of employees who are plan members.

The dollar limit for employer contributions to DPSPs is half of the RPP money purchase limit for the year. Accordingly, the freeze on money purchase limits will affect the dollar limit on contributions to a DPSP. The limit will remain at $6,750 until 2002, rising to $7,250 in 2003 and $7,750 in 2004. The limits will be indexed to the average industrial wage beginning in 2005.

Amounts withdrawn from a DPSP are taxable, but in determining the taxable amount, you may deduct the contributions that you made to the plan (which were permitted before 1991).

You may transfer lump sum proceeds from a DPSP into an RPP, an RRSP or another DPSP, generally tax free.

• Locked-in RRSPs

Holders of RRSPs that are locked-in under a provision of the applicable federal or provincial pension standards legislation are restricted in their maturity options. Historically, only life annuities could be purchased with funds in locked-in RRSPs. Recent changes to the rules permit you to purchase modified RRIFs, plans that are either Life Income Funds (LIFs) or Locked-in Retirement Income Funds (LRIFs). Modified RRIFs include maximum annual withdrawal restrictions that must be adhered to; these are in addition to the annual minimum withdrawal levels imposed by the Income Tax Act.

• RRSP and RRIF administration fees

RRSP and RRIF investment counselling or administration fees paid after March 5, 1996 are not deductible in computing income for tax purposes. These fees were previously deductible as long as they were paid outside of the plan.

Other expenses

Annual dues required to be paid to a professional body, a trade union or similar body are generally deductible. Office rent, salary paid to an assistant and the cost of supplies that an employee is required to pay under an employment contract may also be deductible.

If your office is part of a house or apartment that you rent, you may be able to deduct certain home office expenses, as the table below shows, as long as the required conditions are met.

Home office expenses can be deducted only up to the amount of your employment income for the year. To the extent that you cannot use the full deduction in a particular year, you may carry forward work space expenses indefinitely and deduct them from employment income in future years.

Home office expenses – employees

Deductible (if conditions are satisfied*)	Not deductible
Rent and maintenance attributable to the office. Maintenance expenses include: – fuel – light bulbs – electricity – minor repairs – cleaning materials	– capital cost allowance – mortgage interest
Commissioned sales people only may deduct a portion of these expenses: – taxes – insurance	

* Expenses are deductible only if the workplace is:
- your principal place of employment; **or**
- used by you both:
  - exclusively for the purpose of earning employment income; **and**
  - "on a regular and continuous basis" for meeting customers or other persons in the course of employment.

Reduced employee withholdings

(See page 210 – Interest-free loans to the government?)

✔ Tax Tip 11

If your taxable income will be substantially less than the amount your employer uses to calculate the tax to withhold, possibly as a result of extraordinary deductible expenses that you have incurred, write to your district taxation office requesting a reduction in the amount withheld.

50 | Employees and automobiles

The taxation of automobile benefits and expenses has always been complex. If you own your car, reasonable distance-based allowances for your costs will not be included in your income; other allowances may be. If you received a taxable allowance, you may be able to deduct some of the actual expenses you incurred.

Automobiles – taxable benefits

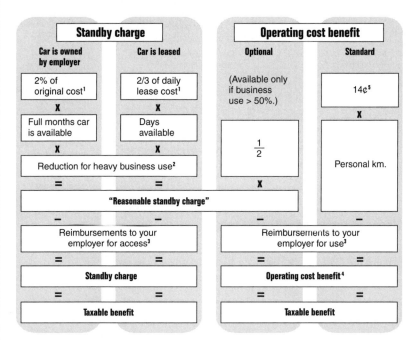

Standby charge		Operating cost benefit	
Car is owned by employer	**Car is leased**	**Optional**	**Standard**
2% of original cost[1]	2/3 of daily lease cost[1]	(Available only if business use > 50%.)	14¢[5]
X	X		X
Full months car is available	Days available	$\frac{1}{2}$	Personal km.
X	X		
Reduction for heavy business use[2]		X	
=	=	=	
"Reasonable standby charge"			
–	–	–	–
Reimbursements to your employer for access[3]		Reimbursements to your employer for use[3]	
=	=	=	=
Standby charge		Operating cost benefit[4]	
=	=	=	=
Taxable benefit		Taxable benefit	

1 Costs include GST and PST.

2 Reduction factor $= \dfrac{\text{personal kilometres}}{1{,}000 \text{ kilometres} \times \text{full months car is available}}$

(Available only if business use is at least 90% and personal kilometres average less than 1,000 per month.)

3 Any operating costs reimbursed to your employer must be paid within 45 days after the end of the year. Reimbursements in respect of standby charges must be paid in the year.

4 Considered to already include a GST benefit component.

5 11¢ for employees whose principal source of employment is selling or leasing automobiles.

If your employer provides you with an automobile (as defined in the Income Tax Act), you are considered to have received two types of taxable benefits: a standby charge (which reflects your access to the car) and an operating cost benefit (which reflects the personal portion of such expenses that are paid for by your employer).

If your employer provides you with a motor vehicle that is not an automobile, you are still considered to have received taxable benefits (i.e., a personal use benefit and an operating cost benefit), but these benefits are calculated differently than the benefits described below.

The standby charge is calculated differently depending on whether the employer owns the car or the car is leased, as the first two columns of the chart on page 50 indicate.

For purposes of calculating the standby charge, original cost and lease payments include the GST, as well as provincial sales taxes. See page 52 for an explanation of how the GST affects taxable benefits relating to automobiles.

✔ Tax Tip 12

The standby charge is calculated on the original cost of the car and does not decrease as the value of the car declines with age. After a few years, it may be cheaper to eliminate the standby charge by buying the car from your employer.

• Operating cost benefit

The federal operating cost benefit formula is simply 14¢ times total personal kilometres (as shown in the chart on page 50). The 14¢ per kilometre rate is reduced to 11¢ per kilometre for employees whose principal source of employment is selling or leasing automobiles (these rates are effective for 1997).

Alternatively, if you use the car more than 50% for employment purposes, you can elect to calculate the benefit as half of the standby charge, less any amounts you reimbursed to your employer.

The operating cost benefit is considered to include a GST component.

✔ Tax Tip 13

If your personal use is less than 50% of the total use and you prefer the alternative operating cost benefit calculation, you must notify your employer in writing before the end of the year.

✔ Tax Tip 14

Minimize your personal use of an employer-provided automobile to reduce your operating cost benefit, and in some cases your standby charge benefit. There may be an advantage if you use your own car for personal purposes.

✔ Tax Tip 15

Reimburse your employer for all personal use operating expenses within 45 days after the year-end (i.e., by February 14) to eliminate your operating cost benefit. In particular, if your employer has paid only a small portion of the operating expenses, consider repaying these amounts before the February 14 deadline so that you will not have a taxable benefit of 14¢ per personal-use kilometre for the entire year.

Tax planning measures may be available to reduce or avoid your operating cost benefit. Your arrangements should be evaluated to identify tax planning opportunities for reducing the benefit.

• Employer-provided automobiles and the GST

If your employer owns the car you use for business purposes, you must include in your income a standby charge based on the actual cost of the automobile, including GST and provincial sales tax (PST).

For example, the table on page 53 shows how the total standby charge added to your T4 slip is calculated.

The same applies to the standby charge for an automobile that is leased: the taxable benefit on a leased automobile must reflect two-thirds of the GST that would be applicable to the lease cost.

	Cost of car	GST*	PST** (assumed 8%)	Total
Components of cost	$25,000	$25,000 x 7% = $1,750	$25,000 x 8% = $2,000	**$28,750**
Standby charge factor	2% x 12 months = 24%			
Components of standby charge	$6,000	$420	$480	**$6,900**

* The GST component must be added to the standby charge even if your employer did not pay GST on the purchase or lease cost of the vehicle.

** In some provinces, PST will be assessed on the GST as well as on the cost of the car.

The amount of any operating cost benefit for an automobile already reflects an estimate of the GST your employer has paid on personal operating expenses.

For purposes of calculating the GST portion of the standby charge benefit, any reimbursement payment that you made to your employer in respect of the benefit is not to be taken into account.

Employee automobile expenses

If you use your own car in carrying out your employment duties, you will have a number of decisions to make. You will have to determine whether any amount you receive from your employer constitutes a reimbursement or an allowance; the tax consequences are different. You will then have to determine whether you are entitled to deduct any car expenses, and then how much.

• Reimbursements

A reimbursement is an amount that you receive from your employer to repay you for amounts (including GST) that you spent on your employer's business. Generally, you do not have to pay tax on a reimbursement unless it is a payment for personal expenses. An allowance, on the other hand, is a payment that you receive from your employer in addition to your salary and wages and that you need not account for. Although the rules dealing with whether or not an allowance has to be included in your income are quite specific, some latitude is nonetheless permitted in applying them.

• Allowances

Essentially, an allowance must be reasonable for it not to be taxable to an employee. An automobile allowance is considered reasonable only if it is computed using an appropriate per kilometre rate that is applied to business driving by an employee. If you receive an allowance from your employer that is solely distance-based, it will ordinarily be considered reasonable, and would not be taxable to you. Accordingly, your employer would not be required to withhold tax in respect of the allowance paid.

If the allowance is determined on another basis, it will not be considered to be reasonable and, therefore, will be taxable to you and subject to withholding at source. A taxable car allowance is not subject to GST. Because the allowance is included in your income, you may be able to claim reasonable business-related expenses.

If the allowance is distance-based and would otherwise be considered to be reasonable, but you believe that the allowance you receive is not reasonable because your business-related expenses exceed the amount of the allowance, you may choose to add the allowance to your income and claim reasonable business-related expenses. The onus is on you, however, to make this decision.

• Deducting automobile expenses

What's the bottom line? You may be permitted to deduct reasonable automobile expenses that you are required to incur in travelling to carry out your employment duties, so long as you are not reimbursed for the expenses and your employer does not pay you an automobile travelling allowance that was excluded from your income. You may deduct a portion of operating expenses, prorated according to the proportion that the distance driven in the course of employment is of the total distance driven. You are also entitled to a prorated portion of capital cost allowance (CCA), as well as leasing costs or interest on funds borrowed to buy the car, subject to certain limits.

If you deduct business-related car expenses on your personal tax return and your employer is a GST registrant, you may be eligible to apply for a rebate of the GST you paid. The rebate is not available if you choose to include an otherwise reasonable tax-free allowance in your income in order to claim business-related expenses.

	Maximum deduction*
Capital cost allowance (CCA) base	$25,000**
Monthly interest charges	$250
Monthly lease payments***	$550**

* For automobiles acquired or leases entered into after 1996.

** Plus GST and PST on $25,000 and $550.

*** Or lesser amount (determined by formula) for certain luxury vehicles.

✔ Tax Tip 16

If you have two cars, consider using one exclusively for business and the other for personal use, to simplify record-keeping.

Loss of employment

In today's economic environment, loss of employment is a challenge that more and more people have to deal with.

In a plant closure, which may take place over a period of months or even a year or more, employees may be in a position to plan for coping with expenses, to rearrange payment schedules for recurring obligations such as mortgages, and to seek other employment without urgency. When termination is unanticipated, however, perhaps because of downsizing or the takeover of an employer by another corporation, employees may find themselves in a difficult predicament, with the need to act quickly.

Little anyone does or says can mitigate the effect of loss of employment. However, you should consider certain things in the unfortunate event that you find yourself without work.

Working with your employer is the first step in the process. Although keeping costs down is a major concern, many of today's more enlightened employers are also concerned with providing employees with tax-effective severance arrangements that do not result in an additional burden to the employer.

Preparing a realistic budget and cash flow schedule with your spouse (and possibly other family members) is another critical element in this process. You need to determine exactly how much money you expect to be coming in and for how long, what your expenses are, which expenses you can defer and which you can cut entirely. If you anticipate a prolonged period of unemployment, don't wait until a major payment is due to the bank, for example, to let them know that you are unemployed. Schedule an appointment with your banker as soon as possible and try to rearrange your payment terms.

Your re-employment counsellor (see page 58) should also be able to give you some suggestions on how to manage your financial position while you are looking for work.

The severance package

• Retiring allowances

The official term "retiring allowance" is a little inaccurate. The definition encompasses a wide range of payments not all of which relate to retirement. A retiring allowance is an amount that you receive:

- upon or after retirement from an office or employment in recognition of long service; or

- in respect of a loss of an office or employment whether or not it was received on account or in lieu of payment of damages, or pursuant to a court order or judgment.

Your severance package may be determined by reference to your current remuneration, including benefits. Although this may seem logical, the way in which your "golden parachute" is structured may prohibit you from making special tax-effective transfers to your RRSP or RPP (see below). Even though you no longer actually report for work, your severance arrangement may provide that in addition to amounts paid to you on termination, certain benefits of employment will also continue for a specified period. If pension accruals continue, Revenue Canada may consider the payments you receive from your former employer to be employment income and not retiring allowances. The greater the extent to which benefits continue, the greater the risk that Revenue Canada will characterize the payments as salary. Consequently, you may not be eligible to transfer these amounts to your RRSP or RPP.

• Transfer to RRSP or RPP

The provisions allowing for the tax-free transfer of retiring allowances to an RRSP are being phased out. You may, however, continue to transfer up to $2,000 per year of service before 1996. There is no change to the rule that allows you to transfer up to $1,500 per year of service before 1989 in which you did not have a vested interest in contributions made by your employer to either a DPSP or an RPP.

Transferring as much as you are able to your RRSP or RPP is a tax-effective strategy. You must also consider your cash flow requirements, however. If you anticipate a prolonged period of unemployment, you may need to reduce the amount of retiring allowance to be transferred to your RRSP or RPP.

• RPPs

If you participate in your employer's RPP, you will have to determine what choices you have regarding contributions that you and your employer have made to your plan. If you are over a specified age and/or have a certain number of years of service with your employer, you may not be able to get at funds in your RPP because they are "locked-in." If that is the case, you may have to wait until you are eligible to receive a retirement pension out of the plan, or you may only be able to transfer the funds directly into a locked-in RRSP or to your new employer's RPP if that plan provides for such transfers.

If your RPP is not locked-in, you may transfer the funds to your RRSP. If this transfer is done directly, then you need not suffer any withholding tax. On the other hand, if you need the funds immediately, your employer will have to withhold tax from the amounts to be paid to you and you will also have to include the amounts in your income for tax purposes in the year you receive them. Of course, any tax withheld at source will be credited to you as a payment of tax.

You should contact your pension plan administrator for details about your plan and the options you have for the funds accumulated in the plan.

• Re-employment counselling/executive search services
As part of your severance package, your employer may provide you with executive search services or the services of a professional re-employment counsellor. Services of this nature that your employer either provides or pays for are not a taxable benefit to you.

✔ Tax Tip 17
When negotiating your severance package, consider having your employer include re-employment counselling or executive search services. The counselling is generally very helpful, and the considerable cost that your employer would incur to provide you with the service is a tax-free benefit to you.

What if you disagree?

• Wrongful dismissal
The definition of retiring allowance is sufficiently broad to include damage awards made by a court in an action for wrongful dismissal.

Accordingly, unless the facts indicate otherwise, an award for damages must be included in your income in the year you receive it.

Awards for damages to compensate for pain and suffering and mental distress, however, may be non-taxable receipts, depending on the facts and circumstances of the particular case. If you have sued your employer for wrongful dismissal and the court has awarded you damages, you should discuss the tax implications with your professional advisor.

• Legal expenses

You may generally deduct legal fees paid to collect or establish a right to salary or wages that are owed to you by your employer or former employer. Legal fees include amounts spent on negotiating your severance package as well as fees for litigation that becomes necessary.

Although amounts that you receive as retiring allowances are specifically excluded from the definition of salary and wages, you may deduct legal expenses associated with retiring allowances, but with a limitation. The deduction is limited to the amount of the retiring allowance actually received in the taxation year that you did not transfer to your RPP or RRSP. For example, if your retiring allowance is $20,000, you transfer $15,000 to an RRSP and your legal expenses are $6,000, you may deduct only $5,000 of legal expenses.

Retiring allowances may be paid over a period of time. Legal expenses may be deducted only to the extent of retiring allowances that you actually receive, but Revenue Canada permits you to deduct legal expenses that you incur to collect retiring allowances over a seven-year period. This means that you can deduct a portion of your legal expenses against the retiring allowances that you receive each year in the carryforward period.

Continuity of benefits

• Loss of disability, medical, dental benefits etc.

Many employers provide attractive benefit packages, such as dental benefits for the employee and his or her family members, medical and travel insurance and disability insurance. Although some severance packages may provide that these benefits continue for a short period after employment ceases, you should evaluate how you will replace these important elements of your compensation package and how much it will cost you to either get insurance coverage yourself, or to pay for services such as dental care out of your own pocket. Of course, if you have other employment lined up, this may not be a concern. If you anticipate a long period of unemployment, however, you should decide which types of expenses can be deferred and which services need to be replaced immediately.

Moving expenses

You may have to relocate to find new employment. If you move to a place in Canada that is at least 40 kilometres closer to your new work location than your old residence was, you may claim eligible moving expenses, to the extent that they are not reimbursed to you by your new employer. You may deduct moving expenses only from income earned in your new capacity. If you move close to the end of the year, you may not have sufficient earnings against which to deduct moving expenses. In these circumstances, you may carry forward your moving expenses and deduct them the following year against income from your new employment.

Employees on temporary assignment

Many employee moves are only temporary. Employees may be moved for various reasons: to a head office for a one- or two-year assignment, to fill a temporarily vacant position, to open a new office or even to carry out a short-term assignment in a desirable location as a perquisite. A temporary period can be anywhere from a few weeks or months to five years.

One of the most important tax issues for employees either coming into or leaving Canada on a temporary assignment is their residency status during the period. Residence is a question of fact; the term "resident" is not defined in Canada's Income Tax Act. The courts have held that an individual is resident in Canada for tax purposes if Canada is the place where he or she, in the settled routine of life, regularly, normally or customarily lives.

Unless the circumstances suggest otherwise, an individual who is absent from Canada for two years or longer is generally considered a non-resident. Revenue Canada has recently been questioning the position taken by taxpayers who are out of the country for two or more years, but who have an intention to return – for example, employees on temporary assignment who are required under their employment contracts to return to Canada once their assignments are over. Revenue Canada has apparently accepted the non-residency status of such individuals, as long as all ties with Canada have clearly been severed during the non-residency period. Problems have arisen, however, when individuals have left homes in Canada that are vacant during their absence. Revenue Canada takes the position that residential ties with Canada have not been severed if a vacant home is available to the individual. Further, a home need not actually be vacant. A dwelling is generally considered to be available if it is leased to a related person, or to an unrelated person if the lease can be terminated with less than three months' notice.

✔ Tax Tip 18

If you are planning to be out of the country on assignment for two or more years, ensure that you have severed all ties with Canada. If you own a home and do not plan to sell it, consider renting it out to an unrelated person. The lease should stipulate that a minimum of three months' notice is required for termination.

Although the two-year rule is one that Revenue Canada generally applies, you may be able to argue that you are a non-resident of

Canada for a period of less than two years if the facts of the particular situation support that conclusion. For example, assume that you leave Canada to take up an assignment that you fully expect to extend beyond two years and you carefully sever all residential ties with Canada. Ten months into your contract, it is terminated for business reasons and you must return to Canada. The court found in favour of a taxpayer in a similar situation; the individual was found to have been a non-resident of Canada for a period less than two years.

✔ Tax Tip 19

If you are to leave Canada on a temporary assignment, discuss the situation with your professional advisor well in advance of your departure. There is a litany of steps you should take to ensure that you have in fact severed your ties with Canada. Do not let your tax planning strategies fail because Revenue Canada considers a few seemingly minor details (which you neglected) to preserve your ties with Canada.

An individual may be deemed to be a resident of Canada even though he or she is not actually a resident. Generally, this means that an individual is resident elsewhere. One of the most common types of deemed resident is a "sojourner." You are a sojourner if you are in Canada for periods totalling 183 days or more in a year. (The 183 figure comes from $365/2 = 182.5$.) If this is the case, you will be considered a resident of Canada for the whole year and will be taxed on your worldwide income. This rule is applied year by year. For example, suppose you live and work in Seattle. In 1997 you spend 192 days in Canada working on a project for your employer. While in Canada, you live in a hotel. You will be considered a deemed resident of Canada in 1997 and will be subject to tax on your worldwide income. In 1998, you continue working on your project, but spend only 110 days in Canada. In 1998, you will not be deemed to be a resident of Canada. You will, of course, be subject to Canadian tax on the income you earn performing employment duties in Canada.

A sojourner is different from an individual who actually takes up residence in Canada, whether or not the individual is present for 183 or more days in the year.

Canada has bilateral income tax treaties with many countries. When an individual appears to be a resident of Canada and another country, the treaties generally provide assistance through tie-breaker rules.

Depending on the circumstances, an individual's residency status and the time residence is taken up may be difficult to ascertain. A discussion with your professional tax advisor well in advance of any move into or out of Canada is strongly recommended.

In the comments below, it is assumed that employees temporarily in Canada are non-residents of Canada, and that employees on temporary assignment outside Canada remain Canadian residents throughout the period spent abroad.

Temporary assignments in Canada

If you are a non-resident of Canada, and you were employed in Canada at any time in the year or in a previous year, you will generally be subject to Canadian tax on your employment income and will be required to file a Canadian income tax return (and a Québec income tax return, if applicable). Depending on your country of residence, your employment income earned in Canada will probably be subject to tax in your home country as well.

The extent to which you will be able to obtain relief from double taxation will depend on whether or not foreign taxes are creditable against the income taxes levied under the laws of your country of residence, or whether Canada and your home country have a bilateral tax agreement.

The treaty rules regarding dependent personal services may provide relief from double taxation to individuals on international assignments. Generally, for remuneration received by individuals temporarily employed in Canada to be taxable in their home country only, the individuals must be present in Canada for less than 183 days and the remuneration must be paid by an employer that neither is a resident of Canada nor has a permanent establishment here. In addition, certain treaties set out a threshold amount of remuneration below which the host country (i.e., Canada) will not impose tax.

⊕ Temporary assignments outside Canada

The courts have held that for tax purposes everyone must be resident somewhere and that an individual can be resident in more than one place at the same time. If a resident of Canada goes abroad, but does not establish a permanent residence elsewhere, the presumption is that he or she remains a resident of Canada. Also, the fact that an individual establishes a permanent residence abroad does not by itself make the individual a non-resident of Canada. In some situations, an individual is resident in Canada and, at the same time, resident in another country according to its laws. Any tax convention or agreement that Canada may have with the other country should help to resolve the problem.

A resident of Canada is taxed on his or her worldwide income. Accordingly, employment income earned during an assignment abroad will be subject to Canadian tax. The same income, however, may be taxable in the foreign jurisdiction as well. Relief from double taxation will generally be available through either a tax treaty between Canada and the foreign country, or the Canadian foreign tax credit provisions or a combination of the two.

✔ Tax Tip 20

If you are a Canadian resident during 1997 and have been or will be employed abroad for more than six consecutive months that begins before the end of the year, you may be entitled to a tax credit designed to limit your Canadian tax liability. Generally, you must be employed by a Canadian resident, or a foreign affiliate of a Canadian resident, in connection with the exploration for or the exploitation of petroleum, natural gas, minerals or similar resources, or a construction, installation, agricultural or engineering activity. The credit, calculated annually, is determined by a formula that provides a tax reduction for overseas employment income that is less than $100,000.

✔ Tax Tip 21

If you are considering a temporary assignment, and your employer has a tax protection or a tax equalization policy, you should become fully aware of the implications of the policy. Determine if you will be protected or equalized on employment-related income only, or on some or all of your income that is not related to your employment. This may be critical if you are earning significant non-employment income.

Giving up Canadian residence

Your departure from Canada may constitute giving up Canadian residence. If so, current rules deem you to have disposed of all of your capital property (except taxable Canadian property, defined below) at its fair market value at that date. That makes you subject to Canadian tax on any capital gains. See page 68 for a discussion of proposed new Canadian emigration rules.

✔ Tax Tip 22

If you have taxable Canadian property that is a share of a QSBC (qualifying small business corporation) or a qualified farm property and you have not used the enhanced $400,000 capital gains exemption, consider selling such properties with accrued capital gains to your spouse. In this way, you can use your enhanced capital gains exemption. Do this before leaving Canada; if you wait until you have terminated Canadian residence, any capital gain will be subject to tax in Canada and you will not be able to shelter any of it with the enhanced capital gains exemption.

You will be required to file a part-year Canadian income tax return in the year in which you leave Canada. Ordinarily, you will report your worldwide income up to your date of departure. Additional Canadian tax liabilities could arise if you continue to carry on business or continue to be employed in Canada after you move away.

Canada's rules relating to a principal residence differ from those of other countries. If you intend to sell your home, your professional advisor can help you decide if you should dispose of it before or after you move. If you wish to rent out your home while you are away, you will be deemed to have disposed of it for proceeds equal to its fair market value, both when you convert your home to a rental property and when you reoccupy it as your principal residence. You may defer tax that would otherwise be payable on a capital gain arising as a result of the deemed disposition rules by electing for there to be no change in the use of your principal residence. Whether this election benefits you will depend on how long you will be outside Canada and if you intend to return.

Before leaving Canada, you should discuss with your professional tax advisor the tax implications of: exercising your Canadian stock options; receiving payments from your former employer after you have left Canada in respect of services rendered in Canada; interest earned in your RRSP etc. The timing of your move will also be critical. The best date will depend on the taxation year of the foreign country as well as on how its tax rates compare with those in Canada.

Taking up Canadian residence

If you are taking up residence in Canada, you will generally be deemed to have acquired all of your capital property (except taxable Canadian property, defined on page 68) at its fair market value on the date you take up residence. Any gain or loss on a subsequent disposition of that property will be calculated with reference to this deemed cost.

In the year in which you take up residence, you will be required to file a part-year income tax return. In that return, you report your world income from the date of taking up residence in Canada, and certain types of income that you received during the part of the year when you were not a Canadian resident. In respect of your non-resident period, you must include: income from business carried on in Canada; income from employment duties performed in Canada; and capital gains realized on the disposition of taxable Canadian property (defined on page 68).

✔ Tax Tip 23

Before taking up Canadian residence, ensure that you and your professional tax advisor have discussed the implications of the types of income you may be receiving both before and after entering Canada, as well as the timing of the receipt of various types of income. In particular, you should review any foreign incentive compensation that might be payable to you. Depending on the circumstances, you might want to arrange to receive income such as bonuses, stock options and payments from profit sharing plans prior to entering Canada.

If you will be selling your foreign residence and acquiring a Canadian one, you will probably benefit more if you sell the former before taking up Canadian residence. If you intend to rent out your foreign home, you will be subject to tax in Canada on the net rental income. If you will also be subject to tax on rental income in your "home" country, you should evaluate the relative benefits of renting out your home to leaving it vacant or even disposing of it.

Also consider the timing of your arrival in Canada. The best date will depend on your tax liabilities in both the country you are leaving and in Canada. Your professional advisor can help you make a detailed estimate.

Taxable Canadian property

Taxable Canadian property includes, among other things:

- real property situated in Canada;
- capital property used in carrying on business in Canada;
- shares of a corporation resident in Canada that is not listed on a prescribed stock exchange (Canadian or foreign);
- shares of a corporation resident Canada that is listed on a prescribed stock exchange if, at any time during the five years immediately preceding a disposition of the shares, the non-resident and other non-arm's length persons held 25% or more of the issued shares of any class of the capital stock of the corporation; and
- shares of a non-resident corporation if certain Canadian content tests are met.

Proposed new emigration rules

Major changes to the income tax rules that apply to individuals leaving Canada were announced in the fall of 1996. Although the measures were still in draft form when *Personal Tax Strategy* was written, once passed, they will apply to departures from Canada after October 1, 1996. Further, information reporting will be required for taxation years after 1995.

Under current rules, a taxpayer who ceases to be a resident of Canada is generally deemed to have disposed of all property and reacquired it at fair market value. This triggers any gains or losses that have accrued up to the date of departure. Taxable Canadian property (defined in the section above), is excepted from the deemed disposition rule. Instead, taxable Canadian property is subject to tax on the full amount of any gains when the property is actually disposed of.

Individuals were permitted to make an election that treated all property as taxable Canadian property as long as acceptable security was provided to Revenue Canada equal to the amount of tax that would otherwise have been payable on the deemed disposition. Careful planning could have resulted in some attractive tax advantages. Although the new rules are still proposed, our understanding is that Revenue Canada will no longer accept such elections and indeed, is proceeding on the basis that passage of the rules is a mere formality.

What does all this mean to you? Individuals who leave Canada after October 1, 1996 will have to calculate their tax as though they had disposed of all their property, other than Canadian real estate, Canadian business property, pension and other rights and stock options. The ability to elect out of the deemed disposition rules has been eliminated. Accordingly, if you depart Canada after October 1, 1996, you will have to pay the tax on any accrued capital gains immediately, or provide the tax authorities with sufficient security for paying it at a later date.

The proposals also provide for an information return that requires a listing of each property owned by an individual at the time Canadian residency ceases. The return will have to be filed by any individual who left Canada after 1995. Personal-use property (clothing, household goods and cars, for example) with a fair market value of $10,000 is excluded. Further, filing of the return is not required if the fair market value of all of your property is less than $25,000.

⚜ **Québec**

If you are a resident in Québec, the comments above generally apply to Québec taxes. However, the following exceptions should be noted:

• **Gain Sharing Plan**

Amounts received by an employee of certain manufacturing corporations under a qualifying gain sharing plan may be deducted in the calculation of Québec taxable income to a maximum of $3,000 per year. A cumulative maximum of $6,000 applies for the five-year period starting in the year of registration of the first plan in which the employee participates.

The plan must have been registered by the Minister of Revenue before January 1, 1996.

• **Tax treatment of certain clothing allowances**

A reasonable allowance given to an employee for the acquisition or upkeep of distinctive clothing required under the employment contract will not be included in income.

Québec Sales Tax

• **Sales tax rate**

The sales tax rate applicable to properties, services and immovables is 6.5% and will be increased to 7.5% as of January 1, 1998. The rates for insurance premiums are 5% or 9%.

• **Property or services acquired in the course of employment**

An individual who is an employee of a registrant or a member of a registrant partnership can claim a rebate of the QST paid in regard to properties or services acquired in the course of his or her employment, if the expense relating to the acquisition is deductible in calculating his or her income. This includes property or services on which the input tax refunds used to be restricted, such as the purchase or rental of an automobile, fuel, telephone services, electricity and meals and entertainment, only if the acquisition is after August 1, 1995 or if the lease contract was entered into after that date.

• QST on taxable benefits
Businesses are required to add QST on the amount of employee and shareholder taxable benefits that are considered QST taxable.

• Purchase of a new home
A rebate equal to 36% of the QST paid on the purchase of a new home costing $175,000 or less is available. A decreasing rebate is also granted on a house costing between $175,000 and $200,000.

Allowance for moving expenses

Starting in 1997, an allowance paid to an employee for moving expenses and relating to an assignment requested by an employer may, in certain circumstances, not be taxable if it does not exceed an amount equivalent to two weeks of the employee's salary.

Refundable child care tax credit

A refundable tax credit for child care expenses is equal to a percentage of the amount paid during the year for child care, to a maximum of $5,000 of expenses per child. The rate of tax credit is based on net family income, as indicated in the table following. The credit has generally to be claimed by the spouse who has the lowest earned income.

A couple will still be eligible to claim child care expenses even if one spouse operates a business generating losses or no income. For this purpose, the amount of child care expenses claimed by the taxpayer with the higher income will be restricted to $150 per child under age seven or who suffers from an impairment, and $90 for other eligible children, multiplied by the number of weeks in the year the taxpayer's spouse operates a business.

	From	To	Tax credit as a % of eligible expenses
Net family income	$0	$10,000	From 75% to 44%
	$10,000	$34,000	40%
	$34,000	$48,000	From 39% to 27%
	$48,000	∞	26.4%

The age limit of a child entitling a taxpayer to the tax credit for child care expenses is 16.

Certain care-givers are required to file information slips (Relevé 24) with Revenue Québec. These information slips will indicate the amount paid for child care expenses and will have to be filed with the tax return of the individual claiming the refundable tax credit for child care expenses.

The tax legislation will be amended to allow heads of single-parent families who are pursuing full-time studies to claim the refundable tax credit for child care expenses, starting in 1996. This measure will also apply to couples in which both spouses are full-time students.

Tuition fees

In 1997, the deduction for tuition fees becomes a 20% non-refundable tax credit (23% in 1998). Tuition fees eligible for the tax credit can be carried forward indefinitely to a year following the year in which they are paid. The definition of eligible tuition fees will be broadened to include specific ancillary fees.

A person upon whom the student is dependent may increase his or her dependent child credit if the student is registered full-time in a post-secondary institution. The person requesting the credit must file form Relevé 8 with his or her Québec income tax return.

Health services fund contribution

Employers pay a health services tax based on employment earnings of their employees. The health services tax also applies to individuals for a contribution limited to $1,000. The tax is paid by individuals resident in Québec on December 31 as part of their overall income tax bill.

The health services tax is payable on notional "total income," including net business income, investment income, pension or retirement income and taxable capital gains. Excluded from the calculation are those items already subject to the employer health tax (e.g., salary or wages), as well as the gross-up on dividends from Canadian corporations, amounts received as Old Age Security benefits, alimony and social security benefits.

Certain deductions are permitted in arriving at "total income," including amounts subject to the federal clawback, expenditures incurred to earn investment income, alimony payments and a general exemption of $5,000.

This contribution entitles a taxpayer to a 20% non-refundable tax credit.

Temporary assignments in Québec

If you are a non-resident of Canada and were employed in Québec at any time in the year or in a previous year, you will generally be subject to Québec tax on your employment income and will be required to file a Québec income tax return.

Temporary assignments outside Canada

If you are a Canadian resident residing in Québec during 1997 and have been or will be employed abroad for 30 consecutive days or more beginning in the year or the preceding year, you may be allowed a deduction in computing taxable income equal to all or part of the employment income earned abroad. A full deduction is available if you are abroad for 12 periods of 30 consecutive days or more. This deduction is available for the same types of employers and activities as those mentioned in this chapter for the federal overseas employment tax credit (see page 64). In addition, the following activities are eligible for this deduction:

- the setting up of an automated office system, data processing system or telephone data system or similar system, if that activity is the principal purpose of the contract;

- scientific or technical services; and

- management or administration related to an activity covered by the deduction for workers outside Québec.

A Québec Court of Appeal decision concluded that in calculating the deduction for an employee working abroad, employment with different employers could be aggregated. This decision is contrary to Revenue Québec's administrative policy of calculating separately each job held with a designated employer. Subject to certain transitional measures, Québec legislation accommodates the effect of this decision.

Québec legislation will also be modified to prevent interposing a Canadian corporation between a foreign employer and a Canadian resident to enable the employee to gain access to the tax deduction for employees working abroad.

Taxable Québec property

Québec has rules similar to those applicable to taxable Canadian property, but they apply only to property situated in Québec that is referred to as "taxable Québec property."

An exception to the general rule is that Québec will remit income tax of an individual who is a non-resident of Canada, does not do business in Canada, and who realizes a capital gain on the sale of shares of a corporation resident in Québec, other than a public corporation. The taxpayer, however, will pay the 52% federal non-resident surtax on basic federal tax.

Québec tax incentives

• Tax holiday for employees of an international financial centre (IFC)

A two-year tax holiday may be granted to foreign employees of an IFC specializing in the field of international financial transactions. In addition, following this two-year period, under certain conditions, these employees may be eligible for an income tax exemption on allowances paid to them, up to a maximum of 50% of their basic eligible salary.

• Tax exemption for employees of international organizations

Employees of international non-governmental organizations that operate in Québec and have signed an accord with the Québec government may be totally exempt from paying income tax if they are not Canadian citizens and if they are permanent residents.

• Tax holiday for foreign researchers

To further encourage research and development specialists to come to Québec, a two-year tax holiday is granted to foreign researchers on their employment income.

• Tax holiday for foreign trainers in an Information Technology Development Centre (ITDC)

The tax legislation will be modified to introduce a deduction for foreign trainers employed by a corporation carrying on a business in an information technology development centre (ITDC), similar to the deduction applicable to foreign researchers, for wages paid to them by the corporation for a period of two years.

Other Québec exceptions

In Québec, receipts for moving expenses and child care expenses must be filed with the tax return.

For salaried employees paid on commission, expenses, which may not be deducted in excess of any commissions paid, must be reduced by an amount not exceeding the lesser of $750 and 6% of total compensation (salary plus commissions).

An individual, other than a trust, has the choice of excluding from his or her income, in the year in which he or she receives it, a retroactive payment of at least $300. Retroactive payments include employment income received as the result of a court judgment or an agreement between parties in judicial proceedings or alimony arrears. This choice will enable individuals to pay any tax related to a retroactive payment as if it had been received in the years to which it applied. This measure applies to amounts received after December 31, 1993.

Québec generally follows the terms of the tax treaties signed by Canada regarding amounts and types of payments that may be excluded from income. The only separate tax treaty that Québec has entered into is with France.

Limitation on meal and entertainment expenses

It was announced that the proposed limitation to 1% of a taxpayer's gross commissions for the year on expenditures for meals and entertainment incurred by an employee who is a commissioned salesperson is suspended. (See page 97 for more details.)

3 Owners/Managers

3 Owners/Managers

What's new?

- No new measures of any significance in the last year affect the tax treatment of owners/managers.

Although the term "owner/manager" is not found in the Income Tax Act, it is a convenient way of referring to anybody who owns and runs a business. This chapter deals first with unincorporated businesses, and then with private companies.

Unincorporated businesses

Carrying on business

The distinction between income from a business and income from employment or from investments is important. If you are indeed in business, you will be able to deduct reasonable business expenses not deductible by an employee or an investor.

For tax purposes, a business includes a profession, calling, trade, manufacture and just about anything else that could possibly be considered a business. Being employed or holding an office, however, is not a business.

If you are self-employed, i.e., you are not an employee and you have not formed a corporation through which you will provide your services, then you must determine whether you are in business. This will not generally pose a problem if you are earning your living from the activity. Generally, you must have a reasonable expectation of profit from the activity for it to be considered a business, and you must pursue the activity in a manner likely to bring you a profit. Although you need not produce a profit immediately, or even have a history of making profits, you must have a reasonable chance of doing so. A recent court case that involves reasonable expectation of profit is outlined on page 13.

An individual can have more than one business, in which case the profits of each must be calculated separately.

Employed versus self-employed

Whether you are employed or self-employed is not always easy to determine. The answer will depend on your particular circumstances, and often boils down to how much control the person paying for your services exercises over your work. For example, if the payer controls your work hours, requires you to work on his or her premises and furnishes you with all the equipment, supplies and office help that you need, you likely would still be considered an employee in the eyes of Revenue Canada. If you provide services to a number of different parties and you determine the nature and degree of service and are in a position to prioritize their demands, you are likely self-employed. Other tests include whether you provide your own tools, whether you have an opportunity for profit and whether you have a risk of loss.

Partnerships

An unincorporated business can be carried on by one person as a proprietorship or by several as a partnership. Each partner is taxed on his or her share of the partnership income in essentially the same way as a proprietor. Based on a predetermined formula, the partnership computes the income that is allocated to each partner. A partner reports the allocated share and deducts expenses incurred personally, such as interest and automobile expenses, to determine his or her net income from the business.

Partnerships with more than five partners are required to file annual financial information. The partnership provides reporting slips to partners for inclusion in their own returns.

✔ Tax Tip 24

A husband and wife, or other family members, can carry on a
business through a partnership. It is generally advisable to have
a written partnership agreement to support the profit-sharing
formula and the basis of contributions to the business in the
event that Revenue Canada raises questions.

Professionals

Professionals may carry on business as sole proprietors, partners or,
depending on the legislation and the rules of the professional bod-
ies, through corporations. Designated professionals (accountants,
chiropractors, dentists, lawyers, medical doctors and veterinarians) are
permitted to elect to exclude the value of work in progress from
income. If they do not make the election, they follow the normal
accrual rules and report income as it is earned.

Instalments

A self-employed individual earning business or professional income
must pay tax directly to Revenue Canada (and Revenue Québec).
Quarterly instalments of tax are due as follows:

No deadlines		Deadline on 15th of month
January	February	**March**
April	May	**June**
July	August	**September**
October	November	**December**

The prescribed rate of interest charged during a calendar quarter
on late or deficient payments of tax is set each quarter. The table
shows the most recent prescribed rates:

Prescribed rate*				
	Other than Québec		Québec	
	General	Owed to Taxpayer	General	Owed to Taxpayer
Quarter of 1997 1st	8%	6%	8%	4.5%
2nd	7%	5%		
3rd	8%	6%		3.25%
4th				

* The rate for deemed interest on employee and shareholder loans is lower than the rates shown (see page 25).

Additional penalties may also be imposed on late or deficient tax instalments if interest in excess of $1,000 is owing.

Calendar year-end requirement

Rules designed to curtail the often significant income deferral opportunities that were achieved by allowing the selection of off-calendar taxation periods became effective for fiscal periods that began after 1994. They require that sole proprietorships, certain partnerships and professional corporations that are members of a partnership report income on a calendar year basis. The rules do provide for some transitional relief, however: the additional 1995 income that would otherwise have been taxed in 1995 may be brought into income via a reserve mechanism over ten years (effectively 5% of the additional income the first year, 10% for each of the next eight years and 15% for the final year).

Taxpayers who cease a particular business but carry on a "similar" business continue to be eligible for the transitional relief. For example, a partner in a law firm who leaves to join another law practice after 1995 will continue to be eligible for transitional relief on his or her 1995 income (assuming that the law practice carries on a similar business).

The ten-year transitional relief reserve is also available to partners who retired in 1995 or who will retire sometime before 2005, as well as existing retired partners who had to report two periods of partnership income as a result of the new legislation.

Professional corporations – corporations that carry on the professional practice of an accountant, dentist, lawyer, medical doctor, veterinarian or chiropractor – that are not members of a partnership are excluded from the calendar year-end requirement.

To accommodate the accounting and reporting requirements for the calendar year-end rules, the deadline for filing income tax returns for individuals with business income from a sole proprietorship or partnership is June 15 (rather than the usual April 30 deadline).

✔ Tax Tip 25

If you are an annual filer for GST purposes and are affected by the rules requiring that you adopt a calendar year for income tax purposes for your business, you will also report GST on a calendar year basis. The GST filing due date for annual filers with a calendar year end is June 15 of the following year. Any net tax owing is due by April 30.

• The alternative method

If you have valid, non-tax reasons for having an off-calendar year-end (for example, because of a natural business cycle or ease of administration), you may be permitted to retain your normal reporting period. You will, however, be required to adjust your earnings to a calendar year basis for tax purposes. The alternative income method may or may not achieve the most favourable results; each situation must be evaluated separately.

Eligible taxpayers may retain off-calendar year fiscal ends if an election adopting an alternative method of calculating income is filed with Revenue Canada. Eligible taxpayers are individuals, and partnerships of which all the members are individuals who are not members of other partnerships.

If income from your business is constant from year to year and earned evenly throughout the year, there will ordinarily be no significant differences between the calendar year calculation and alternative method. If you do not earn your income evenly throughout the year or year by year, the choice between the alternative and calendar year methods becomes more difficult.

If you launched a new business after 1994, or if you are a new partner admitted to a partnership after the end of the fiscal period that ends in the calendar year, under the alternative method you will have no income inclusion in respect of the first year of business. This occurs because the income inclusion under the alternative method is based on the results of the fiscal period that ends in that calendar year. In the first year of business, there are no previous results to extrapolate. Unlike the mechanics of the calendar year method that required the inclusion of two periods of income in 1995 (offset by the reserve), the catch-up occurs in an individual's second year under the alternative method.

If your other sources of income are not significant, it might be advantageous to have at least some part of the income earned in the first year taxed in that year (as opposed to the second year). The rules contain a provision that allows you to designate any amount of income (up to the amount of business or partnership income earned in your first calendar year) in your tax return for the calendar year in which you become a partner or begin a business. This flexibility allows you to make effective use of the lower, graduated rates of tax for two years rather than one. You can also continue to be eligible to contribute to your RRSP, because your contribution is based on your earned income of the preceding year. A caveat, however, is that if you choose to have some income taxed in the first year of your business, your instalment base for the following year will be that much higher.

✔ Tax Tip 26

Choosing the alternative method does offer an element of flexibility. If you are eligible to elect this method, you can request a change to a calendar year-end basis some time down the road.

84

Once this is done, however, you won't be able to switch back to an off-calendar year-end.

This election is effectively for accounting and financial reporting purposes only. For tax purposes, the reported income will have to be adjusted each year to a calendar year-end basis.

Automobiles

The rules for self-employed individuals are not nearly as complex as those for employees who are supplied with a car by their employers. However, restrictions on capital cost allowance claims, monthly interest charges and monthly lease payments that apply to employees claiming automobile expenses apply equally to the self-employed. To make the most of automobile expense claims, keep records of expenses incurred as well as details of personal and business kilometres driven.

✔ Tax Tip 27

You do not have to file supporting vouchers or documents with your income tax return but you should keep them in case they are requested by Revenue Canada. They may turn out to be crucial if you are challenged.

If you use a car partly for business and partly for personal purposes, the deductible amount of car expenses is:

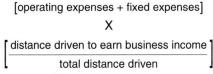

$$[\text{operating expenses} + \text{fixed expenses}]$$
$$\times$$
$$\left[\frac{\text{distance driven to earn business income}}{\text{total distance driven}}\right]$$

Expenses incurred in travelling between different premises of the same business are deductible. Expenses incurred in travelling from your home are not deductible, unless you can establish that your home is the base of your business operations. If you have an office or other fixed place of business located elsewhere, your home will not be regarded as the base of your business operations.

The fact that you render all your services at some other persons' place of business will not necessarily make that place your base, and you may still be able to deduct costs of travelling there from your base at home.

If you are a GST registrant, you may be eligible to claim input tax credits for a portion of the GST you paid on reasonable car expenses.

If you are paying automobile allowances to employees, you may deduct those allowances only to the extent that they do not exceed the limits in the table below. If you choose to pay your employees more than the allowable amounts, you cannot deduct the excess unless the full amount of the allowances is taxable in the employees' hands. If this is the case, you should ensure that your employees keep records of the distance they drive and provide you with their records so that you can support your claims. The employees will be able to deduct their business-related expenses and may be better off than they would have been with a non-taxable receipt.

If you are a GST registrant, you may be able to claim an input tax credit (7/107 of the allowance paid) to the extent the allowance is both reasonable (i.e., not taxable to the employee) and deductible to you.

| | | Maximum deductible automobile allowance (per kilometre) | |
		All provinces	Both territories
Business driving in the year	First 5,000 kilometres	$0.35	$0.39
	Beyond 5,000 kilometres	$0.29	$0.33

Depreciable assets

Although everyday business expenses can be deducted from business income, the cost of capital assets is deductible over a longer period.

86 This is accomplished through the capital cost allowance (CCA) rules, which provide varying rates of write-off, depending on the type of assets involved.

For example, office equipment and furniture are depreciated at a rate of 20% per annum; the rate for general purpose computers and systems software and for automobiles is 30%; and the rate for buildings is usually 4%. All are calculated on a declining-balance basis.

Generally, in the year in which you buy an asset, CCA is limited to half of the rate to which you would ordinarily be entitled. In addition, if your fiscal period is less than a year, you will be required to prorate the CCA amount otherwise determined.

Since CCA is based on the undepreciated capital cost of assets at the end of the year, you will not be able to claim CCA in the year in which you dispose of a business asset unless you continue to own other similar assets that are pooled for CCA purposes with the asset that you sold. On the other hand, you may be entitled to a terminal loss if there is a balance in the class at the end of the year, but no assets.

The CCA rules also permit a taxpayer to elect to place eligible property in a separate class for CCA purposes. Eligible property includes general-purpose electronic data processing equipment, photocopiers and certain electronic communications equipment such as facsimile transmission devices and telephone and related ancillary equipment, if the cost is $1,000 or more.

A separate class election does not change the specified CCA rate on the equipment. Rather, it allows a taxpayer to calculate a separate CCA deduction on one or more particular pieces of equipment. The separate class election ensures that, on the disposition of all the property in the class, any remaining undepreciated cost of the equipment may be fully deductible as a terminal loss. The election benefits taxpayers who acquire eligible equipment that depreciates faster than is implicit in the CCA rate for property of that class. The election must be made in the income tax return for the taxation year in which the property is acquired.

✔ Tax Tip 28

Timing is an important consideration when you purchase and sell capital assets. Try to purchase assets before the end of your fiscal year so that you are at least entitled to claim half of the normal CCA. When disposing of an asset, try to time the sale after year-end so that the full CCA claim is made in the previous year. Generally, you must take delivery of an asset and put it into use in order to claim CCA in the first year.

Office in the home

If you operate an office in your home, you can claim supplies and other expenses that are entirely associated with the business, such as a business phone. Expenses that are shared with the operation of the home, such as utilities, insurance, property taxes, rent and mortgage interest are generally apportioned according to the space used. Depreciation on your home is also deductible, but this will reduce your claim for the principal residence exemption on the sale of your home. Normally, claiming depreciation expense on your home offers little or no advantage.

For your work space to qualify as being used exclusively to earn business income and for regularly and continually meeting your clients, customers or patients, the space set aside for your business must be a room or rooms used exclusively for the business. Setting up a computer and filing cabinets at one end of the living room will not entitle you to claim home office expenses.

If you operate a full-time business out of your home, you will be able to deduct eligible expenses that relate to the work space. If you operate a part-time business, or have other office space out of which you conduct your business, you may be denied a deduction for office in the home expenses.

✔ **Tax Tip 29**

Home office expenses may be deducted only from income earned from the business carried on in the home; they may not be deducted from other sources of income. You may, however, carry excess expenses forward to a future year and deduct them from income generated by the business.

Business meals and entertainment expenses

Half of business meals and entertainment expenses are deductible for tax purposes. A similar restriction applies for purposes of the GST. Accordingly, only 50% of the GST paid on business meals and entertainment expenses may be recovered as an input tax credit.

✔ **Tax Tip 30**

Meal and entertainment expenses specifically identified on your invoice and billed directly back to your clients are not subject to the 50% limitation.

Retirement plans

If you have an unincorporated business, contributions to an RRSP may be the only avenue available to you to accumulate retirement savings. Your net income from the business, i.e., business income after expenses, is considered to be earned income for the purposes of determining the maximum amount that you may contribute to your RRSP. (See page 42 for more details about RRSP contribution limits.)

Salaries to spouse and children

If your spouse or children work in the business, salaries paid to them will be deductible for tax purposes as long as the wages are reasonable in relation to the work performed. Of course, the wages received will be taxable in their hands.

✔ Tax Tip 31

Salaries paid to your spouse or children will enable them to make their own RRSP contributions and to contribute to the Canada or Québec Pension Plans.

Private companies

Setting up the corporation

Unlike a sole proprietorship or a partnership, a corporation is a separate legal entity – an artificial person required to file a tax return and pay taxes quite separately from its owners. You may transfer your business assets to a corporation, generally without tax consequences to you, subject to certain restrictions. In addition to holding shares of the corporation (equity), you may also hold debt.

✔ Tax Tip 32

You will incur expenses in establishing and maintaining a corporation that you would not have with an unincorporated business. You should evaluate carefully both the timing and consequences of incorporating to see if the benefits outweigh the costs.

Tax deferral

The income from an unincorporated business is included in your personal income tax return and, therefore, taxed at your personal marginal tax rate. In contrast, if you incorporate your business, its income belongs to the corporation, and will be taxed at corporate rates. Your personal income tax return will be affected only to the extent that the corporation distributes its earnings to you as salary, dividends or interest.

The rate of corporate tax will depend on the type of income the corporation is earning as well as on the provinces or territories in which it carries on business. For example, up to $200,000 of active business income may be taxed at a combined federal and provincial rate as low as about 18% (even lower if a provincial tax holiday applies). The top marginal rate for an individual earning the same type of income directly would be about triple the corporate rate.

Large private corporations are not entitled to the preferential tax rate. The $200,000 business limit is reduced on a straight line basis for Canadian-controlled private corporations (CCPCs) with taxable capital employed in Canada of between $10 and $15 million in the preceding year. This eliminates the benefit of the small business deduction for those CCPCs with taxable capital of $15 million or more.

If you incorporate your business and retain earnings in the corporation for growth, you will be able to defer tax to the extent that the earnings are not distributed to you.

Integration

If you are the sole shareholder of a corporation, you and the corporation constitute two separate taxpaying entities. Salary that the corporation pays you is an expense that reduces the income of the corporation. For you, it is income.

The corporation will pay tax on its taxable income. Income that is distributed to you from the corporation by way of dividends will be subject to a second tier of tax through the personal tax system. The concept of integration mitigates the effects of this potential double incidence of tax.

According to the integration concept, income earned through a corporation and distributed to an individual shareholder should attract the same amount of tax as if that individual had earned the income directly. In practice, however, integration would work perfectly only if the combined federal and provincial rate of tax were 20% for a corporation and 43.5% for an individual, and if there were no surtaxes.

Because actual corporate and personal tax rates differ from the rates necessary to achieve perfect integration, your total taxes will vary, depending on whether income comes directly to you or through a corporation. The differences will depend on the type of income, your province of residence and the jurisdiction in which the corporation carries on business.

Whether earning income directly or through a corporation is preferable will depend on your personal circumstances. Active business income earned by a corporation, taxed at the small business rate and distributed as a dividend will usually attract less total tax than if you earned the income directly. On the other hand, income taxed at the top corporate rate and subsequently distributed to a shareholder in the top personal tax rate band will suffer some double taxation.

✔ Tax Tip 33

Incorporating your business involves making decisions that are both emotional and practical. Complex issues must be addressed, and the choices you make can be costly to undo. Ensure that your professional tax advisor is involved every step of the way.

Refer as well to the discussion regarding investment holding companies on page 130.

✔ Tax Tip 34

Corporations are not subject to Alternative Minimum Tax (AMT). (Refer to page 198 for details about AMT.) Accordingly,

92

investments that would trigger an AMT liability for an individual can instead be held by a holding company. Be careful, however: moving certain investments into a holding corporation may not be advantageous if you would lose tax shelter deductions associated with those investments.

Salary versus dividends

One of the major decisions for an owner-managed corporation is the split between salary and dividends. Your personal tax position as owner/manager, as well as that of the corporation itself, must be taken into account in determining the optimum compensation package.

Several rules of thumb help determine the best amount to be paid as salary to owners and the amount to be taxed in the corporation and subsequently distributed as dividends. (Refer to the **Integration** section on page 90, as well as to the discussion below.)

The rules of thumb assume that all amounts paid are reasonable in the circumstances, do not take cash requirements for living expenses into account and do not consider a possible sale of the business and the enhanced capital gains exemption discussed below.

✔ Tax Tip 35

Using salary or bonuses to reduce the active business income of the corporation to $200,000 annually will generally be advantageous to the owner-managed corporation.

Consider paying salary, rather than dividends, whenever the combined federal and provincial tax rate of the corporation exceeds 20%. This will generally hold true when the corporation is earning business income that is not eligible for the small business deduction.

This approach should be reviewed annually to ensure that it is still valid in the circumstances. If payroll taxes are substantial, for example, dividends may be preferable to salary. If the corporation is eligible for a provincial tax holiday, has investment tax credits to use up or has losses carried forward to reduce taxable income, the effective rate may be less than the statutory rate, and this strategy may change.

If the corporate rate is 20% or less, paying salary to the owner/manager may be desirable if dividends, when taken with other tax preference items, would subject the owner/manager to AMT.

✔ Tax Tip 36

The salary/dividend mix will affect your tax instalment requirements. Ensure that you and your corporation are remitting the appropriate amounts.

✔ Tax Tip 37

Accrual of a bonus may be preferable to payment of salary. A bonus paid within 180 days of a corporate year-end will be deductible to the corporation. Personal tax will be withheld when the bonus is paid.

✔ Tax Tip 38

Consider paying yourself sufficient salary to enable you to make maximum Canada or Québec Pension Plan contributions, as well as to contribute the maximum to your RRSP. The contribution limit for your RRSP is based on 18% of your earned income in the previous year. The maximum you can contribute to your RRSP in 1997 and 1998 is $13,500, which means that you must have earned income of $75,000 in 1996 and 1997 to make the maximum contributions to your RRSP. (Refer to page 42 for details regarding the freeze on current RRSP contribution limits through to the end of 2003.)

94 | ## Salaries to spouse and children

A corporation may provide an opportunity for income splitting with your spouse or children. Salaries may be paid to family members as long as services are actually performed and the amount of salaries and wages is reasonable. Generally, salaries would be considered to be reasonable if they are representative of an amount that would have to be paid to an arm's length party for similar services.

Paying reasonable wages to family members for actual services rendered has four advantages:

- the salaries will be deductible to the corporation;

- the salaries will be taxed in the hands of the recipients, and depending on the circumstances, probably at rates lower than the top marginal rate;

- the salaries will enable family members to contribute to their own RRSPs; and

- the tuition fee and education tax credits may mean that salaries paid to children attending university may attract little or no tax at all.

Directors' fees

In addition to the role you perform in your own company, you may also be a director, either of another corporation or of your own. If you are a director and earn directors' fees, those fees are considered to be employment income and must be included on your tax return. Directors' fees are earned income for the purposes of determining how much you can contribute to your or a spousal RRSP. Refer to pages 14 and 225 for a discussion of directors' liability.

✔ Tax Tip 39

> When you start a business, keep the business assets in a corpora-
> tion separate from one that holds investment or non-business
> assets.

Shares of Qualifying Small Business Corporations may be eligible
for an enhanced capital gains exemption of $400,000. The amount
is $500,000 if you never used the $100,000 capital gains exemption.
(Refer to page 112 for further details.) A small business corporation
(SBC) is generally defined as a Canadian-controlled private corporation (CCPC), all or substantially all the assets of which (more than
90% according to Revenue Canada) are used in an active business
carried on primarily in Canada. The corporation must be an SBC
when the shares are disposed of and the shares must not have been
held by anyone other than the taxpayer or related persons throughout the immediately preceding 24 months. In addition, throughout
the same period, more than 50% of the fair market value of the
assets of the corporation must be used in an active business it carries
on primarily in Canada.

✔ Tax Tip 40

> Removing any non-qualifying assets from your corporation
> now will help you meet the "all or substantially all" test in the
> definition of an SBC when the shares are eventually sold or
> transferred.

✔ Tax Tip 41

> If the shares in your small business corporation have substantial
> accrued capital gains, consider electing to sell some of the
> shares to your spouse at fair market value, triggering a capital

gain, up to $400,000 of which could be exempt. Professional tax advice is essential because of alternative minimum tax (AMT) and other considerations.

Election for private corporations going public

Although shares of a public corporation do not qualify as small business corporation shares, individuals may benefit from the enhanced capital gains exemption when a small business corporation is about to go public. An individual may elect to be treated as having disposed of all of the shares of a class of the capital stock of the small business corporation immediately before it becomes a public corporation. The individual will have to specify an amount to be the deemed proceeds of disposition. The proceeds may be the adjusted cost base of the shares or any higher amount up to their fair market value. The individual will be treated as having reacquired the shares immediately after the elected disposition at a cost equal to the specified proceeds. These new provisions will enable an individual to claim the enhanced capital gains exemption in respect of the disposition of the qualifying shares.

Planning around your CNIL

A corporation may provide you with some flexibility in arranging your personal concerns. If you will realize capital gains in the year from the disposition of Qualified Small Business Corporation shares that will not be sheltered from tax by the enhanced capital gains exemption because you have cumulative net investment losses (CNILs), consider arranging to receive sufficient interest or dividend income from the corporation to eliminate your CNIL.

This strategy may fully or partially restore your access to the enhanced capital gains exemption (see page 115 for more about CNILs).

If you are an owner/manager residing in Québec, the following differences in the Québec legislation should be noted:

Limitation on home office expenses

The limitation on deductions by employees of home office expenses is extended, effective for fiscal periods beginning after May 9, 1996, to partnerships operated from an individual partner's place of residence. Home office expenses are limited to 50% of the amount previously deductible on specific expenses such as mortgage interest, property taxes and insurance, heating and electricity. Also covered is rent associated with a home office or other work area in the home of an individual who is a member of a partnership, if it would otherwise be deductible. An individual who is a registrant under the QST system may claim an input tax refund (ITR) for such expenditures only if they are deductible under the income tax legislation.

Limitations on meals and entertainment expenses

At present, only 50% of a taxpayer's expenditures for meals and entertainment are deductible. The 1996 Québec budget announced that this deduction was to be further limited to 1% of a taxpayer's gross business income for the year, for taxation years beginning after May 9, 1996. It was announced that the application of this measure is suspended.

Certain expenditures are exempt from the 50% restriction, such as the cost of subscriptions to cultural events held in Québec, including performances of dance, opera, theatre or symphony concerts and certain vocal performances. The minimum number of performances required for a subscription to be eligible is three.

Depreciable assets

Québec has a 100% CCA deduction for:

- computers;
- systems software; and
- machinery and equipment,

used for manufacturing and processing in Québec, without the half-year rule applying. The deduction is 125% for equipment acquired after March 25, 1997.

The same tax treatment is granted for intangible property acquired after May 16, 1989, such as patents, licences, permits (but not trademarks and industrial drawings), knowledge, know-how, techniques, processes or formulae, whether protected or not, acquired in order to implement an innovation or an invention.

Instalments

The Québec prescribed rate of interest charged on late or deficient instalments of tax for the fourth quarter of 1997 is 8%. Additional interest at the rate of 10% per annum is payable on any late or deficient instalment that is less than 90% of the required instalment.

Health services fund contribution

For more information about this contribution, please refer to page 73.

Annual information forms and registration

An annual partnership information return, separate from the federal information return, must be filed with Revenu Québec. In addition, to do business in Québec, every partnership, sole proprietorship and legal person must register with the Inspecteur général des institutions financières, who can be reached at (418) 643-3625.

Deduction for artists

Artists may claim a maximum deduction of $15,000 in calculating taxable income. This deduction is reduced by 1.5 multiplied by the artist's entire income for the year in excess of $20,000 from copyrights of which he or she is the first holder. Therefore, no deduction may be claimed if the income derived from the distribution of works created by the artist exceeds $30,000 for the year. Income from royalties does not include income earned from performances by a performing artist.

An artist can benefit from the deduction if he or she comes within the definition of an artist in the *Act respecting the professional status and conditions of engagement of performing, recording and film artists*, which deals with the professional status of artists in the visual arts, arts and crafts and literature and their contracts with promoters. Formal membership in a recognized artists' association is not necessary.

4 Investors

4 Investors

What's new?

- The $100,000 general lifetime capital gains exemption has now been eliminated.

- Measures designed to restrict or eliminate the benefits of tax shelter investments are still in draft form.

- Complex rules that may deny losses on transfers of property among affiliated persons are still in draft form.

- No new tax measures of any significance in the last year would affect the tax treatment of investors.

You are an investor even if you do not have an extensive portfolio. If you own your home or maintain a bank account you should review this chapter.

Astute investors never lose sight of the fact that the after-tax result of their activities is what matters, not the nominal yield on their investments. Tax is only one element in the complex process of making investment decisions. The investment's yield and risk should always be considered ahead of income tax aspects. Although tax itself seldom should motivate a particular transaction, it can be a crucial factor when deciding among alternative investments with similar pre-tax yields.

Financial rewards from investment fall into two broad categories for tax purposes: investment income and capital gains. This chapter covers both, along with tax shelters (investments with a significant tax reduction component).

Investment income

Interest and dividends

Interest and dividends are taxed differently. All interest income you received and generally all interest income that accrued to you during the year is fully taxable in your hands. Even a small amount of interest on your savings account for which you did not receive a T5 slip from the bank is taxable.

Dividends from taxable Canadian corporations are included in your income along with a 25% "gross-up" of the amount you received. You can claim a federal dividend tax credit of 16⅔% of the actual dividend (equivalent to 13⅓% of the grossed-up amount) in

How the gross up and dividend tax credit reduce taxes at top marginal rates
(Illustration for a ficticious province or territory)

Without gross-up and dividend tax credit

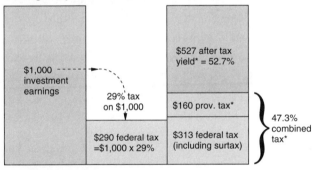

With gross-up and dividend tax credit

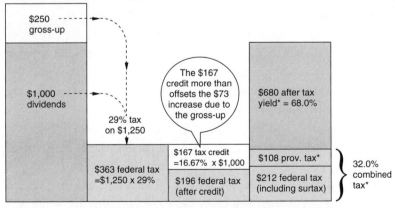

* Provincial tax, and therefore the after-tax yield, will vary depending on actual provincial tax rates. This example assumes provincial taxes are 55% of federal taxes (before the federal surtax).

arriving at your basic federal tax. You may claim the dividend tax credit only in the year the dividend was received.

Once the federal surtax is accounted for, the net effect is a reduction in tax of about 15 percentage points, depending on the province or territory of residence.

The bar charts compare the income tax on $1,000 of dividends under the gross-up/credit arrangement and under ordinary rules (i.e., as if no gross-up or credit applied) for a taxpayer at the top rate. The 32.0% combined tax that results from the gross-up and dividend tax credit is about 15 percentage points less than the 47.3% calculated without them.

This approximate 15 percentage point effective reduction in the tax on Canadian dividends means that in 1997, an individual in the top marginal tax bracket would require a gross yield of only about 6% on a dividend to generate the same net after-tax yield as an investment earning 8% interest. (For more information about tax rates on Canadian dividends, see Appendix 3, page 262).

Annual accrual rules

Generally, all interest that accrued in the year on investments you acquired after 1989 must be included in your income for tax purposes, even if you did not actually receive the income. The types of investments to which this rule applies include compound interest debt obligations, deferred annuities and certain life insurance policies. The amount to be reported is the interest earned or accrued during each complete investment year.

For example, if you made a long-term investment on September 1, 1996, the first year's interest must be calculated to the end of August 1997. This amount, whether you receive a T5 slip or not, must be reported on your 1997 income tax return. Similarly, interest accrued on that investment from September 1, 1997 to August 31, 1998 will have to be reported on your 1998 return.

An investment will be treated as having been acquired after 1989 if, after that year, it has been materially altered, for example, by extending its term. Of course, these rules do not apply to interest earned in a statutory deferred income plan such as your RRSP.

Before 1990, you had the choice of reporting accrued interest income from the above-noted securities annually, or deferring tax for up to three years by reporting accrued income every third calendar year after the year of purchase. Accordingly, you may continue to report accrued interest using the method you have used in the past (i.e., annually or in the third calendar year after purchase and every three years thereafter) if:

- you purchased a debt obligation before 1990 (but after November 12, 1981, when the rules changed), and

- the terms of the security have not changed materially.

✔ Tax Tip 42

If you currently hold certain "locked-in" compound interest securities that were acquired before November 13, 1981, you may want to keep them. This type of security is not subject to the accrual rules. You don't have to pay tax on the earnings until the contract matures and you actually receive the interest.

Debt obligations that are held in connection with a U.S. Individual Retirement Account (IRA) are excluded from the accrual rules.

✔ Tax Tip 43

Bonds and other debt instruments that mature should be cashed and reinvested promptly, because they pay no interest after the maturity date. Canada Savings Bonds should be reviewed every October.

106 | Life insurance policies

Life insurance could be an important part of your personal financial planning.

Traditionally, life insurance has often been used as an investment vehicle as well as a means of providing funds to an insured's estate or beneficiaries on the insured's death. Nevertheless, many people opted for "pure" or "term" life insurance policies, which simply paid a stipulated amount on the insured's death, but had no investment component. This preference often reflected the expectation of low investment returns or at least uncertainty about the return available on non-term policies. In recent years, however, the investment aspect has taken on new importance and has become more attractive. One of the major reasons for this is the favourable tax treatment provided for "exempt" policies. Any investment income earned in an exempt policy is exempt from tax. Furthermore, any amounts paid out under an exempt policy on the death of the insured are also exempt from tax. In a sense, the investment element of an exempt policy is a perfect tax shelter, in that the investment income can be earned and paid out without ever having been subject to tax.

To be "exempt," a policy must satisfy certain complex rules covering the relationship between the "pure" insurance portion of the policy and the investment portion. In effect, these rules require that a certain portion of your premium be used by the insurance company to provide pure insurance coverage, rather than being invested on your behalf. Whether a policy meets these requirements is essentially under the control of the insurance company. Any income accruing on the savings component of a non-exempt policy would be subject to the annual accrual rules referred to in the preceding section.

The other development that has made life insurance more attractive as an investment is that insurance companies have become more willing to disclose mortality and administrative costs, and even to guarantee minimum interest rates. This makes insurance policies easier to understand and makes their investment merits easier to assess.

The tax shelter aspect of an exempt policy has several potential uses, particularly after other tax shelter opportunities (e.g., RRSP contributions) have been exhausted. For example:

Some tax shelter uses of exempt insurance policies

		Comments
Uses of exempt insurance policies	To fund a retirement compensation arrangement	Retirement compensation arrangements are formally provided for under the Income Tax Act. They are a way for an employer to set aside funds for the retirement of employees. Investment income earned on those funds is normally subject to tax.
	To fund supplementary retirement benefits	An exempt life insurance policy with a savings account element may be used to supplement your other retirement benefits or to finance long-term objectives. Capital is typically built up over the longer term. Careful planning can increase the tax-free component of returns.
	As a vehicle for making charitable contributions.	A donation tax credit is available for the value of a policy assigned to a charity or for premiums paid on a policy on your life owned by a charity.
	In connection with corporate buy-sell arrangements	If you have a private corporation that owns a policy on your life and pays the premiums, any proceeds the corporation receives increases its capital dividend account (CDA). The balance in a corporation's CDA can be paid out as a tax-free dividend to the corporation's shareholders. Review new and existing buy-sell arrangements to determine if they are adversely affected by proposed new stop-loss rules. These rules will significantly reduce the tax advantages of many succession strategies.

You may also be able to get at the tax-sheltered earnings through taxable draws on the cash surrender value of the policy or by pledging the policy as collateral for a loan.

Another possible advantage is protection of your assets. The investment portion of an exempt policy may be excluded by law from the reach of creditors. For more information on this aspect, you should consult your legal advisor.

As with any other tax shelter, an investment in an exempt policy should be assessed on its merits. The insurance business is competitive, so you should shop around before making a decision.

Spouse's Canadian dividends

You may elect to include your spouse's taxable Canadian dividends in your income if that lets you claim or increase your married status tax credit. All of your spouse's dividends must be transferred. You cannot pick and choose to maximize tax savings.

This strategy works because the tax saving that results from increasing your married status tax credit may more than offset the extra tax that you must pay on the dividends, taking into account the reduced tax on dividends as a result of the dividend tax credit described above.

Be careful. If adding the dividends to your earnings pushes your net income above the threshold at which Old Age Security benefits are reduced or eliminated (see page 150) you may be worse off, and should not make the transfer.

✔ Tax Tip 44

Check to see whether transferring your spouse's Canadian dividends to your tax return will yield significant tax savings. In some cases the saving may amount to several hundred dollars.

Other investment income

Rental properties are a common investment. In some cases, income from an interest in a partnership is reported as investment income.

• Rental income

Net rental income is taxable. To calculate net rental income, current expenses you incur to earn that income are deducted. Most common are interest, heat, electricity, property taxes, water bills, insurance, labour and materials for routine repairs and maintenance, and the cost of advertising for tenants. Condominium management fees are also deductible.

Capital expenditures can be claimed only through the capital cost allowance (CCA) system. Your CCA claim cannot be used to create or increase a loss on the rental property.

• Partnership income

If you have an interest in a partnership or limited partnership in which you are not actively engaged, you must report your share of net income or loss on Schedule 4 of your tax return. Normally, you receive a tax reporting package from the general partner that sets out the amount. You should attach this information to your tax return.

If you are a limited partner and a portion of a partnership loss is allocated to you, the investment may be a tax shelter subject to the at-risk rules. (See page 124 for more information about at-risk rules and about recent changes to the provisions dealing with partnership interests.)

You may deduct partnership losses allocated to you only to the extent of your at-risk amount. This means that you cannot deduct losses that exceed the cost of your interest in the partnership, plus profits (or less losses) and other adjustments.

If you have not received a tax reporting package from the general partner, or are uncomfortable with the required calculations, you should talk to your tax advisor.

Deductible interest expense

In general, interest paid or accrued on funds borrowed to earn investment or business income is deductible for tax purposes.

In this context, investment income includes interest and dividends, as well as other sources of income, such as royalties and "passive" rental income. Although investment income in this context does not include capital gains that may be realized on capital property, many investments – such as shares and mutual funds – have the potential of paying dividends or earning income at some future date even if they do not currently. Accordingly, interest expense is generally deductible on funds borrowed to acquire these types of investments.

What happens if you sell the source of your business or property income at a loss? The courts have traditionally held that interest ceases to be deductible when the source of income to which the interest related no longer exists or is sold and the borrowed money cannot be traced to a replacement income-producing source. However, in certain circumstances interest on borrowed money may continue to be deductible even if the source of the income from business or property is no longer held.

For example, assume that you borrowed $4,500 in 1996 to acquire shares for your investment portfolio. The shares cost a total of $6,000. They decline in value and you sell them for $3,600 in 1997. You no longer have the shares, but you still owe money to the bank. You may be able to continue to deduct all or a portion of your interest expense, depending on what you do with the $3,600 proceeds.

• If you use the $3,600 proceeds to buy another corporation's shares, you will be able to deduct the full amount of your interest on the original borrowing. Here's how it works: because you sold the first shares for 60% of their cost ($6,000 - $3,600), 60% of your $4,500 original borrowing (i.e., $2,700) is considered to have been used to acquire the new shares. You used the proceeds to buy income-producing property, so the interest on the $2,700 is tax-deductible. The new rules will deem the $1,800 balance of the original borrowing to continue to be used to earn income. You will be able to continue to deduct interest on the $1,800. The result? You may deduct the full amount of interest on the $4,500 that you borrowed.

• Keep the facts the same as above, but this time you use the $3,600 to pay down your credit card balance. What happens to your interest expense? In the same way as in the scenario above, interest on $1,800 continues to be tax-deductible. Interest on the $2,700, however, is no longer deductible because you used that portion of the borrowed funds for personal reasons and not for an income-producing purpose.

The rules will also apply if you borrowed money for the purpose of earning income from a business and the business ceases. In this situation, you may continue to deduct all or a portion of the interest on money you borrowed for your business depending on how the business is liquidated.

✔ **Tax Tip 45**

If you must borrow, try to borrow for investment or business purposes before you borrow for personal reasons. Conversely, when repaying debt, always repay loans on which interest is non-deductible before you repay those on which the interest is deductible.

✔ **Tax Tip 46**

If you are buying Canada Savings Bonds on a payroll savings plan, don't forget to claim a deduction for interest expense. Essentially, you have purchased the bonds at the first of November with borrowed funds and you repay the loan with interest during the year.

Capital gains and losses

Capital gains and losses are realized when you dispose of a property. The word "dispose" is used because even if you have not sold the property (in the ordinary sense) special rules could deem you to have disposed of a property.

For example, when the use of a property changes from non-income producing to income producing, the property is deemed to have been disposed of for proceeds equal to its fair market value at the time of the change. The property is then deemed to have been reacquired immediately after for a cost equal to that fair market value. Special rules apply if the property is your principal residence and you make an election to continue to treat the property as a non-income producing one.

Property includes real estate, shares in a corporation, an interest in a partnership, depreciable property such as cars or a building, rights or options to purchase or sell property, and even personal property such as antiques, books or boats.

With the demise of the capital gains exemption (see the next topic), generally three-quarters of your realized capital gains are subject to tax. Appendix 3 (page 262) compares the tax payable on capital gains to that on other forms of income.

Capital losses are also multiplied by the three-quarters to determine your allowable capital loss. Allowable capital losses realized in the year must first be used to reduce all taxable capital gains realized in the year. Any balance remaining can then be carried back to the three immediately preceding years to reduce taxable capital gains. Any further balance may be carried forward indefinitely and likewise be used to reduce taxable capital gains.

If you realize significant capital gains you could become liable for alternative minimum tax (AMT). For more details about AMT, see page 198.

✔ Tax Tip 47

Unused capital losses that have been carried forward from years before 1985 may be applied at a rate of $2,000 per year to reduce income from any other sources.

Enhanced capital gains exemption

Although the $100,000 lifetime capital gains exemption has been eliminated, an enhanced $400,000 exemption is available for gains realized on the disposition of shares of a Qualifying Small Business Corporation (QSBC) or on the disposition of a qualified family farm operation.

When the expression "enhanced capital gains exemption" is discussed or referred to in this book, the amount of the exemption will be taken to be $400,000. This assumes that the general lifetime capital gains exemption has already been claimed. For individuals who never used their $100,000 capital gains exemption in respect of other property, the enhanced exemption will be $500,000.

For the disposition of shares of a corporation to be eligible for the additional $400,000 exemption, the company must be a small business corporation (SBC) at the time of sale. An SBC is generally a Canadian-controlled private corporation (CCPC) that uses all or substantially all of its assets in an active business carried on primarily in Canada by the corporation or a related corporation. Also included are CCPCs whose assets or debts are of "connected" SBCs. "All or substantially all" generally means 90% of fair market value.

The corporation must also comply with restrictive requirements concerning the nature of its assets throughout the relevant holding period (usually two years prior to the date of sale). More than 50% of the fair market value of the assets must be attributable to: assets used in active business carried on by it or by a related corporation primarily in Canada; and/or shares or debt of connected CCPCs that satisfy certain holding period and asset tests. (See page 96 for the exemption when a business goes public.)

Suppose a disposition is deemed to have occurred as a consequence of a shareholder's death and the corporation fails to meet the "all or substantially all" test immediately before the time of death. A measure that is intended to provide relief in such situations could preserve the opportunity to use the enhanced $400,000 capital gains exemption that otherwise may have been lost. A share that is deemed to have been disposed of on a shareholder's death may constitute a QSBC share at the time of the disposition if it met the "all or substantially all" test at any time within the 12-month period preceding the disposition.

Sometimes a corporation holds a life insurance policy under which a shareholder of that corporation is the life insured. In that situation, an increase in the value of the policy could cause the corporation to fail the asset tests in the definitions described above. This could prevent the enhanced gains exemption from being available on the deemed disposition of the shares on the taxpayer's death. For the purposes of the definitions of a QSBC share and a share of the capital stock of a family farm corporation (see below), a relieving provision deems the fair market value of the policy at any time prior to the shareholder's death to be its cash surrender value.

A farm property qualifying for the enhanced $400,000 exemption may be operated as a corporation or as a farm partnership. The property must be actively farmed by the taxpayer or family members immediately before the sale to qualify for the exemption. All or substantially all the assets of the business must be devoted to farming. To qualify, the property may have to meet holding period requirements similar to those for QSBC shares.

The definition of "share of the capital stock of a family farm corporation" clarifies that the property of a family farm corporation need not be used in the course of carrying on the business of farming at the time of the disposition of the share. Provided that the other conditions in the definition have been satisfied, prior use of the property throughout any 24-month period ending before the disposition will suffice. A similar clarification exists for an interest in a family farm partnership.

✔ Tax Tip 48

Eligible farm property can be transferred to your children at your cost, so there are no immediate adverse tax consequences, unless an AMT liability arises (see page 198). If you are not going to otherwise use your enhanced $400,000 capital gains exemption, consider electing to transfer the property at a higher value and claiming the exemption. This strategy would "step up" your child's cost base for the farm. He or she will be liable for a much smaller capital gain on any eventual sale.

Reserves

If you sell a capital property at a profit and do not receive the full proceeds at the time of sale or before the end of the calendar year, you may be eligible to claim a reserve. The reserve represents the portion of the gain related to the sale proceeds that are not due until after the end of the year. The reserve is available if you secured the unpaid balance of the purchase price by way of a note payable or a mortgage.

The tax on your gain can be postponed for no longer than five years on most types of capital property. (The reserve limit is extended to ten years for qualified farm property or shares in a small business corporation sold to your children, grandchildren or great-grandchildren.) Each year, beginning with the year of sale, you must bring into income the greater of:

- your capital gain times the proportion of the proceeds actually received prior to the end of the year, less the amount previously recognized; and

- one-fifth (or one-tenth, if appropriate) of the capital gain for each year from the year of sale to the current year.

Amounts brought into income each year under the reserve mechanism are treated as capital gains. The amounts to be included in your income are based on the capital gains inclusion rate in effect in the year the reserve is brought into income.

Cumulative net investment losses (CNILs)

The CNIL rules were designed to prevent investors from claiming deductions for interest and other investment expenses as well as the capital gains exemption. The elimination of the general life-time capital gains exemption means that the CNIL will be relevant only in limited circumstances. Net capital gains eligible for the enhanced capital gains exemption on qualifying small business corporation shares or on qualified family farm property must be reduced by your CNIL.

✔ Tax Tip 49

If the enhanced capital gains exemption is still available to you and you believe that you might be using it in a particular year, be careful not to get tripped up by a CNIL balance. Your CNIL is calculated to the end of the year. Accordingly, if you plan to claim the enhanced capital gains exemption in 1997 for example, you have until the end of that year to "cure" any CNIL problems.

Your CNIL is computed at the end of a year as the amount by which your investment expenses accumulated after 1987 exceed investment income also accumulated after 1987. Investment income includes the following types of income reported on your tax return:

- interest, the taxable amount of dividends and other income from investments;

- your share of net income from a partnership in which you are not an active member;

- income from property or from the renting or leasing of rental property; and

- 50% of income relating to the recovery of exploration and development expenses.

Investment expenses generally include the following expenses claimed on your tax return:

- interest and carrying charges relating to investments that yield interest, dividends and rent;

- interest and carrying charges relating to your interest in a partnership in which you are not an active member;

- your share of a loss in a partnership in which you are not an active member;

- 50% of exploration and development expenses claimed; and

- any loss for the year from property or from renting or leasing rental property.

Your interest expense and other eligible investment expenses and losses remain deductible and your access to the enhanced capital gains exemption is merely delayed, not eroded.

✔ Tax Tip 50

If possible, borrow for business purposes rather than investment purposes. The interest expense on funds borrowed to carry on a business or profession does not enter into the calculation of your CNIL account.

Special rules for capital gains and losses

• Transfers of losses – proposed new rules

Extensive new rules dealing with losses are still in draft form. Although the new provisions primarily affect transfers of losses within corporate groups, individuals may also be affected.

The draft legislation introduces the concept of "affiliated persons." As an individual, you are considered to be affiliated with yourself and with your spouse, but not your children. By virtue of the new affiliated persons concept, you may also find that you are affiliated with a corporation or a partnership. What does this mean to you? Generally, a loss will be denied on transfers of property between affiliated persons. Further, losses will be denied on the redemption of shares of an affiliated company. The new rules generally will apply to dispositions of property that occur after April 26, 1995.

This is a complex area. Where transactions dealing with just about anything other than general portfolio investments are concerned, be careful not to end up with unintended results. In particular, if you are acquiring or disposing of capital property that involves corporations, trusts or partnerships in which you have an interest, professional advice is a must.

• Identical properties

When you acquire securities that are exactly the same – Class A common shares of ABC Corp. for example – the shares are pooled for purposes of determining your cost when you sell a portion of your holdings.

Assume, for example, that you buy 200 shares today at $5 each (total cost $1,000) and 100 shares next week at $8 each (total cost $800). Your cost per share for tax purposes is $6 (300 shares for a total cost of $1,800). If you then sell 200 shares at $7 each, your capital gain is $200 ($7 minus $6, times 200 shares).

✔ Tax Tip 51

When determining which of your losers to sell prior to year end, ensure that you indeed have accrued losses on the specific securities and that you will not be tripped up by the identical property rules.

• Pre-1972 capital property

Capital gains were not subject to tax before 1972. If you acquired a property before 1972 and you still own it, the portion of any gain accruing to December 31, 1971 is not subject to tax. To determine the portion of the total post-1971 capital gain, you must know the value of the property on V-Day (Valuation Day, basically December 31, 1971) or you may have to have the property valued as of that date, which could be costly. A published list gives V-Day values for publicly traded securities.

If you own identical properties, some of which were acquired before 1972, on a disposition you will be deemed to have sold the pre-1972 properties before those acquired after 1971. Two separate pools will determine the cost of the properties sold; one comprising the properties acquired before 1972, another for those acquired after 1971.

✔ Tax Tip 52

Before having a property evaluated for purposes of determining the non-taxable pre-1972 gain, ensure that the cost of the valuation will be more than offset by the expected tax saving.

• Superficial losses

If during the year you realized capital gains that will be taxable, you may be tempted to dispose of some of your losers to offset the gains. In so doing, however, be careful not to run afoul of the superficial loss rules. A superficial loss arises if you repurchase a security identical to the one you disposed of within 30 days before or after the original sale.

A loss realized on the original sale will be denied if it is a superficial loss. The amount of the loss will simply be added to the cost base of the newly acquired identical property. A similar result occurs if your spouse or a corporation that you control purchases the identical security.

• Denial of capital losses

In two specific situations you are not permitted to recognize a loss for tax purposes:

- Losses arising on the sale of capital property to your own or your spouse's RRSP or RRIF will be denied in their entirety. You would be better off selling the property to an arm's length party and making a cash contribution to your RRSP.

- If you sell capital property to a corporation that is controlled by you or your spouse, the property will be considered to have been transferred to the corporation at your cost, even if you sell the property to the corporation at a loss. If you or your spouse are con-templating a transaction that involves the sale or transfer of prop-erty, ensure that you consider the new rules affecting transfers of losses among "affiliated persons" (see the discussion on page 117).

• Settlement date

Transactions involving publicly traded securities take place at settle-ment date: three days after the trading date in the case of Canadian stock exchanges.

✔ Tax Tip 53

Don't undermine your planning strategies by ignoring the set-tlement date. In 1997, December 22 is probably the last day on which a sale executed through a Canadian stock exchange will be considered a 1997 transaction. Your broker can tell you if foreign exchanges have different settlement dates.

Allowable business investment losses (ABILs)

Losses incurred on the sale of shares or debt in a Small Business Cor-poration (SBC) are treated differently from ordinary capital losses. An SBC is a Canadian-controlled private corporation (CCPC) that uses all or substantially all of its assets in an active business carried on primarily in Canada (based on a fair market value test). Included are CCPCs whose assets are shares in qualifying SBCs.

An ABIL is calculated in the same manner as an allowable capital loss: three-quarters of the business loss is the ABIL.

An ABIL is a reduction in computing net income, unlike an allow-able capital loss, which may be used only to reduce taxable capital gains. Any portion of an ABIL not used may be carried back three years and forward seven, the same as normal business losses. After that time, business investment losses become ordinary capital losses.

Bear in mind that:

- your business investment loss may be reduced by dividends paid after 1971 if you owned the shares before 1972; and

- any ABILs realized will reduce your $400,000 enhanced capital gains exemption.

✔ Tax Tip 54

Although you should consider delaying the realization of an ABIL until you have exhausted your enhanced capital gains exemption, by delaying the recognition of an ABIL, you may be prepaying tax on other income.

✔ Tax Tip 55

The allowable portion of losses realized on the disposition of shares or debt in an SBC may qualify as business investment losses. Therefore it may be offset against income from all sources. Remember, however, that any post-1984 losses reduce your enhanced capital gains exemption.

Principal residence

• What is a principal residence?

The home you occupy is your principal residence. It can be a house, condominium, cottage, mobile home, trailer or even a live-aboard boat – as long as you occupy it for a portion of the year. A principal residence need not be located in Canada.

Included in the definition of principal residence is the land on which it is situated. Only the amount of land necessary to the enjoyment of the home is included in the definition. Usually that is no more than half a hectare. A hectare is 10,000 square metres or about two and one-half acres.

Where zoning bylaws required a larger parcel of land to be included with your house at the time of purchase, more than half a hectare of land may be included in the principal residence definition.

• Capital gain on disposition

Gains on the sale of a principal residence are generally tax-free. The principal residence exemption is available to a family unit (you, your spouse and your unmarried children under the age of 18) on only one home, in any particular year or part year, for gains arising since the beginning of 1982. For gains arising after 1972 and before 1982, each individual is entitled to the principal residence exemption for one house.

• Change in use

If you start to rent out part or all of your principal residence, an election is available to preserve the principal residence status for up to four consecutive years. You must report as income the rent received, net of out-of-pocket expenses. If you claim capital cost allowance (depreciation) on the home while it is being rented, Revenue Canada will consider that you have rescinded the election and deem a disposition to have occurred.

In addition, to claim the principal residence designation, you must continue to be a Canadian resident for the period during which you do not occupy the home.

Foreign residences

Any home that you normally occupy, even seasonally for only part of the year, may qualify as your principal residence. This includes a home in another country. You must be a Canadian resident in the years in which you designate your foreign home as your principal residence.

Even though the gain under Canadian rules is tax-free, you may incur a foreign tax liability when you sell your foreign home.

If you estimate that the foreign tax liability will be significant and that you will be entitled to foreign tax credits on your Canadian tax return for foreign taxes paid, you may be better off not claiming the principal residence exemption. Professional advice is essential in this situation.

• Farm property

A farm house is eligible for the principal residence exemption. When you sell the farm, you may prorate the proceeds between the farming property and your principal residence, including no more than half a hectare of land as part of your principal residence. Alternatively, you may elect to reduce the full amount of the gain on disposition by $1,000 plus another $1,000 for each year of ownership after 1971.

Tax shelters

Tax shelters are investments or business opportunities that offer various types of income tax savings in addition to the potential economic benefits of a successful investment. In most cases, initial tax savings will be complemented by long-term realization of income, if the investment is successful. If the investment does not succeed, the initial tax savings may compensate for part of the economic loss.

The federal government applies specific provisions to restrict or eliminate the benefits of tax-shelter investments, including at-risk rules for limited partnerships, reporting requirements for tax shelter promoters and capital cost allowance (CCA) restrictions. Other measures may reduce or limit the tax value of tax shelters for some investors. For example, the alternative minimum tax (AMT) limits the benefit of "tax preferences."

Every promoter of a tax shelter is required to obtain an identification number from Revenue Canada. Prior to investing in a new tax shelter, to preserve your right to the deductions available to reduce your taxes, you should confirm that an identification number has been obtained.

New tax shelter rules, still in draft form, ensure that investors' deductions are limited to funds fully at risk. They enhance compliance by ensuring that all tax shelters are appropriately identified. The new rules extend the base of alternative minimum tax to include partnership losses allocated to limited partners and to certain passive partners, tax shelter losses, as well as carrying charges associated with any of these investments.

✔ Tax Tip 57

Evaluate the investment potential of a tax shelter in the same way as any other investment. It does not make any economic sense to invest in a shelter if there is little chance of either earning income on your investment or recovering the amount you have at risk, i.e., the amount you invested net of the tax benefits.

Limited partnerships – at-risk rules

Special rules define and limit the extent to which limited partners can use partnership losses and investment tax credits to shelter other income. Losses of a partnership allocated to a limited partner are deductible only to the extent of the partner's at-risk amount at the end of a particular year. A limited partner's at-risk amount at any time is essentially the cost of his or her partnership interest, plus profits or minus drawings and losses, and other adjustments.

The partnership at-risk rules have been extended recently. The adjusted cost base (ACB) of property that you own reflects your cost of the property and is taken into account in computing a capital gain or loss when you sell the property. In certain circumstances, the ACB of your property may become negative, in which case you would be treated as having realized a capital gain. This rule, however, generally does not apply if the property is a partnership interest. The exception to the rule recognizes that a partner's negative ACB may result from legitimate, and possibly temporary, circumstances, for example, when losses of the partnership are allocated to a partner for tax purposes.

Some tax shelters have been structured to use the exception to the negative ACB rules. To ensure that the at-risk rules cannot be circumvented, limited partners and certain other passive partners are required to report as a capital gain any negative ACB in their partnership interest at the end of a fiscal period of the partnership.

Although the new rules apply to fiscal periods of partnerships ending after February 22, 1994, transitional rules defer the application of the new rules to the fifth fiscal period of the partnership ending after 1994 in the case of film partnerships satisfying certain criteria.

Draft legislation contains numerous changes to the limited partnership rules, including amendments to the "at-risk amount" and an extended definition of "limited partners." Other proposals accommodate changes that arise as a result of the new affiliated persons rules (refer to page 117) and changes required by the elimination of the $100,000 capital gains exemption.

Real estate

Investment in real estate as a tax shelter is not as attractive as it once was, because rental losses on real estate cannot be created or increased by claiming capital cost allowance (CCA). In addition, most costs related to the construction period of a project, particularly property taxes and interest expense, must be added to the cost of the land or building. Therefore, they become deductible as depreciation over time, at best, rather than in the first year or two of the investment. Certain soft costs, however, such as rental commissions, guarantees and landscaping, may be deductible in the early years of a project.

Canadian films

Capital cost allowance (CCA) in respect of investments in certified films is limited to a rate of 30% on a declining-balance basis. The rule that normally limits CCA to half the amount that you could otherwise claim in the year of acquisition does not apply. Additional CCA may be claimed up to the lesser of the undepreciated capital cost of certified film productions and the income (net of expenses and the basic 30% CCA) from all certified productions in the year.

For eligible films produced by qualified taxable Canadian corporations, the capital cost allowance tax shelter incentive is replaced with a fully refundable tax credit to be known as a "Canadian film credit." The investment tax credit is 25% of qualified salaries and wages. Eligible salaries and wages are limited to 48% of the cost of an eligible production, however. Accordingly, the credit provides assistance for up to a maximum of 12% of the cost of the production [25% times 48%]. An eligible production will require a certification as such by the Minister of Canadian Heritage.

Existing CCA incentives will be retained for Canadian certified productions that were acquired before 1996, the principal photography of which was completed before July 1, 1996. Film productions from 1995 can qualify either for the existing incentives or for the Canadian film credit, but not both.

Farming

The attractiveness of a farm shelter from a tax point of view lies primarily in the potential for claiming losses against other sources of income. The key to a farm shelter is the business aspect: to deduct any loss at all, you must have a reasonable expectation of earning a profit from the farming operation. If farming is not at the centre of your livelihood, you may be restricted to $8,750 of losses in a year.

Qualified farm property may be eligible for the enhanced $400,000 capital gains exemption.

Provincial tax shelters

A number of provinces encourage investment in specified areas or industries through various incentive initiatives. Stock savings plans provide tax deductions or credits and venture capital programs are intended to foster investment in small to medium-sized corporations.

Income splitting

Income splitting is having income that normally would be taxed in the hands of the highest income family member taxed at lower rates in the hands of another family member. Tax may even be eliminated if the family member has very little or no income. If you earn income that is taxed at a top marginal rate of say 48% and can arrange to have your spouse earn some of the income so that it is taxed at say 28%, your family will save $20 for every $100 of income earned. Not surprisingly, rules have been established to limit the circumstances in which income splitting may be effective.

Attribution rules

A variety of rules discourage income splitting. Essentially, if you transfer or lend assets to your spouse or a child under 18 years of age, in virtually any manner, the investment income (including interest, dividends, rental income etc.) will be attributed to you. That means it will be taxed in your hands, rather than in the hands of your spouse or child. As well, capital gains or losses realized by your spouse on the sale of transferred property will be attributed to you. Attribution of capital gains does not apply on assets transferred to children under 18 years old.

Attribution continues to apply when assets are substituted for the original assets transferred. However, income earned on reinvested income is not attributed to the transferor (see Income on income, page 129).

Although attribution of income ordinarily ceases when a child turns 18, income earned on an investment made by a child age 18 or over (or any other non-arm's length person) using borrowed funds is subject to the attribution rules if one of the main reasons for the loan is to reduce or avoid tax by having the investment income taxed in the child's hands.

The attribution rules may apply not only to loans, but to all situations in which an individual becomes indebted to another non-arm's length individual. Accordingly, the attribution rules will apply when, for example, the unpaid balance of a purchase price is satisfied by a non-interest-bearing note and one of the main reasons for incurring the indebtedness was to avoid tax by having income included in the hands of the debtor.

In spite of the attribution rules, a number of ways to split income among family members still work. For example, the rules in the Income Tax Act generally do not apply to attribute business income or losses. Income from a partnership is usually income from a business. However, in certain circumstances the attribution rules may apply to structures designed to split the partnership income among family members.

Income that results if a loan is made at commercial interest rates and the interest is actually paid within 30 days of year end is also excluded from the attribution rules. Similarly, sales to a spouse at fair market value are not subject to the rules if you receive adequate consideration in return. Because transfers of property between spouses are generally considered to be made at the adjusted cost base of the property, if you want to use this approach, you must elect on your tax return that the transfer take place at fair market value rather than at the adjusted cost base. A contribution to a spousal RRSP is still one of the best income-splitting techniques.

If you are in a higher marginal tax bracket than your spouse, you might consider paying off any balances on your spouse's credit cards. The attribution rules will not apply as long as the credit card debt was not used to acquire income-producing property.

If your income is taxed at a higher marginal tax rate than your spouse's, the family will benefit if your spouse earns investment income and you pay family expenses such as credit card balances. Although these payments could be considered gifts to your spouse, no attribution would apply, because the funds are used to pay ordinary costs of running a family and not to generate investment income.

✔ Tax Tip 58

Investment income may be shifted to a child 18 or over by an outright sale or gift of the income-producing property.

✔ Tax Tip 59

Because capital gains on property transferred to children under 18 years of age are not attributed, consider buying capital property with a low yield but high capital gains potential in the names of your children. The income will be attributed to you, but any future capital gains will be taxed in the children's hands, presumably at lower tax rates.

Income on income

Income earned on property that you transfer to your spouse or a child under 18 is generally subject to the income attribution rules and is included in your income for tax purposes. However, if he or she reinvests the income, income earned on the reinvested income (e.g., interest on interest) is not attributed to you.

Common-law spouse

Two individuals of opposite sex are considered to be spouses of each other when they are cohabiting in a conjugal relationship and they either:

- have so cohabited throughout the preceding 12 months; or

- are the parents of the same child.

Common-law couples are eligible for the married tax credit and may make contributions to spousal RRSPs. Common-law couples are subject to the attribution rules and many other provisions that apply to married couples, including rules that deny losses on the disposition of property to a spouse. Common-law spouses must combine their incomes for the purposes of determining the GST tax credit and the monthly payments under the Child Tax Benefit system (see page 199). The deductibility of child care expenses may be adversely affected. A common-law couple is subject to the same rules that limit a married couple or a family unit to one principal residence.

How does the government monitor common-law couples who choose not to live by the new rules? When does a common-law relationship begin and end? Although marriage, divorce and separation are legally defined by registration, divorce decrees, separation agreements etc., whether two people are in a common-law relationship is often unclear. They may even disagree between themselves.

Common-law couples must be careful that they do not fail to anticipate the substantial income tax consequences that may arise as a result of the conduct of their private lives. For example, a legally married individual who leaves his or her spouse, begins living with another person and has a child with that person, may not only have two spouses, but may also inherit an unusually large group of related persons.

Investment holding companies

The tax system contains special rules that are meant to eliminate some of the biases between income earned by an individual and income earned by a corporation. Some of these are designed to ensure that the after-tax return on income realized through a corporation, and subsequently distributed to the shareholder, is roughly the same as if the shareholder had received the income from the investments directly. The system is imperfect, because surtaxes are imposed on individuals in certain provinces and provincial income tax rates vary. In any case, earning interest, dividends and capital gains in a corporation has usually been advantageous as long as the income is retained in the corporation and the second incidence of tax on distribution is postponed.

Changes to the integration system in recent years make holding investments through a corporation less attractive. In general terms, taxes payable by corporations on investment income have been raised.

Every situation is unique and requires a separate analysis. Nevertheless, you should consider some general guidelines when you assess your strategies.

- If the corporation has a large amount of undistributed income or property with accrued gains, the holding company should be retained (due in large part to the amount of tax that would be payable on a wind-up).

- Generally, the largest deferral opportunities remain with dividend-producing assets, rather than interest.

- Larger portfolios generally will be less affected by annual costs of administering a corporation, such as legal and accounting bills, because as a portfolio gets larger, the dollar value of the deferral will increase more rapidly than annual costs.

- Individuals eligible (or about to become eligible) for OAS benefits and whose personal income (excluding investment income) does not exceed $50,000, may still come out further ahead by keeping their investments in a corporation.

- The cost of capital tax must be considered for investment holding companies in most provinces. Of course, the federal Large Corporations Tax must be evaluated for all investment holding companies as well.

✔ **Tax Tip 60**

A regular review of your tax situation, including an annual look at your portfolio, is the best way to determine the most advantageous tax structure in light of any tax rate changes, new legislation and changes to your business.

Is it still worthwhile to incorporate an investment portfolio?

Traditionally, one of the main tax reasons for using a holding company has been the ability to defer income tax. The deferral opportunity has generally been eliminated as a result of measures aimed at closing the gap between corporate and personal tax rates on investment income. In some cases, earning investment income through a holding company actually creates a disadvantage, particularly once administrative costs incurred to use a corporation have been considered.

Non-tax factors should also be evaluated, however. Refer to the section below for some issues you should consider.

Should you retain an existing investment holding company?

A shareholder of a holding company has a choice: the holding company can continue to hold existing investments or it can be wound-up. The decision should not be made on tax considerations alone; there may be sound business and other reasons for choosing one route over another. Accordingly, you should discuss your situation with your professional advisor, whether you intend to make changes or live with the status quo. In any event, a variety of factors require your careful consideration, including:

- residency of the individual and the company

- portfolio mix

- continuing costs

- tax consequences of associated corporations

- creditor proofing

- probate fees and estate planning

- cost of winding-up the company

✔ Tax Tip 61

You can use an investment holding company as a discretionary source of dividend income to reduce the balance in your cumulative net investment loss (CNIL) account, if and when necessary.

⊕ International investors

Canadians investing outside Canada

Canadian residents are taxed on their worldwide incomes. Accordingly, income you earn on investments made in foreign jurisdictions is subject to tax in Canada and must be reported on your income tax return. Whether the funds are deposited into your Canadian bank account or into a bank account in a foreign country is irrelevant.

Generally, you may use the average exchange rate for the year to convert to Canadian dollars both the amount of income to be reported on your tax return and the amount of foreign tax withheld. However, you may use the actual rates at the time the income was received if that is more beneficial. Tax may be withheld in the foreign country from funds remitted to you. You must include in income the gross amount of earnings, i.e., the amount you received plus the withholding tax. The 25% dividend gross-up rule does not apply, nor is a dividend tax credit available in respect of non-Canadian dividends.

Any foreign tax withheld (up to 15% of the gross foreign investment income) should be used in the foreign tax credit calculation to determine the amount of foreign tax that may be deducted from your Canadian tax liability. Foreign tax withheld in excess of 15% may be deducted in arriving at net income for tax purposes.

Foreign source investment income is subject to the same reporting requirements as Canadian investment income. That is, interest income accrued but not received must be included in income on an annual basis for investments acquired after 1989 (at least every three years for pre-1990 investments).

✔ Tax Tip 62

A foreign tax credit may be claimed only when amounts are actually paid and foreign taxes withheld. Consequently, no foreign tax credits may be claimed in respect of investment income accrued but not received. Consider filing a waiver with Revenue Canada to keep "open" years in which unpaid interest is reported. This should ensure that the related foreign tax credit will be allowed when amounts are actually received. Be careful to limit the waiver, which is filed on Form T2029, to the accrued investment income reported.

⊕ Non-resident investors in Canada

If you are a non-resident of Canada receiving income from Canadian sources, you may be subject to federal tax in Canada.

If you receive passive investment income such as interest, dividends, royalties, rents and pensions, you are not ordinarily required to file a Canadian income tax return. Instead, the Canadian payor of these types of income is required to pay tax on your behalf by withholding and remitting the appropriate amount of tax at source. The general rate of withholding tax on payments to non-residents is 25%, but the rate may be reduced to between zero and 20%, depending on the type of income and whether a bilateral tax treaty is in force between Canada and the country in which you reside.

If you are a non-resident of Canada and you received certain types of income (for example, alimony payments, pension or super-annuation benefits, retiring allowances, or RRSP and RRIF payments) that are otherwise subject to the withholding of tax at source, you may elect to file a Canadian income tax return if the tax reported would be less than the amount withheld. If you do, the election must be made within six months of the end of the calendar year, and you must report all income from Canadian sources. You may generally claim deductions that relate to income reported on the return. In addition, you may be able to claim personal tax credits (discussed in the next paragraph). Any Canadian tax that has been withheld from income reported on this elective return will be refunded to you if your return shows an overpayment of tax.

Personal tax credits are generally available to an electing non-resident only if more than half of the individual's income is taxable income earned in Canada. In addition, the amount of credits that may be claimed is limited. If you receive rental income from Canada, withholding tax is imposed on the gross amount of rent. You may, however, elect to file a Canadian income tax return and report the rental income and claim related expenses (including capital cost allowance). Again, you would make this election if it reduced your tax liability. You may not claim any other deductions or personal tax credits (i.e., the only income and expenses reported on this type of return must be related to the rental property). However, there is a catch: you will have to file a return for the year in which you dispose of the property and pay tax on any recaptured depreciation or taxable capital gains.

A non-resident of Canada is also subject to Canadian tax on dispositions of taxable Canadian property. Taxable Canadian property includes, among other things:

- real property situated in Canada;

- capital property used in carrying on business in Canada;

- shares of a corporation resident in Canada that is not listed on a prescribed stock exchange (Canadian or foreign);

- shares of a corporation resident in Canada that is listed on a prescribed stock exchange if, at any time during the five years immediately preceding a disposition of the shares, the non-resident and other non-arm's length persons held 25% or more of the issued shares of any class of the capital stock of the corporation; and

- shares of a non-resident corporation if certain Canadian content tests are met.

A non-resident will use the same rules to determine taxable capital gains and allowable capital losses as a Canadian resident. Although non-residents are not generally subject to provincial income tax on taxable capital gains, a federal surtax applies to income earned outside a province. The rate is 52% of basic federal tax.

✔ Tax Tip 63

If you are a non-resident and you are considering investing in Canada, depending on the type of investment and the magnitude of funds to be invested, you may benefit from holding your investment through a corporation, rather than directly. You should discuss your plans with your professional advisor.

✔ Tax Tip 64

If you are a non-resident and plan to become a resident of Canada, consider seeking professional advice regarding opportunities to minimize or defer tax as well as potential liabilities to avoid in the course of relocation.

⚜ Québec

If you are an investor resident in Québec, the comments throughout this chapter apply for Québec tax purposes, except for the following:

Reporting requirement for renovations and maintenance

Taxpayers, including partnerships, must file prescribed form TP-1086.R.23.12 with their Québec tax return if they incur expenditures for renovating or maintaining a building, structure or land that is situated in Québec and used in a business or to derive income from it.

Investment income

You may claim a Québec dividend tax credit of 11.08% of the actual amount of dividends (equivalent to 8.87% of the grossed-up amount) in the calculation of your Québec taxes.

Capital gains or losses

Unused losses that have been carried forward from years before 1985 may be applied at a rate of $1,000 per year to reduce income from any other source.

Safety deposit box

Safety box rental fees paid to a financial institution will no longer be deductible, starting in 1998.

Cumulative net investment losses (CNILs)

To encourage Québec investments, Québec excludes from the calculation of CNIL deductions:

- the Québec stock savings plan (QSSP);
- the Cooperative investment plan (CIP);
- Québec business investment companies (QBIC);

- R&D venture capital corporations;

- exploration expenses incurred in Québec; and

- the additional deduction for Québec exploration.

⊕ International investors

If the foreign tax credit that may be claimed in calculating your federal tax liability is limited, the balance could be claimed in the calculation of your Québec income taxes. Foreign tax withheld in excess of 15% may be deducted in arriving at net income for Québec tax purposes. For Québec purposes, the strategy of filing a waiver to keep open years in which unpaid interest is reported (see Tax Tip 62, regarding foreign tax credits, on page 134) may not be available. Revenue Québec's position is that only they can initiate waivers to keep years "open."

⊕ Non-resident investors in Canada

Special elections allowed under federal tax legislation dealing with:

- certain types of income (for example, alimony payments, pension or superannuation benefits, retiring allowances, RRSP or RRIF payments) paid or remitted to a non-resident; and

- rental income received by a non-resident of Canada,

do not apply for Québec tax purposes because Québec does not levy tax on such income.

For Québec tax purposes, any individual who has not resided in Canada at any time during the year but who has:

- been employed in Québec;

- conducted a business in Québec; or

- disposed of a taxable Québec property during the year,

will generally be subject to Québec tax. In such a case, the federal surtax of 52% of basic federal tax, normally applicable to income earned outside a province, does not apply.

Québec tax shelters

Québec encourages investment in specified areas or industries through various incentives. Stock savings plans provide tax deductions and venture capital programs are intended to foster investment in small to medium-sized corporations.

The following are considered to be "Québec tax shelters":

- the Québec stock savings plan (QSSP);

- the Cooperative investment plan (CIP);

- Québec business investment companies (QBIC);

- R&D venture capital corporations; and

- exploration expenses incurred in Québec.

• Québec stock savings plan (QSSP)

A taxpayer who:

- is resident in Québec on the last day of a taxation year; and

- has acquired qualifying shares,

may deduct a portion of the cost of the shares in computing taxable income. The last day of the contemplated taxation year is always December 31, rather than any other taxation year end under tax legislation, such as when a taxpayer ceases to reside in Canada.

The settlement date for acquisition of qualifying shares cannot be later than December 31. The deductible portion of the cost of qualifying shares is known as the "adjusted cost" and does not include brokerage, safekeeping or loan fees related to the shares. The adjusted cost of shares corresponds to a deduction varying between 50% and 100% of the actual cost of the shares, depending on the type of corporation, type of shares and type of investor.

The deduction that may be claimed each year with respect to QSSP shares is limited to 10% of "total income" of a taxpayer. In this context "total income" means net income minus social benefits and any capital gains deduction claimed in the year.

• QSSP Investment Fund (QIF)

Purchases of QSSP investment fund (QIF) securities allow an individual to take advantage of QSSPs. Generally, to be eligible for a QSSP deduction, the funds collected by the QIF must be invested in QSSP qualified shares, either as part of a public share offering or a private investment made by a qualifying corporation. Rules for QSSPs generally apply to investments in a QIF.

• Cooperative investment plan (CIP)

Rules for the deduction for shares of a cooperative investment plan (CIP) are similar to those for shares in a QSSP. Employees of a cooperative who purchase shares in their cooperative under a CIP may benefit from a basic 100% deduction. An additional deduction of 25% is available for investments under specific programs. An additional 25% will be given for special qualified plans in place after May 16, 1989, raising the deduction levels to 125% or 150%.

Eligible CIP investors also include individuals employed by a partnership in which an eligible cooperative that issues securities eligible for a CIP holds an interest at the time of issue, if the cooperative's share in the revenues or losses of the partnership exceeds 50%.

• Québec business investment companies (QBICs)

Québec business investment companies (QBICs) are special financing vehicles whose activities consist of investing in small and medium-sized private corporations. A QBIC must be registered as such with the Société de développement industriel du Québec (SDI).

A taxpayer who purchases ordinary shares with full voting rights in a QBIC is entitled to a deduction equal to the lesser of:

- 30% of total income; and

- 125% of the amount invested.

The deduction can reach 150% when a QBIC makes an investment in a designated region. Also, if you are an eligible employee of the corporation in which the investment is made, the deduction will be raised to 150% or 175%, depending on whether or not the investment is made in a designated region.

Any amount not claimed in the year may be carried forward to the five subsequent taxation years.

• R&D venture capital corporations

A deduction of 100% of the cost of the share will be granted to shareholders of an R&D venture capital corporation when the scientific research and experimental development expenditure is made by or on behalf of the eligible corporation. The basic deduction is limited to 30% of total income.

Any unused deduction may be carried forward into the five subsequent taxation years.

• Exploration expenses incurred in Québec

To maintain and enhance tax incentives of strategic importance to Québec's economy, the Québec government allows a 25% deduction with respect to certain exploration expenses incurred in Québec (in addition to the 100% regular deduction). An additional deduction of 50% can be obtained for surface mining exploration expenses. As a result, a deduction up to 175% of the original investment may be allowed.

It was announced that the 175% deduction will also apply to other expenses, such as expenses incurred for drilling or completion of an oil or gas well, construction of a temporary access road to that

142

well and site preparation for the well, provided the expenses qualify as Canadian exploration expenses.

• Disposition of certain Québec resource property

A special capital gains exemption is available for certain resource property acquired after May 14, 1992. It can be obtained by filing Form TP-726.20.2-V.

5 Retired Persons

5 Retired Persons

What's new?

- A Seniors Benefit will replace the existing OAS/GIS benefit system in 2001 (proposed).

- Tax treatment of U.S. social security payments received by Canadians to change again (proposed).

Retirement is no longer simple to define. Even if you are actively working and earning income, you should read this chapter if you (or your spouse) receive any pension or similar income, or if you are at least 64 years old. If you are a director of a corporation and are earning directors' fees, those fees are considered to be employment income and must be included on your tax return. Accordingly, you should look at Chapter 2, **Employees** (page 23), to see if anything pertains to you. For example, directors' fees are considered to be earned income for the purposes of determining how much you can contribute to your own RRSP or a spousal RRSP (although see page 146 for details about the reduced age limit for maturing your RRSP). Refer to pages 14 and 225 as well for a discussion concerning directors' liability.

The OAS/ GIS (Guaranteed Income Supplement) benefit system is to be replaced by a Seniors Benefit in 2001. If you were 60 or more on December 31, 1995, you and your spouse, no matter what age, will be guaranteed no less than your current pension entitlement. You will, however, have the choice of moving to the new system or keeping your monthly benefits as currently structured, whichever is more advantageous to you. You will not have to make the choice until the new system is about to be introduced in 2001. Refer to page 239 in Chapter 10, **Looking Ahead**, for further details about the proposed new system.

Pension income

You must include in income for tax purposes all of the following payments received during the year:

- benefits from your registered retirement savings plans (RRSPs), whether in the form of periodic payments or a lump sum payment;

- amounts received under your registered retirement income funds (RRIFs);

- income from an annuity;

- superannuation or pension benefits;

- Old Age Security (OAS) benefits;

- Canada Pension Plan (CPP) or Québec Pension Plan (QPP) benefits;

- benefits from a deferred profit sharing plan (DPSP);

- foreign pensions;

- retiring allowances; and

- death benefits.

Subject to some phase-out rules, an individual may no longer make a tax-free transfer of retiring allowances to an RRSP. Some grandfathering provisions permit individuals to continue to transfer up to $2,000 per year of service before 1996, plus $1,500 for each year before 1989 in which they earned no pension or DPSP benefits.

A death benefit is generally an amount paid to a spouse or other beneficiary in recognition of the deceased's employment service. If you received a death benefit, you must include the amount received in your income. If the deceased person was your spouse, $10,000 of death benefits are exempt from tax. If you received part of the death benefit in one year and the balance in the next, you may still deduct only $10,000 in total.

You may make tax-free transfers of lump sum amounts from an

RPP or DPSP to your RRSP (provided the amounts are transferred directly and subject to limits if the transfer is from a defined benefit RPP). However, periodic retirement or pension payments cannot be transferred to an RRSP tax free.

You may also contribute a lump sum amount received from a U.S. Individual Retirement Account (IRA) to your own RRSP or RPP.

Registered retirement savings plans (RRSPs)

The age at which you must arrange to receive a retirement income stream from the funds accumulated in your RRSP has been reduced from 71 to 69. You will not be permitted to contribute to retirement plans or accrue pension benefits after the end of the year in which you turn 69. Further, you will have to begin receiving retirement income out of these plans or your RRSP will be deregistered in the following year and the entire amount will be included in income and taxed at your normal tax rates.

If you have RRSP deduction room after age 69, you will be able to contribute to a spousal RRSP up until the end of the year in which your spouse turns 69.

The new rules do not apply if you were 70 or more at the end of 1996; you will be able to mature your plan as if the age limit were still 71. If you turned 69 in 1996, you will have to accelerate maturity by one year, i.e., your plan will have to mature by the end of 1997, the year in which you turn 70. Individuals who were under 69 at the end of 1996 will have to comply with the new rules and mature their RRSPs before the end of the year in which they turn 69.

By converting your RRSP into a program that provides you with retirement income, the tax shelter benefits of an RRSP are partially retained. Only the amount you actually receive each year is included in your income. Generally, you have two options:

- You can arrange to receive a life or a fixed-term annuity. The fixed-term annuity extends to age 90 and may be based on your

age or your spouse's age if he or she is younger than you. Various **147**
issuers may offer different features and prices, so allow yourself
some time in your 68th year for shopping around, when the time
comes to convert to an annuity.

Both types of annuities may be indexed in a variety of ways so
that payments increase each year. Life annuities may be guaranteed
for specific periods. Joint annuities based on the lives of both you
and your spouse may be arranged. You can also purchase an
annuity that may be commuted at your option (the annuity
options may be restricted if your RRSP has received a transfer
from an RPP, however).

• You can choose to establish a registered retirement income fund
(RRIF) with the funds accumulated in your RRSP (see below).

Registered retirement income funds (RRIFs)

A registered retirement income fund (RRIF), as indicated in the
RRSP section above, is one of the alternatives you have when converting your mature RRSP to a retirement income stream. As you
will see below, you may also establish an RRIF at any time.

Transfers from an RPP as well as an RRSP may be made to an
RRIF of which you are the annuitant (the person who will receive
payments). Transfers from an RPP to an RRIF of which your
spouse is the annuitant will also qualify if your spouse became the
annuitant as a result of marriage breakdown or your death.

You may have more than one RRIF and you may transfer funds
from an RPP or RRSP to your RRIF plans at any time. Since your
RRSP must mature (i.e., must be converted to some type of retirement income stream) by the end of the year in which you turn age
69, that is technically the latest time that you can transfer funds from
your RRSP to an RRIF. You may also contribute a refund of
premiums from a deceased spouse's RRSP to an RRIF tax free.

The RRIF rules allow payments to continue until the death of the annuitant or his or her spouse. Although a specific minimum amount must be paid to you each year (and taxed in your hands, of course), you may withdraw as much as you want at any time. The income tax regulations prescribe the minimum amount that must be withdrawn each year. There is no minimum amount for the year the plan is established. The minimum amounts are based on a complicated formula beginning at age 71. The formula for minimum RRIF payments if you are under 71, however, is quite simple: one divided by 90 minus your age. For example, if you set up an RRIF in the year in which you become 66, you would have to receive payments equal to at least 4.35% [1/(90-67)] of the value of the plan at the end of that year, but not until the next year, i.e., in the 67th year. At age 71, when the more complicated formula comes into effect, the minimum payments for that year are equal to at least 7.38% of the value in the plan at the beginning of the year. The minimum percentages that must be withdrawn increase each year until the annuitant (or his or her spouse) reaches the age of 94. For years following, the minimum payment is 20% of the value of the fund at the beginning of each year.

The new rules for maturing your RRSP reduce the age limit to 69, so the minimum payments that you will receive out of an RRIF established at age 69 will be based on the simple formula described in the preceding paragraph, although the first payment need not be withdrawn until the year in which you reach 70 years of age.

The rules apply to all RRIFs to which funds are transferred after the end of 1992. For most RRIFs that were purchased before the end of 1992 ("qualifying RRIFs"), lower minimum payment percentages apply for ages up to 77. The new minimum payment percentages apply to all RRIFs for ages above 77, regardless of the date of purchase.

Of course, the payments you receive are taxable in your hands. You may have a self-directed RRIF, a mutual fund RRIF or an RRIF that guarantees to pay a specific interest rate over the life of the plan.

✔ Tax Tip 65

If you have an RRIF from which you receive minimum annual payments based on your age, and you have a spouse who is younger, consider setting up a new RRIF. Minimum payments from the new RRIF can then be based on your spouse's age. The payments will be smaller but will stretch out over more years. (You may not alter the terms of your current RRIF to accommodate the smaller payments.) The minimum payments are just that; you can choose to take out more.

✔ Tax Tip 66

If you are receiving OAS benefits, withdrawals from your RRSP or payments from an RRIF may result in OAS benefits being reduced or eliminated (see page 150).

Pension income credit

The pension income tax credit is 17% of pension income or qualified pension income, depending on your age. The federal credit is limited to $170, which translates into $1,000 of pension income. If you are age 65 or over, pension income includes periodic payments from pension plans (including foreign funds or plans), annuities, profit sharing plans, RRSPs and RRIFs.

If you are under age 65, you may be eligible for the pension income credit if you receive qualified pension income. Qualified pension income includes life annuity payments from a superannuation or pension plan and certain amounts received as a consequence of the death of your spouse (including a common-law spouse): payments from an RRSP, RRIF or DPSP. Lump sum payments do not qualify in any event, nor do CPP or OAS benefits.

The pension income tax credit is transferable to your spouse if you are unable to use all or a portion of it.

| ## Age credit

You are entitled to claim an age credit if you are age 65 or over. The federal age credit is $592 in 1997, which is 17% of the "age amount" of $3,482.

The age credit is subject to an income test. The age amount on which your credit is based will be reduced by 15% of your net income exceeding $25,921 (in 1997). If your income is more than $49,134, you lose the credit entirely. These income thresholds are subject to the same indexing factor as your other personal claim amounts.

The age amount is not reduced if the credit is transferred from your spouse.

Old Age Security (OAS) clawback

Before July 1996, if your OAS benefits were subject to the clawback rules, you had to repay the benefits that you received through a special calculation on your income tax return. OAS benefits for a particular year are now determined with reference to your net income as reported on the income tax return that you filed for the previous year. If your net income in 1996 was less than $53,215, you should be receiving OAS benefits in 1997 as you did in the past. On the other hand, if your net income in 1996 was above $53,215, your OAS benefits for 1997 have either been reduced or eliminated entirely, depending on how much your net income exceeds the threshold. For example, based on OAS benefits of $4,370 (the maximum in 1996), you would continue to receive at least a portion of the OAS benefits as long as your net income was less than about $82,300. The $53,215 threshold is indexed in the same way as personal tax credits and tax brackets.

If you are no longer resident in Canada and are otherwise entitled to receive OAS payments (i.e., your net income falls below the current threshold), to continue receiving your benefits, you must file a statement of worldwide income.

✔ Tax Tip 67

If you are just over the $53,215 threshold and your spouse's net income is below it, consider splitting your CPP benefits if that will bring your net income below $53,215.

✔ Tax Tip 68

If you are considering making the election to include all of your spouse's taxable Canadian dividends in your income (see page 108), ensure that in so doing you are not subjecting yourself to reduced OAS benefits.

⏀ Foreign pensions

A foreign pension, including a pension from a U.S. Individual Retirement Account (IRA), must be included in your income and is therefore subject to tax in the same way as a Canadian pension.

Canada has social security agreements with a number of countries. These agreements coordinate benefits from each country and are intended to ensure that an individual is not subject to social security taxes of two countries. If you receive a pension from a country with which Canada has entered into a social security agreement, the taxation of your pension benefits may be affected. You should either seek professional advice or contact your local Health and Welfare Canada office for further information.

Under the most recent Protocol to the Canada-U.S. Tax Treaty, if you receive retirement or survivor benefits under the social security programs of either country, your benefits will be taxed only in the country that pays them. Residents of Canada who receive U.S. social security payments will pay U.S. tax and will not be subject to Canadian tax on the payments. Similarly, Canadian OAS or CPP payments to a person resident in the U.S. will be subject to Canadian withholding tax and will not be subject to U.S. tax.

Representatives from Canada and the U.S. have agreed to a draft Protocol to the Canada-U.S. Treaty that will change the rules dealing with the taxation of social security benefits once again. Under the proposed new rules, only the country where the recipient lives will be able to tax benefits received. This means that only Canada will be able to tax U.S. benefits paid to residents of Canada, and vice versa.

Once ratified, the change will be retroactive to January 1, 1996. Any excess tax collected since that date will be refunded retroactively to social security recipients in both countries. See page 173 of Chapter 7, **Taxpayers with U.S. Connections**, for further details about the draft Protocol and how it affects social security benefits.

Special expenses

Retirement does not trigger any special tax treatment of expenses that some retired people may face. However, the credit for medical expenses may apply more broadly than many people realize. In addition to payments to medical practitioners, payments for prescription drugs and various medical aids, the costs of one full-time attendant at home, full-time care in a nursing home, travelling expenses to obtain medical treatment in your area and home renovation costs to enable you to get around at home may be deductible. (See page 187 for additional information about the medical expenses tax credit.)

⚜ Québec

If you are a retired person resident in Québec, you should note the following Québec differences.

Health services fund

For more information about the health services fund contribution, please refer to page 73.

Special tax credit for retired persons

Québec's income tax system provides various refundable and non-refundable tax credits available to retired or elderly persons. Chapter 8, **Calculating Your Taxes** (page 203), provides more information on these credits.

Death benefits

Third parties who receive QPP death benefits after May 9, 1996 are no longer taxed on these amounts. The death benefits will be taxable in the estate of the deceased.

6 Separated or Divorced Persons

6 Separated or Divorced Persons

What's new?

- Tax treatment of child support payments changes in 1997.
- The Child Tax Benefit is to be replaced with an expanded National Child Benefit System (proposed).

People who are separated or divorced face a special set of tax issues. Those who anticipate separation or divorce must deal with issues that will have tax consequences for many years. These involve the possible distribution of property to satisfy family law requirements, as well as alimony and maintenance payments, income attribution rules, personal tax credits, retirement savings arrangements and the family's principal residence.

This chapter deals first with issues regarding past marriage breakdowns, and then with issues that are important at the time of marriage breakdown.

For income tax purposes, the definition of "spouse" has been extended to a common-law spouse. Two persons of the opposite sex will be considered to be spouses of each other if they are cohabiting in a conjugal relationship and either: (a) have so cohabited throughout the preceding 12 months; or (b) are the parents of the same child. Accordingly, the broad range of provisions in the Income Tax Act that govern the fiscal relations between spouses extends to common-law couples.

The rule means that common-law spouses are entitled to the married status tax credit and are permitted to contribute to spousal RRSPs. It also means that the attribution rules apply, and that common-law spouses must combine their incomes for purposes of the GST credit and the Child Tax Benefit.

For simplicity, in this chapter, "spouse" includes a former spouse.

In the past few years, the tax rules regarding alimony and maintenance payments have been redefined, largely as a result of court cases. The spouse making payments and the spouse receiving payments are both affected. Changes in the family law of several provinces have also made the division of assets on marriage breakdown more complex.

✔ Tax Tip 69

Counsel provided by a professional tax advisor may be as important on the breakdown of a marriage as legal advice from a divorce lawyer. The repercussions of failing to consider tax issues involved in a divorce or separation agreement can be very costly.

After marriage breakdown

Alimony and maintenance

Alimony or maintenance payments you make to your spouse are deductible for tax purposes if they meet certain criteria. (However, see the discussion below regarding the new treatment of child support that is generally effective May 1997.) Conversely, if your spouse can deduct payments to you, you must include them in your income. In general, the reverse is also true: if your spouse cannot deduct the payment, you need not include it in your income.

To be deductible, payments must:

- be periodic (lump sum payments do not qualify, even if made by instalment);

- be for the maintenance of the spouse and/or children; and

- generally be made pursuant to a decree, court order or judgment, or pursuant to a written agreement.

In addition, the spouses must be living apart at the time payment is made and throughout the remainder of the year.

The recipient must have complete discretion over how the payments are to be used, except in the case of third-party payments (e.g., mortgage payments made directly to a bank) and payments singled out in the divorce or separation agreement to be devoted to a particular use. Generally, the amount of the payment must be specified. However, indexed payments may qualify for a deduction, as may certain third-party payments of no specific amount. Indexed payments will qualify only if the formula for adjustment is an acceptable one (for example, payments adjusted in accordance with changes in the Consumer Price Index).

Periodic payments made before the date of a court order or written agreement are generally deductible to the payor if the payments are made in the same year as the order or agreement, or in the preceding year, and if the order or agreement specifically provides that the payments will be included in the income of the spouse and will be deductible by the payor.

Payments made directly to third parties may be deductible if the decree, court order, judgment or written agreement provides that the payments will be treated as income to the recipient and will be deductible to the payor.

Payments to your estranged spouse for specific purposes, and provided for in more recent decrees, written agreements etc., may also be deductible, depending on the date of your order or agreement and the purpose of the payment. These must be included in your spouse's income as well.

✔ Tax Tip 70

If you must take legal measures to enforce payment of alimony or maintenance, your legal costs are generally deductible for tax purposes. The legal costs associated with the separation and divorce, however, are not deductible.

You may be able to deduct maintenance payments for your former partner or your children made under a court order on the breakdown of a common-law relationship. Provided that a court order has been issued, the requirements for deductibility by the payor and taxability to the recipient are similar to those discussed for separation or divorce.

Changes to the tax treatment of child support payments came into effect in 1997. Child support payments paid pursuant to an agreement or court order made on or after May 1, 1997 are neither to be included in the income of the recipient for tax purposes, nor are they to be deducted in computing the income of the payor.

Child support paid pursuant to an agreement or court order made before May 1, 1997 will have to be included in the income of the recipient and will continue to be deductible to the payor. Parents with existing agreements may change to the new regime with relative ease by filing a joint election with Revenue Canada to apply the new tax treatment. The new tax treatment will also apply if an agreement or order is varied after April 30, 1997 to change the amount of child support. Further, the new tax treatment will apply (but not before May 1, 1997) in cases where after March 6, 1996, an agreement or order provides for the new treatment to apply to payments in respect of child support obligations that arise on or after a specified date.

The tax changes do not apply to spousal support. Periodic spousal support payments paid under a written agreement or court order will remain deductible from income by the payor and must be included in the income of the recipient for income tax purposes.

At the time of marriage breakdown

Income tax is unlikely to be the prime concern of a couple whose marriage is breaking down. Nevertheless, ignoring the tax consequences can be expensive when negotiating future financial arrangements and the division of property.

Lump sum payments or payments of capital are not deductible. Settlements at the time of divorce cannot be deducted by the payor and do not have to be included in the income of the recipient.

While the down payment on a home to be occupied by the spouse is not deductible, payments on account of principal and interest on the mortgage are, up to 20% of the original amount of the debt in any one year, provided the payments and tax consequences are specified in the agreement. The spouse benefitting from these payments has to include this amount in income, but may not receive any cash from the payor with which to satisfy any resulting tax liability.

Attribution rules

Income attribution rules (discussed on page 127) cease to apply upon separation or divorce, as long as the spouses are living apart as a result of their marriage breaking down. However, the spouses must jointly elect for capital gains not to be attributed. This election is intended to prevent one spouse from shouldering the unexpected tax liability that could occur if a capital asset were sold for a sizeable gain, most of which accrued during the marriage.

Capital property transferred to a spouse in settlement of rights that arise out of marriage, or to an individual pursuant to a prescribed court order, will be deemed to be transferred at the adjusted cost base of the property, so that no taxable capital gain will result. However, the transferor may elect otherwise in his or her return for the year of the transfer, and therefore govern the taxation of future capital gains. This should be taken into account in negotiating the settlement.

Personal tax credits

In the year of marriage breakdown, you may either claim the married status credit to which you normally would be entitled, or deduct your alimony or maintenance payments. You cannot do both. In either case, the spouse receiving the payments must include them in income. Of course, if the new rules dealing with child support payments apply to you, there will be no deduction or income inclusion for the payments. As long as you are not deducting amounts paid in respect of child support *in the year of marriage breakdown,* you may claim the married status tax credit.

Beginning in 1997, if you are separated throughout the year and provide any periodic support amount for your children or a former spouse, you may not claim any personal tax credits for any person covered by the payments. This is the case whether the payments are deductible to you or not.

✔ Tax Tip 71

Calculate your tax liability using both methods to determine which works out better in your particular situation. Remember that one method involves a deduction, the other a tax credit.

Equivalent-to-married credit

The equivalent-to-married credit is currently available to a single, separated or divorced parent of a child under the age of 18. Typically, the recipient of child support, rather than the payor, claims the credit.

This treatment will continue to apply under the new rules dealing with child support payments. The approach is consistent with the new federal child support guidelines and is based on the assumption that it is the recipient spouse who claims the equivalent-to-married credit.

The provision relating to the equivalent-to-married credit was modified recently to clarify that the credit may be claimed by an individual who was otherwise entitled to the married tax credit but did not claim it. For example, in the year in which an individual divorces or separates, he or she may claim either a married tax credit in respect of their former spouse or an equivalent-to-married tax credit for a dependent child residing with the individual.

Child Tax Benefit

Under the Child Tax Benefit system, the mother of eligible children ordinarily receives the non-taxable monthly payments. For the purposes of determining the amount of the payments, family earnings and income are combined. On marriage breakdown, the spouse with whom the child or children will be living may elect within 11 months following the month of breakdown that the former spouse's income be ignored for the purposes of computing the Child Tax Benefit for each subsequent month.

Refer to page 199 in Chapter 8, **Calculating Your Taxes**, for information about the proposed new National Child Benefit System that was announced in the 1997 federal budget.

Retirement plans

A tax-free transfer of funds from your RRSP or RRIF to your spouse's or common-law spouse's plan(s) is permitted if the transfer is made pursuant to a decree, court order or judgment or a written separation agreement, and the transfer relates to a division of property.

Retirement income payments eventually made will be taxed in the hands of the spouse who is the annuitant under the plan. As well, attribution rules that discourage one spouse from withdrawing the contributions he or she made to a spousal RRSP do not apply in the case of RRSP transfers or withdrawals on the breakdown of a marriage.

Special tax-free transfers are also allowed in the same circumstances from registered pension plans to other RPPs or RRSPs. Often, benefits from a plan are split between the spouses, including common-law spouses. Each spouse would receive the appropriate pension payments directly from the plan and be taxable on amounts received.

Canada Pension Plan (CPP) benefits may also be split between estranged spouses. Each spouse would be taxable on the amount received. To use this arrangement, you and your spouse must have been legally married and living together for a minimum of 36 consecutive months.

Principal residence

If you and your spouse own only one home at the time of marriage breakdown, the tax-free status of any accrued gain on the family home will generally be maintained. If one spouse continues to live in the home, he or she will be able to designate the home as a principal residence for each of the years it was occupied during the marriage and after the breakdown. The other spouse could acquire a principal residence after the marriage breakdown, and any gain on its disposition would be sheltered by the principal residence exemption.

The situation is more complex where two homes are owned at the time of marriage breakdown. If each home is sold at some point after a divorce, each spouse will want to claim the principal residence exemption for the years during which they were married.

However, only one home may be designated by a married couple for years after 1981. One spouse would have to forego designating his or her principal residence for the relevant years of marriage. Alternatively, ownership of one of the houses may be transferred at the time of the marriage breakdown and the available principal residence exemptions used at that time (see page 121).

If two houses eligible for principal residence designation are owned at the time of separation or divorce, careful planning will permit maximum use of the principal residence exemption and the greatest deferral of tax.

⚜ Québec

If you are a separated or divorced person resident in Québec, please note the following Québec differences:

Legal costs

In addition to the federal rules regarding the deductibility of legal costs, you may be able to deduct (for Québec tax purposes only) the legal or extra-legal expenses you paid, as plaintiff or respondent, for a review of the right to receive, or the obligation to pay, alimony or maintenance allowances if certain criteria are met.

However, legal or extra-legal expenses paid to establish the initial right to receive, or obligation to pay, an alimony or maintenance allowance are not deductible.

Attribution rules

The Québec income attribution rules are similar to the federal rules. Specific rules in the Civil Code of Québec, that favour economic equality between the spouses, can create some tax complications on death or marriage breakdown. Professional advice is recommended.

Exclusion of spouse's income after a separation

A spouse's income after separation will not reduce the married person's tax credit and will not have to be added to the total income used to determine tax benefits such as the income tax reduction for families, the property tax refund and the refundable tax credit for the QST.

Personal tax credits

In the year of marriage breakdown, Québec generally allows you to claim the married and dependent credits in addition to the deduction of alimony payments.

Alimony paid in respect of prior years

A recipient of alimony paid in respect of prior years may elect to pay the tax owing on the payments as if the alimony were received in the years to which the payments relate, rather than in the year of receipt. If an election is made, the payor will also have to claim the deduction in the years to which the payments relate.

Support payments

Specific legislation provides that, in certain cases, individuals making periodic support payments, must make their payments directly to the Minister of Revenue who will, in turn, remit the payments to the person entitled to the payments.

Child support payments

Similar to the federal changes, child support payments paid pursuant to an agreement or court order made on or after May 1, 1997 are neither to be included in the income of the recipient for tax purposes nor deducted in computing the income of the payor. Spousal support payments will continue to be included in income of the recipient and deductible to the payor in keeping with current tax rules.

7 Taxpayers with U.S. Connections

7 Taxpayers with U.S. Connections

What's new?

- The draft Protocol to the Canada–U.S. Treaty contains changes that will affect the taxation of social security benefits and certain capital gains (proposed).

If you are a Canadian working, investing, living or doing business in the U.S., if you own property in the U.S. or if you have or expect to have coverage under U.S. social security, then you may have a U.S. connection for tax purposes. If you are a U.S. citizen with comparable ties to Canada, you should review this chapter as well.

Special issues regarding employees on temporary assignment in or from another country are dealt with elsewhere in this book (see page 60).

A draft protocol to the Canada-U.S. Treaty was signed in the summer of 1997. The draft protocol contains proposed new measures that will change the rules for capital gains on company shares whose value is attributable to real estate and will amend yet again the rules dealing with the taxation of social security benefits.

Canada–U.S. Tax Treaty

Rules for the taxation of income earned in one jurisdiction by a resident or citizen of another are complex and depend on the nature, and in some cases the magnitude, of income received from U.S. sources, among other things. As a Canadian resident, non-U.S. citizen, you would not ordinarily be required to file a U.S. income tax return if you are receiving interest from deposits in a U.S. bank or if you are receiving dividends from some U.S. shares. (That income may, however, be subject to withholding tax at source.) On the other hand, if you are providing services in the U.S. in the capacity of an employee, or if you own property in the U.S., you may have to file a U.S. income tax return, even though you may ultimately not have any tax to pay.

Various provisions in the Canada–U.S. Tax Treaty may be significant to you. The table below shows a few types of payments you might be receiving from the U.S. Bear in mind that individual states may not recognize treaty benefits, particularly on employment and pension income.

U.S. Withholding rates on payments to individuals

			% of payment or proceeds withheld in the U.S. (in general)
Received from the U.S.	Rents and royalties		0% or 10%
	Interest		10%
	Dividends		15%
	Pension payments	Periodic	
		Lump sum	30%
	Capital gain realized by Canadian resident on disposition of U.S. real property*		10%
	Alimony and maintenance		Exempt
	Employment income earned in the U.S.	Within treaty exemption limits**	
		Non-exempt	Applicable federal and state rates

* May apply for withholding certificate. Gain is also subject to tax at applicable federal (and possibly state) rates.

** Exempt by treaty if:
- remuneration is less than US$10,000; or
- the individual was present in the U.S. for less than 184 days and remuneration was not borne by an employer who is a resident of, or has a permanent establishment in, the U.S.

✔ Tax Tip 72

Under U.S. domestic law, interest earned on deposits with U.S. banks is generally free of tax when paid to a non-resident. If withholding tax is deducted at source, you should advise the bank immediately. You may have to provide a Certificate of Foreign Status.

170 | Capital gains on real estate

Under the Canada–U.S. Treaty, Canada can tax capital gains realized by a resident of the U.S. on the disposition of shares of any corporation, trust or partnership whose value is made up primarily of Canadian real estate. Similarly, the U.S. can tax gains realized by a resident of Canada on what is known as a "United States real property interest."

A result of changes to the definition of "taxable Canadian property" for Canadian tax purposes is that Canada may tax non-residents' gains on shares of non-resident corporations and interests in non-resident trusts, if most of the value of the shares or interests is attributable to Canadian real estate or resource property.

The proposed changes to the treaty will limit the application of the new definition of taxable Canadian property in the case of U.S. residents. Canada will agree not to tax U.S. residents' gains on shares of corporations that are not resident in Canada and the U.S. will agree that "United States real property interests" will not include shares of corporations that are not resident in the U.S. The change will apply as of April 26, 1995.

What does the change mean to you? If you invest in U.S. real estate through a Canadian company, you will continue to pay Canadian tax, rather than any possible future U.S. tax, when you sell your shares down the road. In the same manner, U.S. investors in U.S. companies that hold property in Canada will still pay U.S. tax, rather than Canadian tax, when they dispose of their shares.

Canadian income tax rules are complex enough on their own, without having to take into account the tax rules of another jurisdiction. You should discuss any transborder issues with your professional tax advisor.

U.S. estate tax

U.S. estate tax is levied on the fair market value of U.S. "situs property" owned by a deceased as of the date of death. U.S. situs property includes: real estate (a vacation condominium, a private house or U.S. real estate used or held in connection with a U.S. business venture); shares of a U.S. corporation (whether public or private); debt obligations issued by U.S. residents (including debt obligations issued by the U.S. government); and other personal property situated in the U.S. (including furnishings, cars, boats, jewellery and even the value of a membership in a U.S. club). Non-recourse debt attributable to U.S. assets, as well as a portion of other liabilities, may be deducted to arrive at the net taxable value of an estate. Deposits with U.S. banks or savings and loan associations, as well as proceeds from life insurance policies, are excluded from the U.S. taxable estate of a non-resident, non-citizen decedent.

With an almost invisible border between Canada and the U.S., it is not unusual for Canadians to own substantial property in the U.S. With estate tax rates ranging from 18% to 55%, Canadians who die owning U.S. situs property could face significant estate tax liabilities. Fortunately, the 1995 Protocol to the Canada-U.S. Treaty contains some relieving provisions (see below).

Canada has no estate tax. Instead, Canadian income tax law deems a disposition of the decedent's property on death and income tax is levied on the accrued capital gains. Canadian income tax on accrued gains on property that passes from the decedent to the surviving spouse or to a spousal trust can be deferred until the death of the surviving spouse. The opportunity for a Canadian to defer U.S. estate tax until the death of a surviving spouse is more limited. In fact, property bequeathed by an individual to a surviving spouse may be subject to U.S. estate tax twice – once on the death of the individual and again on the death of the spouse.

The 1995 Protocol to the Canada-U.S. Treaty provides for relief from U.S. estate tax and offers protection against double taxation. In the case of an individual resident in Canada (other than a U.S. citizen), determination of a U.S. estate tax liability rests with the value and situs of the assets of the individual's estate. If the value of the worldwide gross estate of a Canadian resident does not exceed US$1.2 million, the estate will be subject to federal U.S. estate taxes

172   only in respect of property whose sale would yield a gain that would
be taxable to an individual as a result of the provisions in the treaty
that deal with gains. This property would include real property,
resource property and business property of a permanent establishment.

Further, under the Protocol, the U.S. estate tax liability of a non-
U.S. citizen Canadian will be determined taking into account the
US$600,000 exemption that is otherwise available to U.S. citizens. The
mechanics of the exemption are achieved through a "unified credit"
of US$192,800. The credit, however, is based on the percentage of a
Canadian individual's total worldwide estate that is located in the U.S.
For example, if all of your assets are in the U.S., your estate would be
entitled to the full credit. If only half of your assets are in the U.S., only
half the credit would apply, and so on. The unified credit so calculated is then reduced by any credit for gifts previously made by the
deceased. An additional marital property credit (of up to US$192,800)
is also available in respect of spousal bequests of U.S.-situated property.

To the extent that a deceased individual has a U.S. estate tax liability, the tax would be eligible for foreign tax credit treatment in
Canada. The U.S. estate tax is based on the total value of the property in question; Canadian taxes are exigible on appreciation of the
same property, i.e., tax is levied on gains arising as a result of the
deemed disposition of property on death. A deceased's estate will pay
the greater of the Canadian tax on the gain and the U.S. tax on the
value, generally the latter.

✔ Tax Tip 73

Canadians with real property interests in the U.S. or significant
U.S. investments should still review their portfolio arrangements
with a view to taking advantage of U.S. estate tax planning
techniques. If you are concerned that you might have a U.S.
estate tax problem despite the relief available under the Protocol,
you might consider some of the following suggestions for
reducing your U.S. taxable estate:

- Split property with your spouse and/or among your children. Every individual is entitled to his or her own estate tax credit.

- Refinance. (Non-recourse loans secured by U.S. situs property reduce the net taxable value of an estate.)

- Rent rather than buy personal use property, such as cars, boats and vacation properties.

- Change your investment portfolio and reinvest in Canada or elsewhere.

- Consider using a Canadian corporation to hold your U.S. property.

- Evaluate the cost of life insurance as a means of funding a possible U.S. tax liability.

Professional tax advice is a must before you attempt to implement any strategy to reduce or eliminate your exposure to U.S. estate tax.

U.S. social security payments

Under current rules, which became effective January 1, 1996, social security benefits are taxed only in the country that pays them. Accordingly, residents of Canada who receive U.S. social security payments are subject to U.S. tax and are not liable for Canadian tax on the amounts received. Similarly, Canadian OAS and CPP benefits paid to a person resident in the U.S. are subject to Canadian withholding tax and are not subject to U.S. tax.

Amendments proposed under the most recent draft Protocol to the Canada-U.S. Treaty will grant an individual's country of residence the exclusive right to tax social security benefits.

What does this mean to you? If you are a resident of Canada, a non-U.S. citizen and are receiving U.S. social security benefits, only Canada will be able to tax the amounts you receive. (Currently, U.S. social security benefits that you receive are subject to U.S.

withholding tax of 25.5%.) Once the protocol is signed and ratified, the new rule will apply as of January 1, 1996.

Once the new rules are in place, the U.S. will stop withholding tax. The benefits you receive will be taxed on your Canadian income tax return. Only 85% of the benefits, however, will be taxed, because you will be able to deduct 15% of the amount you receive in calculating your income that is subject to tax.

What happens for 1996 and 1997?

Because the draft Protocol has not yet been ratified, the U.S. cannot stop withholding income tax from payments that you are currently receiving. Once the amendments are passed, you will receive a refund of the tax withheld by the U.S. At the time of writing, refunds are not expected until sometime in early 1998. Both governments intend that you will not have to make applications for refunds of the withholding tax. Rather, refunds of the appropriate amount of withholding tax will be based on exchanges of information between the two countries.

Similar rules will apply when U.S. residents are receiving OAS or CPP benefits from Canada.

Beneficiaries of retirement arrangements

Canadian-resident beneficiaries of U.S. retirement arrangements and U.S.-resident beneficiaries of Canadian retirement arrangements are allowed to elect to defer Canadian or U.S. taxation, respectively, until funds are received from the plans.

Gambling

The 1995 Protocol permits Canadian residents who gamble in the

U.S. to offset gains with losses resulting from wagering transactions, for the purpose of computing their U.S. tax liability.

Canadian "snowbirds"

Many Canadian "snowbirds" are required to file a special statement with the U.S. tax authorities.

A Canadian citizen and resident will also be considered to be a U.S. resident for tax purposes by the Internal Revenue Service (IRS) if he or she meets a "substantial presence" test. The individual is deemed to meet this test if he or she is present in the U.S. for 31 days during the year and, if pursuant to the following formula, he or she is present in the U.S. for 183 days or more: one-sixth of the days in the U.S. in the second previous year plus one-third of the days in the U.S. in the previous year plus all of the days in the current year. Canadians who spend just over four months a year in the U.S. will generally meet this test.

If an individual is considered to be a resident according to the test above, but spends fewer than 183 days in the U.S. in the current year, has a tax home in a foreign country and a "closer connection" with the foreign country, the individual will not be considered to be a U.S. resident and will not have to file a U.S. resident tax return as long as he or she files a statement with the IRS.

A tax home is generally considered to be the country where the individual reports for work or where the individual has his or her regular place of abode. Certain factors are considered in determining whether a "closer connection" exists. These include the location of the individual's permanent home, family, social and economic ties. The IRS will also consider the location in which the individual holds a driver's licence, voting registration and country of residence designated on forms and documents.

To claim the "closer connection" exemption, an individual must file Form 8840 or a prescribed statement under penalties of perjury. The statement must contain the following information:

- the individual's name, address, U.S. identification number and visa number, if any;

- the individual's Canadian passport number;

- the year for which the statement is to apply;

- the number of days of presence in the U.S. during the past three years;

- whether the individual has taken steps to obtain permanent resident status;

- the facts that would indicate a "closer connection" to a foreign country; and

- sufficient evidence to show that the individual has filed a return as a Canadian resident.

The "closer connection" statement must generally be filed by June 15 with the IRS in Philadelphia, Pennsylvania. If a U.S. tax return is otherwise required, the statement should be filed with the return. Failure to file the statement could result in the individual's being treated as a U.S. resident subject to U.S. tax.

Apart from the Canada–U.S. Tax Treaty, a Canadian resident who does not meet the "closer connection" test, (i.e., who has a U.S. "green card" [permanent residence status] or who spends 183 or more days in the U.S. in a year) will be considered to be a U.S. resident for tax purposes and required to file a U.S. tax return. However, such an individual may be considered a resident of Canada under the treaty. As a resident of Canada, the individual will generally be able to exclude non-U.S. income from the U.S. return. The individual will, however, be required to file a treaty-based disclosure form (see below) and disclose his or her world income.

In view of the serious implications, you should consult your professional tax advisor if you regularly spend time in the U.S. or if you have a vacation or retirement home there.

Disclosure of treaty-based filing positions

Canadian individuals who benefit from the Canada–U.S. Tax Treaty may have to file a statement disclosing the fact that a treaty provision has been used to reduce or eliminate U.S. tax that would otherwise be payable. In cases in which no U.S. tax return is filed, a disclosure statement may still have to be filed if a taxpayer relies on a treaty-based benefit.

The reporting requirement is waived when the return-based position pertains to, among other things:

- treaty-reduced withholding payments such as interest, dividends, rents or royalties paid to unrelated parties; and

- a reduction or modification of taxation of income derived from wages and salaries, pensions, annuities and social security payments.

Other situations will require disclosure too. For example, if a Canadian resident does not meet the "closer connection" test (see Canadian "snowbirds" on page 175) and is relying on the Canada–U.S. Treaty to exclude non-U.S. income from a U.S. return, disclosure will generally be required. When a Canadian relies on a provision of the Canada–U.S. Treaty that reduces or modifies the taxation of a gain or loss from the disposition of U.S. real property interests, or claims application of the non-discrimination clause of the treaty, disclosure will also generally be required.

Although it is not a required form, IRS Form 8833 may be used to provide the necessary information. The form, or other similar disclosure statement, should be filed with an individual's tax return. Fairly detailed information must be reported, including the taxpayer's name and address, the nature and amount of the gross receipts on which the treaty benefit is claimed and a statement of facts relied upon to support each separate position taken.

Penalties for failure to disclose a treaty-based position are stiff. For an individual, the fine is $1,000 per position not disclosed.

178   Canada–U.S. Social Security Agreement

The reciprocal Social Security Agreement between Canada and the United States coordinates the social security programs that provide old age, disability, survivor and death benefits of the two countries. It protects the social security rights that Canadian and U.S. migrant workers have earned through a combination of residence status and social insurance contributions. It also provides for continuity of coverage and ensures that a worker will not be contributing to both countries' social security schemes for the same work.

⚜ Québec

If you are a Québec resident with a U.S. connection for tax purposes, or if you are a U.S. citizen with comparable ties with Québec, the federal rules generally apply.

8 Calculating Your Taxes

8 Calculating Your Taxes

What's new?

- Tax incentives for charitable giving to be enriched (proposed).

- List of medical expenses eligible for tax credit to be broadened (proposed).

- Education and tuition fee tax credits to be increased; other measures relating to tax assistance for education and training enhanced (proposed).

- National Child Benefit System will replace the existing Child Tax Benefit (proposed).

Ultimately your tax has to be calculated – first by you or your advisor, then by Revenue Canada. Even after all the elements in your tax return are determined, calculating your tax can be a confusing exercise, even when you are using the tax schedules provided in the Revenue Canada Guide, or a commercial computer program.

This chapter, along with information that Revenue Canada provides, will help guide you through the many steps involved in calculating your tax. Throughout the chapter you will encounter references to the personal tax flowchart (developed especially for this book to show how the various elements in a tax calculation are related). The flowchart appears twice (pages 183 and 196). The second version has an extra section that deals with alternative minimum tax (AMT) that includes boxes referred to by letter (e.g., flowchart box D). All the other boxes are numbered (e.g., flowchart box 4) and are the same in both versions. The chapter, however, will still make sense even if you prefer to ignore the flowcharts.

The appendices (especially Appendix 2 on page 256) can help you estimate the amount of tax you will be required to pay.

As in other chapters, material at the end highlights important additional information and differences for Québec taxpayers.

Taxable income

From total income to taxable income

Your total income includes income from employment, investments, taxable capital gains, pensions and business income [**flowchart box 1**]. These have been discussed in other chapters of this book.

After working out your total income, you calculate your taxable income in two stages. Your total income less certain deductions and adjustments equals net income. Net income less other deductions gives you your taxable income.

Deductions

The first set of deductions includes RRSP and RPP contributions, union or professional dues, child care expenses, ABILs, moving expenses, alimony or maintenance payments and interest and carrying charges for investments [**flowchart box 2**]. Another deduction in arriving at net income is the social benefits repayment ("clawback") discussed later in this chapter [**flowchart box 14**].

Subtracting these deductions from your total income yields your net income [**flowchart box 3**]. Net income is used in a number of preliminary calculations, such as the "equivalent-to-married" credit.

A second set of deductions [**flowchart box 4**] includes the capital gains deduction (if applicable), the employee home relocation deduction, stock option and share deductions and deductions for net capital and non-capital losses from previous years.

Subtracting this second set of deductions from net income produces your taxable income [**flowchart box 5**].

Taxable income and net income are used in some provinces' flat tax calculations – a form of surtax (see Appendix 5, page 270).

182 | Federal tax

Federal tax is calculated using your taxable income and the federal marginal rates **[flowchart boxes 5 and 6]** found in Appendix 4 (page 266) or in Schedule 1 of your 1997 tax return. Once you have determined your federal tax, you will have to subtract some tax credits and add the federal surtax. As well, you will have to make a number of other adjustments and calculate provincial (or territorial) income tax before arriving at your actual tax liability for the year.

Non-refundable personal, dividend and other tax credits

From the amount you have calculated, you deduct your personal and other non-refundable tax credits **[flowchart box 8]**, including self-employed CPP contributions **[flowchart box 13]**. These credits are based on amounts you claim. Every taxpayer claims the basic personal amount; other claims depend on individual circumstances: Are you married? Are you age 65 or over? Did you have substantial medical expenses? Did you make any charitable donations?

Your credit is calculated as 17% of the total of these claims, except that higher charitable donations are credited at 29%.

Sufficient non-refundable credits could reduce your basic federal tax **[flowchart box 9]** to zero, eliminating your federal and provincial income tax liabilities. They cannot produce a negative amount that would create a refund, unlike some other credits, which are refundable (discussed later).

Appendix 6 (page 276) sets out the various personal tax credits.

• Personal tax credits

Personal tax credits **[flowchart box 8]** are the first non-refundable tax credits. They reduce your federal tax. Personal tax credits are equal to 17% of your "claim amounts." For example, as noted above, everyone is entitled to claim the basic personal amount, which

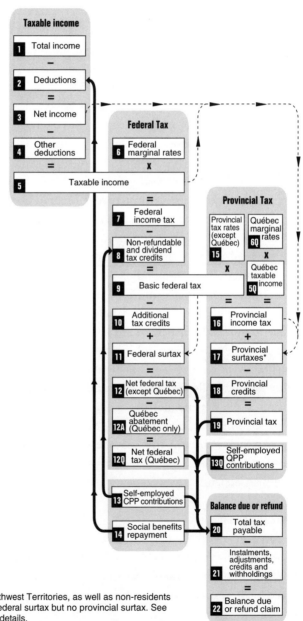

Taxable income

1 Total income

−

2 Deductions

=

3 Net income

−

4 Other deductions

=

5 Taxable income

Federal Tax

6 Federal marginal rates

X

=

7 Federal income tax

−

8 Non-refundable and dividend tax credits

=

9 Basic federal tax

−

10 Additional tax credits

+

11 Federal surtax

=

12 Net federal tax (except Québec)

−

12A Québec abatement (Québec only)

=

12Q Net federal tax (Québec)

13 Self-employed CPP contributions

14 Social benefits repayment

Provincial Tax

15 Provincial tax rates (except Québec)

6Q Québec marginal rates

X

5Q Québec taxable income

X

=

=

16 Provincial income tax

+

17 Provincial surtaxes*

−

18 Provincial credits

=

19 Provincial tax

13Q Self-employed QPP contributions

Balance due or refund

20 Total tax payable

−

21 Instalments, adjustments, credits and withholdings

=

22 Balance due or refund claim

* Residents of the Northwest Territories, as well as non-residents of Canada, pay the federal surtax but no provincial surtax. See Appendix 5 for more details.

is $6,456 for 1997. At 17%, the claim translates into a credit of $1,098.

If you are married, you may claim an amount in respect of a spouse you are supporting. The claim, and hence the credit, will be reduced dollar for dollar if your spouse's net income is more than $538, dropping to zero at a net income of $5,918.

You may claim an equivalent-to-married credit if you are single, widowed, separated or divorced and you wholly support a person related to you by blood, marriage or adoption. Except in the case of a dependent child, the person you are supporting must reside with you in Canada. The person you support must be under 18 years of age, unless that person is your parent or grandparent, or unless the person was dependent on you because of a mental or physical infirmity. The amount of the equivalent-to-married credit is the same as the married credit. Further, only one equivalent-to-married credit may be claimed per household.

Although you may claim only one equivalent-to-married credit, you may also claim credits for dependents (your or your spouse's children, grandchildren, parents, grandparents, brothers, sisters, aunts, uncles, nieces, nephews and in-laws) who are totally dependent on you for support. The dependents must be at least 18 years old and must be physically or mentally handicapped. The claim amount is $2,353 if the dependent's net income is less than $4,103, dropping to nil at a net income of $6,456. Special rules apply to determine the maximum amount that may be claimed if an infirm dependent qualifies for both the equivalent-to-married credit and the credit for an infirm dependent.

• Disability credit

If you are severely disabled, a disability tax credit is available. The disability tax credit for 1997 is $720. Generally, your daily living activities must be markedly restricted and the impairment must have lasted or be expected to last for a continuous period of at least 12 months.

A medical doctor or optometrist must certify the disability on a prescribed form, the Disability Tax Credit Certificate, which must be filed with your return when you first make your claim. The 1997 federal budget proposes to allow audiologists to certify eligibility for the credit in respect of hearing impairments.

A taxpayer may also claim the unused part of a dependent's disability credit. You may claim the credit for a person in respect of whom you claimed the equivalent-to-married credit, or for a dependent child or grandchild who is at least 18 years of age and who has a mental or physical handicap.

Certain non-refundable credits that your spouse does not require to reduce his or her tax payments to zero may be transferred to you. The age, disability, tuition and education fees and pension income credits are all transferable.

• EI, CPP or QPP credits

If you paid employment insurance (EI) premiums or contributed to the CPP or QPP, you are entitled to credits based on your contributions and the maximum required.

• Pension income credit

If you receive various types of pension income, you are entitled to a pension income credit of 17% of eligible pension income, to a maximum credit of $170 (or $1,000 of pension income). The credit is transferable to your spouse to the extent that you are unable to use it. (Refer to page 149 for the types of pension income that are eligible for the credit and strategies to ensure that you will be entitled to use it.)

• Age credit

You are entitled to claim an age credit if you are 65 or over. The federal age credit is $592 in 1997, which is 17% of the "age amount" of $3,482.

The age credit is subject to an income test. The age amount on which your credit is based will be reduced by 15% of your net income exceeding $25,921 (in 1997). If your income is more than $49,134, you will lose the credit entirely. These income thresholds are subject to the same indexing factor as your other personal claim amounts.

The age amount will not be reduced if the credit is transferred from your spouse.

• Tuition and education tax credits

The federal tuition credit is 17% of the portion of eligible tuition fees that exceeds $100. The 1997 federal budget proposes to increase the education credit to 17% of $200 (from $100), for each month or part of a month that the student was enrolled in a qualifying educational program as a full-time student at a designated educational institution. The increase will be phased in, rising to $150 in 1997 and to $200 for 1998 and subsequent taxation years. The student need only be enrolled in a qualifying program; he or she need not be actually attending the designated educational institution. This ensures that the credit is available to students participating in long-distance education programs or correspondence courses. Entitlement to both credits must be supported by Form T2202 or Form T2202A, which the educational institution will provide. Enrolment in either a Canadian or foreign educational institution may entitle the student to a credit.

✔ Tax Tip 74

The tax credits may be transferable from the student to a supporting person (generally a parent, grandparent or spouse). Only the amount that the student is unable to use to reduce his or her federal tax to zero can be transferred. The total of tuition and education credits that can be transferred is $850. This corresponds to $5,000 of tuition fee and education amounts that may be transferred.

The tuition and education tax credits must be claimed by the student or transferred to a supporting individual in the taxation year to which they relate. In certain circumstances, students are unable to fully use or transfer the credits. For example, students may have low incomes, high tuition fees, no supporting individual or a supporting individual with low income in the year. The 1997 federal budget proposes to allow students to take full advantage of the tuition and education credits by permitting students to carry forward indefinitely, unused amounts on which the credits are based until they have sufficient tax liability to use them. The proposed measure is effective beginning with the 1997 taxation year.

Tuition fees may be claimed only on a calendar year basis. On your 1997 return, for example, you may claim only fees paid for courses taken between January 1 and December 31, 1997.

Fees eligible for the tuition credit include the basic costs of instruction as well as other charges, such as library and laboratory facilities and mandatory computer service fees. Increasingly, other ancillary fees are being imposed on students. Accordingly, effective for the 1997 taxation year, the federal budget proposes to expand the list of fees that may be included in the base on which the tuition credit is calculated. Mandatory ancillary fees imposed by universities, colleges and other post-secondary institutions – fees for health services, athletics and various other services – will be eligible for the tuition credit. Student association fees and ancillary fees at institutions certified by the Minister of Human Resources Development, however, are specifically excluded from the list of eligible fees.

• Medical expense tax credit

You may claim a tax credit for medical expenses paid within any 12-month period ending in the year. Expenses for which you are reimbursed, either by your employer or a private or government-sponsored health care plan, are not eligible for the credit. However, few plans reimburse 100% of expenses, and the difference between the amount you actually pay and the amount received from the health plan is a medical expense.

The list of eligible medical expenses is extensive and includes fees paid to a private health or dental plan. Although most of us are quite good about keeping our receipts for doctor, dentist and pharmacy bills, we tend to forget about receipts for premiums paid to private plans. Make sure that you and your spouse (and other family members, if appropriate) keep them. The receipts must be attached to your tax returns to be eligible for the credit.

Total eligible medical expenses must first be reduced by the lesser of 3% of your net income and $1,614 in 1997. This amount is indexed annually in the same way as personal tax credits. The $1,614 cap takes effect if your net income is more than $53,800. The tax credit is 17% of the amount remaining.

✔ Tax Tip 75

Carefully select the 12-month period for medical expenses. Keep your receipts for 1998 if some 1997 expenses are not claimed on your 1997 return.

Up to $5,000 of part-time attendant care expenses that are not otherwise deductible in computing income qualify for the medical expense tax credit. Eligible expenses are those incurred by or on behalf of a disabled person who qualifies for the disability tax credit in respect of an attendant who is not related to the disabled person.

The 1997 federal budget proposes to increase the maximum amount of remuneration for part-time attendant care eligible for the medical expense tax credit to $10,000 from $5,000 and to $20,000 from $10,000 for the year in which an individual dies.

The budget also contains proposals that will expand the list of medical expenses eligible for the medical expense tax credit. Effective for the 1997 taxation year, eligible expenses include:

• 50% of the cost of an air conditioner for individuals with severe chronic ailments, diseases or disorders (to a maximum of $1,000);

• 20% of the cost of a van that is adapted, or that will be adapted within six months, for the transportation of an individual using a wheelchair (to a maximum of $5,000);

- sign language interpreter fees;

- expenses incurred for moving to accessible housing (to a maximum of $2,000); and

- reasonable expenses relating to modifications to the driveway of an individual's principal residence to facilitate access to a bus if the individual has a severe and prolonged mobility impairment.

• Refundable medical expense tax credit

Effective for the 1997 taxation year, the 1997 federal budget proposes to introduce a refundable tax credit for low-income working Canadians with higher than average medical bills.

The refundable credit, which will be based on eligible medical expenses, will be available to workers with at least $2,500 in earned income. The credit, calculated as the lesser of $500 and 25% of the allowable portion of expenses that can be claimed under the medical expense tax credit, will have to be reduced by 5% of family net income in excess of $16,069.

Individuals who claim this credit will also be able to claim the medical expense tax credit.

• Charitable donation tax credit

Donations that you make to registered Canadian charities translate into tax credits on your income tax return. The amount of donations that may be claimed in any one year is limited to a percentage of your net income, but donations in excess of the limit may be carried forward for five years.

Tax incentives for charitable giving were enriched in each of the 1994, 1995 and 1996 federal budgets. Generally, the changes are intended to encourage larger donations to charitable organizations and to facilitate donations of gifts capital property ("gifts in kind").

Currently, the annual limit on charitable donations is 50% of net income. Donations to registered Canadian charities as well as donations to specified foreign universities are eligible for the tax credit. Donations to U.S. charities or foreign charities in countries with which Canada has a tax treaty also qualify, but normally only to the extent that you have income from the foreign jurisdiction. More generous rules deal with qualifying donations to the Crown or donations of certified Canadian cultural property and to gifts in kind.

The 1997 federal budget proposes further changes. Beginning in 1997, the annual net income limit on which the charitable donation tax credit is based will be 75%. The limit will apply to all charitable gifts, including gifts to the Crown (currently, the credit for donations to the Crown is limited to 100% of net income). Donations in the year of death and the preceding year, as well as donations of ecologically sensitive land and Canadian cultural property, will continue to be eligible up to 100% of net income.

For income tax purposes, making a gift in kind has two consequences. First, you are normally considered to have made a gift to the charity in an amount equal to the fair market value of the property. Second, you are considered to have disposed of the property and, if it has appreciated in value, to have realized a capital gain.

The federal budget proposes to increase the 75% net income limit by a further 25% of any taxable capital gains arising from the donation of appreciated capital property. This is intended to offset any tax liability arising from the donation of such property in the year the donation is made. The budget also proposes to halve the income inclusion rate on capital gains arising from certain donations by individuals to charities (other than private foundations) to 37.5% from 75%. Donations of securities (such as shares, bonds, bills, warrants and futures that are listed on a prescribed stock exchange) will be eligible for the reduced capital gains inclusion rate, provided the donation is made between February 18, 1997 and the end of the calendar year 2001. Prescribed stock exchanges include Alberta, Montreal, Toronto, Vancouver, Winnipeg and a number of foreign stock exchanges.

An example best illustrates the budget proposals. Assume that you wish to donate some bonds to a favourite charity (and the bonds are eligible for the proposed reduced capital gains inclusion rate). The bonds cost $40,000 and have a current fair market value of $120,000. You would be considered to have made a charitable gift of $120,000 and the charity would issue a receipt to you in that amount. You would also have to include in income a taxable capital gain of $30,000 [($120,000 – $40,000) x 37.5%]. Assume further that your net income, including the taxable capital gain, is $100,000. The tax credit for your $120,000 gift in that year would be based on $82,500, with the excess $37,500 available for carryforward to be claimed in any of the next five years. The $82,500 maximum is based on the limit of $75,000 [75% x $100,000 of net income] plus an additional $7,500, which is 25% of the taxable capital gain arising on the disposition of the bonds to the charity [25% x $30,000].

The budget also contains proposals to encourage donations of depreciable assets such as buildings and equipment by adjusting the amount of donations the donor can claim as a percentage of net income. The budget proposes to increase the net income limit by 25% of any capital cost allowance (CCA) recapture arising from donations of depreciable capital property for taxation years commencing after 1996.

✔ Tax Tip 76

The effect of this last proposal is that donors of depreciable assets will have sufficient tax credits to more than offset the tax arising from the recapture of CCA. Accordingly, this proposal will be of particular benefit to you if you are considering making a donation of buildings, equipment or other similar assets.

You must file official tax receipts with your tax return. (Cancelled cheques are not acceptable.) Otherwise, the tax credit may be disallowed.

The tax credit for charitable donations is two-tiered. The credit is 17% of the first $200 of charitable donations plus 29% on any excess. Either spouse may claim the donations of the other, no matter whose name is on the official receipt.

✔ Tax Tip 77

If you and your spouse donate more than $200 in any one year, the tax credit will be larger if one spouse claims the entire amount. For example, if you and your spouse each donate $200 and claim a tax credit on your own returns for the donations made, your tax credit would be $34 each [$200 x 17%], for a family total of $68. On the other hand, if one of you included the entire amount of donations on your return, the tax credit would be $92 (200 x 17% + $200 x 29%).

Tax advantages are just an added benefit of charitable giving; as with your investment decisions, tax is only one factor. A donation that offers little or no tax benefit should not be rejected on that ground alone.

✔ Tax Tip 78

Watch the timing of your donations. If you donate $400 this year, $200 of your tax credit will be calculated at 17% and $200 at 29%. If, instead, you donate $200 in December and another $200 in January of the following year, your tax credit will be determined using 17% in both years, and your tax credit will be $24 less.

• Dividend tax credit

In addition to deducting non-refundable tax credits from federal tax on taxable income, you are also entitled to a dividend tax credit if you reported dividends from taxable Canadian corporations [**flowchart box 8**]. On your tax return, the actual amount of your dividend is grossed up by 25%. The dividend tax credit is 13⅓% of this grossed-up or taxable amount of dividends that you reported (see also page 103).

At this point, the amount of basic federal tax [**flowchart box 9**] is preserved for computing provincial income taxes and the federal surtax, and for comparison with AMT. However, further adjustments enter into the calculation of federal income tax.

The remaining steps in your tax calculation are the same whether you have to pay AMT or not. The only differences are that if you have to pay AMT:

- the basic federal tax [**flowchart box 9**] is replaced by the "minimum amount" from the AMT calculation; and

- the additional tax credits [**flowchart box 10**] are replaced by a special foreign tax credit.

Additional tax credits

Foreign tax credit

You may reduce tax payable by claiming a non-refundable tax credit for income or profits taxes paid to a foreign government [**flowchart box 10**]. The credit is equal to the lesser of the foreign tax paid and Canadian tax payable on that income. A separate calculation must be made for each foreign country. A separate calculation is also required for business income taxes and non-business income taxes paid to each foreign country. Unusable foreign business income tax credits may be carried back three years and forward seven.

Non-business income taxes do not enjoy the same treatment. However, to the extent that foreign tax on your investment income exceeds 15% of the foreign income, the excess is deductible in computing income subject to tax.

You may also be able to claim a provincial foreign tax credit, to the extent that you were unable to claim the entire foreign tax credit on your federal return.

• Political contribution tax credit

You may claim a tax credit on your federal income tax return for contributions made to federal political parties **[flowchart box 10]**. Official receipts must be filed with your return. Most provinces have similar credits for political contributions to provincial parties.

The credit is calculated as follows: 75% of the first $100; 50% on the next $450 and 33⅓% of any contributions more than $550. The maximum credit allowed in any one year is $500, which means that you get no credit for political contributions in excess of $1,150.

✔ Tax Tip 79

Consider spreading your political contributions out over two years. For example, if you contribute $700 in 1997, your federal tax credit will be $350. If instead you contribute $350 in 1997 and $350 in the following year, your tax credits will be $200 each year, a $50 increase.

Federal surtax

The federal individual surtax **[flowchart box 11]** has two levels, both based on basic federal tax.

The first level applies to everyone: it is 3% of basic federal tax.

The second, the "high-earner" surtax, is determined as 5% of any basic federal tax more than $12,500. A taxpayer resident in Canada with the fewest and smallest possible credits and no deductions will begin paying the second-tier surtax after earning approximately $62,195. At that level the federal marginal rate is 29%, so at 8% of basic federal tax the federal surtax adds 2.32% [8% × 29%] to the marginal rate. For more on the calculation of the federal surtax, see Appendix 4, page 266.

The total federal surtax is added to the federal component of your income tax.

Provincial, territorial and non-resident taxes

Provincial, territorial and non-resident taxes provide a tier of income tax that adds roughly 45% to 69% of federal tax **[flowchart boxes 9 and 15 to 19]** to your tax bill, before any provincial surtaxes are added. Except for Québec, provincial taxes are determined by applying the appropriate provincial rate to basic federal tax (see Appendix 5, page 270). In addition, most provinces have their own systems of surtaxes and tax reductions (see Appendix 5). Outside Québec you do not file a separate provincial tax return. Instead, you calculate the provincial tax owing and remit it, along with your federal income tax return and federal balance payable to the government of Canada, which allocates it to the appropriate province.

Québec's tax system is more complex. Rather than calculating tax as a percentage of the federal level, Québec has a parallel system that resembles the federal one, but requires a separate return and payments directly to the provincial government **[flowchart boxes 5Q to 16]**. For further details about that province's tax regime, refer to the various Québec sections of this book (at the end of each chapter).

If you are filing a Québec income tax return, your federal return will also be affected. In recognition of the fact that Québec collects its own taxes, a refundable Québec abatement, based on your basic federal tax **[flowchart box 12A]**, is deductible in calculating your net federal tax **[flowchart box 12Q]**. This abatement is simply a credit of 16.5%.

The Yukon and Northwest Territories also impose taxes comparable to provinces other than Québec.

A Canadian-resident individual typically pays provincial tax to the province or territory of which he or she is a resident on December 31. Non-residents of Canada who receive income from Canadian sources

196 | **Personal tax flowchart – with AMT**

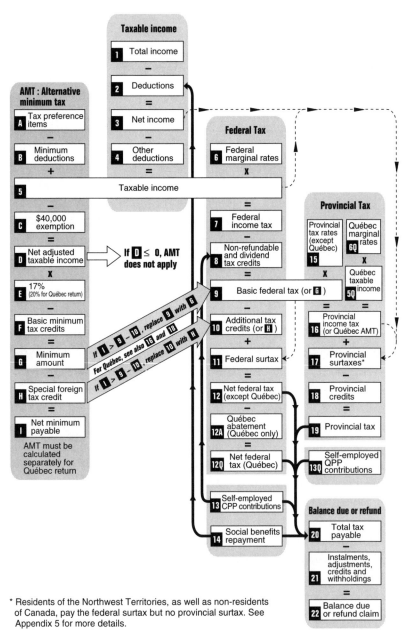

Taxable income

1 Total income

−

2 Deductions

=

3 Net income

−

4 Other deductions

=

Taxable income **5**

AMT : Alternative minimum tax

A Tax preference items

−

B Minimum deductions

+

5

−

C $40,000 exemption

=

D Net adjusted taxable income

⇒ If **D** ≤ 0, AMT does not apply

X

E 17% (20% for Québec return)

−

F Basic minimum tax credits

=

G Minimum amount

−

H Special foreign tax credit

=

I Net minimum payable

AMT must be calculated separately for Québec return

Federal Tax

6 Federal marginal rates

X

=

7 Federal income tax

−

8 Non-refundable and dividend tax credits

=

9 Basic federal tax (or **G**)

−

10 Additional tax credits (or **H**)

+

11 Federal surtax

=

12 Net federal tax (except Québec)

12A Québec abatement (Québec only)

12Q Net federal tax (Québec)

13 Self-employed CPP contributions

14 Social benefits repayment

If **I** > **9** − **10**, replace **9** with **G**
For Québec, see also **16** and **18**
If **I** > **9** − **10**, replace **10** with **H**

Provincial Tax

15 Provincial tax rates (except Québec)

6Q Québec marginal rates

X

5Q Québec taxable income

=

16 Provincial income tax (or Québec AMT)

+

17 Provincial surtaxes*

=

18 Provincial credits

=

19 Provincial tax

13Q Self-employed QPP contributions

Balance due or refund

20 Total tax payable

−

21 Instalments, adjustments, credits and withholdings

=

22 Balance due or refund claim

* Residents of the Northwest Territories, as well as non-residents of Canada, pay the federal surtax but no provincial surtax. See Appendix 5 for more details.

(for example, rental income, pensions, annuities, alimony and capital gains) may be subject to federal tax. Although non-residents will not ordinarily be subject to provincial income tax, because they are not resident in a province or territory, they may be subject to a federal surtax that applies to income earned outside a province. This surtax has the effect of putting a non-resident in a position comparable to that faced by a resident. Of course, non-residents earning Canadian source employment or business income may have to pay provincial or territorial tax on that income.

Social benefit repayment ("clawback")

If you received employment insurance (EI), you may have to repay a portion, depending on your income. If your net income exceeded $60,840, you must repay a portion of the EI benefits you received **[flowchart box 14]**. That repayment is deductible **[flowchart box 2]**. The rules dealing with OAS benefits are discussed elsewhere in this book (see page 150).

Balance due or refund claimed

To calculate your total tax payable **[flowchart box 20]**, add:

- the net federal tax **[flowchart box 12]**;
- any self-employed CPP contributions you are required to make **[flowchart box 13]**;
- the "clawback" **[flowchart box 14]**; and
- total provincial tax **[flowchart box 19]**.

Only a few more items **[flowchart box 21]** need to be considered before the tax calculation is complete.

You subtract any tax you have already paid, particularly amounts that have been withheld at source, any instalments of tax that you have made throughout the year, and overpayments of CPP or EI premiums. The refundable tax credits, including the investment tax credit and any provincial tax credits, are also subtracted **[flowchart box 21]**.

At last you know how much you owe Revenue Canada, or how much Revenue Canada owes you as a refund **[flowchart box 22]**.

Alternative minimum tax (AMT)

If your calculation of taxable income **[flowchart box 5]** reflects "tax preference items" **[flowchart box A★]** that lower your tax bill, you should calculate your net adjusted taxable income **[flowchart box D★]** and your minimum amount **[flowchart box G★]** to determine if you are liable for alternative minimum tax (AMT).

Tax preference items in adjusted taxable income for this calculation include certain deductions, and income that is subject to special rules. The most common tax preference items are:

- contributions to RPPs, RRSPs, DPSPs (less lump sum receipts);

- CCA claimed on certified film properties (less income before CCA);

- resource expenditures, depletion and resource allowances (less resource income); and

- the non-taxable portion of capital gains.

A non-arm's length sale to realize capital gains may result in a minimum tax liability.

Your minimum amount **[flowchart box G★]** is calculated by applying a federal rate of 17% **[flowchart box E★]** to net adjusted taxable income **[flowchart box D★]**. If your net adjusted taxable income is zero or less, you need not go any further: AMT does not apply to you. Although no refundable credits or dividend tax credits are available (although the dividend gross-up is excluded from

---

★ Refer to the Personal tax flowchart – with AMT, page 196.

income), you may deduct basic minimum tax credits **[flowchart box F★]** to arrive at your minimum amount **[flowchart box G★]**.

You should not have to pay AMT unless your tax preference items exceed the $40,000 exemption **[flowchart box C★]**. Even then, the 17% rate may be lower than your "regular" tax rate, which means you won't be subject to AMT.

From your minimum amount, you may deduct a special foreign tax credit **[flowchart box H★]**, leaving you with your net minimum payable **[flowchart box I★]**. The special foreign tax credit is similar to the regular foreign tax credit, discussed above.

Your net minimum payable **[flowchart box I★]** is compared to your basic federal tax less additional tax credits **[flowchart box 9 less box 10]** and the larger amount is used in subsequent tax calculations. Accordingly, if you are liable for AMT, your federal surtax and provincial tax will increase.

AMT is a complex calculation, and there are other more unusual elements to consider. Revenue Canada has provided Form T691 for calculating AMT. You are even better off if you use one of the available computer programs for preparing your return; the calculation will be done automatically.

If you are required to pay AMT, you are entitled to a credit in future years when your basic federal tax **[flowchart box 9]** exceeds your AMT minimum amount **[flowchart box G★]** for that year. The credit is the excess of AMT over your regular liability. The carryforward period is seven years, and the credit each year cannot reduce your liability below your AMT amount for that year.

Child Tax Benefit system

The Child Tax Benefit program currently provides for monthly tax-free payments to eligible Canadian families with children and is generally paid to the mother. The benefit is calculated by the

---

★ Refer to the Personal tax flowchart – with AMT, page 196.

government on the basis of tax information from the previous year. The basic benefit of $1,020 per child may be supplemented by:

- $75 for the third and each subsequent child in a family; and

- $213 per child under age seven, when no child care expenses are claimed.

Low-income working families with children also receive an earned-income supplement. The supplement is reduced when family adjusted income exceeds $20,921.

The Child Tax Benefit does not have to be included in your income, nor is it recovered on your tax return. The amount of the benefit is, however, reduced by a factor based on net family income and the number of children in the family. In particular, the benefit is reduced by 2.5% of family income in excess of $25,921 for families with one child and 5% of the same amount for families with more than one child.

A separate paper, "Working Together Towards a National Child Benefit System," was tabled with the 1997 federal budget documents. The paper discusses a new initiative: the creation of the Canada Child Tax Benefit, a combination of the existing Child Tax Benefit, the Working Income Supplement (WIS) plus additional funding. The objective is for the provinces to redirect provincial resources towards improved income support and children's services for low-income working families. The projected date for the expanded and redesigned Canada Child Tax Benefit system is July 1998. In the meantime, interim measures have been proposed that will restructure the WIS from a family basis to a per-child basis. The modified WIS is scheduled to be introduced in July 1997.

⚜ Québec

Québec residents do not calculate their provincial taxes as a percentage of federal tax (see Appendix 5, page 270). Instead, Québec has a parallel tax regime that closely resembles the federal system but requires a separate provincial return in addition to the one you file for federal purposes. The calculation of Québec taxable income is slightly different **[flowchart box 5Q]** (page 183 or 196) as are the marginal rates that are applied to Québec taxable income **[flowchart box 6Q]** to determine your Québec tax liability.

If you pay your federal tax by instalments, you may have to remit instalments of tax to Québec as well (see pages 214 and 226).

Credits and deductions

Although most of the federal tax credits **[flowchart box 8]** are available in Québec, the amounts and types of credits differ somewhat.

Changes in the determination of net income

- Child care expenses are treated as refundable tax credits in Québec, although they remain a deduction in determining income for federal tax purposes.

- Union and professional dues or dues to a recognized artistic association are treated as a non-refundable tax credit for Québec purposes, although they remain a deduction in determining net income for federal tax purposes.

Non-refundable tax credits

• Reduction of certain tax credits

Three credits are reduced progressively depending on the taxpayer's net income: credit for persons living alone, age credit for those 65 or over and the credit for retirement income. For 1997 and subsequent taxation years, the reduction will be 15% of each dollar of a taxpayer's net income in excess of $26,000. If the age tax credit and the tax credit for retirement income are transferred from one spouse to the other, they will not be subject to these recovery rules.

• Amount for a person living alone

A credit of $1,050 may be claimed in Québec by a person living alone and who:

- during all of 1997, maintained and ordinarily lived in a self-contained domestic establishment in which no other person lived during the year, with the exception of a person for whom an amount for dependent children (i.e., under 18 or a full-time student) could be claimed;

- was not married at any time in 1997 or, if married, was not living with or supporting his or her spouse; and

- did not have a common-law spouse at any time in 1997 or, if he or she did, was not supporting the common-law spouse.

The fact that a person made alimony payments giving rise to a deduction does not in itself mean that the person is considered to have been supporting a spouse or common-law spouse.

This credit cannot be claimed in the income tax return of a deceased person.

This credit is subject to the recovery mechanism stated above.

• Married person tax credit

A spouse's income after separation does not reduce the married person's tax credit and does not have to be added to the total income used to determine tax benefits such as the income tax reduction for families, the property tax refund and the refundable tax credit for the QST.

• Tax credit for dependent children

In 1997, the amount of the tax credit for a child is $2,600 and $2,400 for a second and each subsequent child.

• Tax credit for the elderly

Taxpayers aged 65 or over are entitled, for Québec income tax purposes, to a non-refundable tax credit equal to 20% of $2,200, which reduces the amount of income tax they have to pay by up to $440.

As noted earlier, this credit is subject to the recovery mechanism.

• Tax credit for political contributions

The Québec tax credit for contributions to a political party is $250 for 1997.

• Medical expenses

In 1997, taxpayers will be permitted to claim only medical expenses exceeding 3% of net income. For a couple, the 3% applies to combined net income of both spouses. The legislation will be modified to broaden the definition of eligible medical expenses for handicapped persons.

• Dues

As of 1997, deductions for union and professional dues or dues to a recognized artistic association will be converted into non-refundable tax credits of 20%. This change applies to both employees and independent contractors. However, the portion of professional dues relating to professional liability insurance will continue to be allowed as a deduction. Also, an amount for professional liability insurance needed to maintain a professional status recognized by law will be allowable as a deduction in calculating an employee's income.

• Credit for retirement income

Taxpayers may claim a tax credit for certain eligible retirement income received in the year for up to $1,000, for a maximum credit of $200. This credit, as stated above, is subject to a recovery mechanism.

• **Fonds de Solidarité des Travailleurs du Québec (FSTQ) or Fondaction**

Shares issued by workers venture capital funds provide for a tax credit of 15% with a maximum annual share acquisition of $3,500.

Refundable tax credits

• **Tax credit for elderly persons housed by others**

Québec grants a refundable tax credit to persons who lodge the elderly. The amount on which this tax credit is based is $2,750, which corresponds to a credit of $550 for each adult lodged in 1997. To be eligible for this tax credit, the housed person must be aged 70 or over and must have lived with the taxpayer for a period of at least 365 consecutive days, including at least 183 days in 1997, or must be aged 60 or over and suffering from a prolonged, severe mental or physical disability.

• **Tax credit for adoption expenses**

The 1997 refundable tax credit for adoption expenses is equal to 20% of eligible adoption expenses incurred for a child and paid by the individual or by his or her spouse. It may not exceed $2,000 per child for a maximum of $10,000 in eligible expenses. This measure applies to final adoption orders handed down after December 31, 1993. A copy of the final adoption order or proof of its registration at the Court of Québec, as the case may be, will have to be forwarded with the income tax return of the taxpayer claiming the tax credit.

• **Handicapped persons**

A new refundable tax credit for medical expenses (with a maximum credit of $500) is available starting 1997 for low-income workers who are handicapped.

• **Refundable child care credit**

The refundable child care credit is discussed under the relevant heading in Chapter 2, **Employees** (page 71).

• Charitable donations

Québec will not follow the rules proposed in the 1997 federal budget relating to the reduced inclusion rate for capital gains from gifts of securities, the annual income limitation for charitable donations and gifts to the government and to the increase in this limitation in certain cases.

The tax credit for donations in Quebec equals 20% of the amount of donations, up to 20% of the net income of a taxpayer. One spouse can claim a credit for donations made by the other spouse.

Additional contributions or taxes

• Health services fund contribution

The health services fund contribution is discussed under that heading in Chapter 2, **Employees**, on page 73.

• Self-employed Québec Pension Plan

If you are self-employed in Québec, you will need to add self-employed Québec Pension Plan (QPP) premiums to your Québec tax liability **[flowchart box 13Q]** and remit this amount to the province, instead of remitting self-employed CPP premiums to the federal government as you would in the case of the other provinces and territories. **[flowchart box 13]** For 1997, premiums under the QPP and CPP are not identical.

• Alternative minimum tax (AMT)

The Québec AMT is calculated at a rate of 20% (23% in 1998) **[flowchart box E★]**. The adjusted taxable income **[flowchart box D★]** on which Québec AMT is calculated can also be different, because net income for Québec tax purposes may be different from federal net income.

The basic exemption for alternative minimum tax in Québec is

★ Refer to the Personal tax flowchart – with AMT, page 196.

$25,000 in 1997. Also, a retiring allowance transferred to an RRSP is not added to adjusted taxable income for the purposes of minimum tax.

To ensure that high-income taxpayers are required to contribute to the financing of public expenditures on the basis of their ability to pay, the strategic investments for the Québec economy account has been eliminated as of the 1994 taxation year for purposes of the alternative minimum tax. Thus, a taxpayer who formerly benefited from preferential tax treatment in Québec will have to include all of his or her strategic investments when determining whether or not he or she is subject to the alternative minimum tax. However, individual deductions included in this account will continue to be eligible deductions in the determination of a taxpayer's taxable income.

• Québec surtaxes

In Québec, a surtax equal to 5% of the provincial tax that exceeds $5,000 and another 5% of the tax that exceeds $10,000 must be added. However, Québec has a tax reduction equal to 2% of the excess of $10,000 over tax payable after deducting non-refundable tax credits.

In 1998, both surtaxes and the 2% reduction will be eliminated because they will be reflected in the new tax rates following personal tax reform.

• Contribution to poverty fund

In 1997, Quebec taxpayers have to contribute an amount equal to 0.3% of their tax payable for the year to a special fund to combat poverty in Québec. This new tax was generally reflected in source deductions as of January 1, 1997. Effective for the 1997 taxation year, individuals who remit their tax by instalments must also include the new tax in their payments.

• Gifts of works of art to charitable organizations

A tax credit or deduction is not available for a gift of a work of art to a charitable organization unless the work of art is sold by the charitable organization within five years. This rule is to ensure that the tax advantages that a donor may obtain are those envisaged by the legislation. The measure will not apply to a work of art acquired by a charitable organization as part of its primary mission.

9 Filing Returns and Paying Your Taxes

Filing Returns and Paying Your Taxes

What's new?

- Penalties will be charged for non-compliance with new rules for reporting ownership of foreign property.

You can save time, money and aggravation by being careful about how and when you file and pay your taxes, and how you deal with Revenue Canada. This chapter will help you handle these matters effectively, before you file, when you file and after you file your tax return.

One of the easiest ways to save money is to observe Revenue Canada's payment and filing requirements. Interest and penalties can leave you with a significant and avoidable bill. Daily compounding can quickly double your tax liability. There is little point in conscientious tax planning if you fail to file or pay your taxes on time.

✔ Tax Tip 80

The interest provisions are a two-way street: refunds due to you from Revenue Canada as a result of overpayments of tax will earn interest, although to a much lesser degree than they used to. You begin to accrue interest on an overpayment only 45 days after the later of April 30 or the date you actually filed your return. Although filing your return as early as possible won't necessarily earn you any interest from Revenue Canada, you should get your refund cheque sooner. Accordingly, the funds will be available sooner for you to invest or to use for other purposes.

Improving your cash flow

Interest-free loans to the government?

When you filed your income tax return in the spring, were you thrilled to find that you were getting a large refund from Revenue

Canada? A tax refund is a mixed blessing. Expecting and getting a cheque in the mail is pleasant, but a large tax refund normally indicates that your cash management could be better. In effect, you are making an interest-free loan to the government, because:

- you are making excessive instalment payments; or

- your employer is withholding too much tax.

Instead of having your money to use and invest throughout the year, you have been giving it to Revenue Canada for its use, for what could amount to an entire year or more. When you overpay your tax, you don't get your own money back until after you have filed your tax return for a particular year and it is processed. Nor will you earn a year's interest on the money that you've "advanced." As mentioned above, Revenue Canada has an "interest-free processing period" that runs 45 days from the later of April 30 and the date the return is filed. That means that if you file your return on time – on April 30 – no interest will be paid on refunds until after June 14. The same treatment applies when you make excessive instalment payments: you won't begin earning interest on an overpayment until 45 days after the overpayment arose.

Steps to take

To a large extent, you can avoid the problem and improve your cash flow.

If you pay your tax by instalments, you should be reviewing your instalment requirements throughout the year. If you made a large, perhaps unexpected, contribution to your RRSP mid-year, recalculate your tax liability. It may be significantly lower than the estimate you made in March because of the RRSP contribution. Your instalments for the remainder of the year should be reduced accordingly.

If you are employed, most of your tax liability is likely satisfied through withholdings at source. Consider writing to the Chief of Source Deductions at your local District Taxation Office for a waiver from, or reduction in, withholdings if you:

- incur business or investment losses;
- have significant deductible interest expense;
- make RRSP contributions;
- pay deductible alimony or maintenance to a former spouse; or
- have some other deductible expenditures.

If your request is approved, your employer will receive a letter from Revenue Canada authorizing a reduction in the amount of tax withheld from your income. This could increase your cash flow and allow you to use or invest the funds that otherwise would not be available until you get your tax refund.

The rules that employers must follow regarding source deductions have been eased to permit reduced withholdings from employee remuneration. If your employer deducts amounts that are being paid directly into your RRSP, or if you are paying deductible alimony or maintenance payments, your employer may base the tax deductions at source on the net amount, without having to obtain a waiver of withholding letter from Revenue Canada. Note that CPP and EI contributions must still be based on your gross remuneration.

✔ Tax Tip 81

If you are going to be making a lump sum contribution to your RRSP, for example, from a bonus that you have earned, consider asking your employer to make the contribution directly to your RRSP on your behalf.

Some numbers will illustrate how attractive the option in Tax Tip 81 can be:

Assume that your top marginal rate is 52% and that you will be receiving a bonus of $10,000. If the bonus is paid to you, you will receive $4,800 ($10,000 net of $5,200 of tax). You then contribute the $4,800 to your RRSP, generating a refund of $2,496 ($4,800 x 52%) some time after you file your tax return for the year. If you wanted to make an additional RRSP contribution, you might have to borrow the funds, the interest costs on which would not be tax deductible. If instead you direct your employer to make an RRSP contribution on your behalf of all or a portion of the bonus, you would have a larger amount in your RRSP, no interest to pay and little or no tax, depending on whether you contributed the entire bonus.

Before you file

Social Insurance Number

If you lived or worked in Canada during the year and you file an income tax return, you must include your Social Insurance Number (SIN) on your return. You should also indicate your spouse's SIN on your return.

If you are requested to provide your SIN to a person preparing information returns and fail to do so, you may be liable for a fine of $100 each time you do not provide it. If you do not have a SIN, you have 15 days to apply for one from the time you are requested to provide it, and a further 15 days to supply the number.

✔ Tax Tip 82

Writing your SIN on any documents you submit with your tax return is a good idea (if it is not already printed on the document). If something goes astray at Revenue Canada, it can be readily returned to your file.

| **Instalment requirements**

If you are earning employment income and have no other major sources of income, the amount of tax withheld at source by your employer will generally leave you with either a small refund or a small balance owing on April 30. If you have other sources of income, however, you may have to make instalments of tax during the year.

Instalments for a particular year are due quarterly, as follows:

No deadlines		Deadline on 15th of month
January	February	**March**
April	May	**June**
July	August	**September**
October	November	**December**

Any final balance is due when you file your return. Late or deficient instalments could result in onerous interest and penalty charges (see Interest and penalties, page 217).

You are required to make quarterly payments if the difference between your tax payable and amounts that have been withheld at source is greater than $2,000 in both the current and either of the two preceding years.

Tax payable includes combined federal and provincial income tax. For Québec residents, the threshold amount is $1,200 of federal tax payable after federal tax withholdings.

Revenue Canada notifies individuals required to remit instalments of the amount of each instalment determined on the basis of tax information from prior years.

Individuals who are required to pay quarterly instalments should have received two notices from Revenue Canada in 1997, one in February with the March and June instalments and one in August with the September and December instalments. Here is how Revenue Canada determines the amounts:

- The first two instalments are based on your tax liability from two years ago, i.e., for 1997, each of your first two instalments would be based on one-quarter of your 1995 tax liability.

- The third and fourth payments are based on your liability for the preceding year, i.e., 1996 for 1997 instalments, with an adjustment to ensure that the total of the four instalments equals your prior year's liability.

If you choose to follow this method and pay the exact amounts specified by Revenue Canada on time, you will not be charged interest and penalties, even if your instalments are short.

Of course, the two other existing options are also available to you if you prefer to continue with the method you have used in the past:

- Divide your prior year's tax liability by four and pay that amount each quarter.

- If you are confident that your current year's liability will be less than that of the previous year, estimate the liability and pay 25% of that amount each quarter. In this case, review your situation before each payment to make sure that your original estimate is still valid.

If you choose this latter option and you estimate incorrectly, interest may be charged on the deficient instalments.

✔ Tax Tip 83

Interest charges on late or deficient instalments can be significant. You can cure a deficient or late instalment payment by early payment or overpayment of the next instalment. Because interest is levied only to the extent that debit interest exceeds any credit offset, you should be able to reduce or eliminate interest charges on late or deficient instalments.

The rate of interest charged on overdue taxes (see pages 217-18) is 2% higher than the rate Revenue Canada pays on refunds owing to you. For purposes of the interest offset, however, the same rate of interest will apply to overpayments and underpayments. Accordingly, the new higher interest rate will be charged only on net deficient instalments.

When you file

Filing on the most favourable basis

Tax laws and regulations are sometimes ambiguous. When filing your return, you should choose the most favourable, reasonable interpretation. For example, file your current year's return reflecting the results of a favourable court decision. If your position is challenged, possibly because the case you followed is under appeal, you may have to protect the position you have taken by filing a Notice of Objection. This should enable you to sustain the claim if Revenue Canada eventually agrees with the court's decision. If the decision is subsequently overturned, at least you are in the same position you would have been in had you not made the claim. You should be out of pocket only for some interest charges.

Filing returns

Your income tax return each taxation year must generally be filed by April 30 of the following year. Unless a demand is made for your return, the penalty for late filing is based on the amount of tax payable. If you owe tax but cannot pay it on the due date, the late filing penalty will be avoided if you file your return on time. Conversely, you should face no late filing penalty if your tax is paid in full by April 30, even though you do not file the return until later.

Income from an unincorporated business or a partnership is reported in your personal return. The partnership will have to file information with Revenue Canada and provide you with a reporting slip to enclose with your return. If the business or partnership has a non-calendar year end, income from it must be included in your return for the calendar year in which the fiscal year of the business or partnership ends.

Sole proprietorships, professional corporations that are members of a partnership and certain partnerships are required to have their fiscal periods end on December 31. This rule is described in greater detail on page 81.

The annual filing deadline is extended to June 15 for individuals (other than trusts) reporting business income (other than only from limited partnerships). Tax owing will still be payable on April 30 and interest on unpaid taxes will continue to be charged from that date.

Paying your taxes

If you have a balance of tax owing for a particular year, it is due on April 30 of the following year. This payment due date applies whether your return must be filed by April 30 or by June 15. If you do not pay the balance by April 30, interest will be charged on the outstanding amount (see Interest and penalties, below).

If you are unable to pay taxes owing by April 30, you should include a letter with your return explaining the situation, or contact the Collections Section of your district office. Revenue Canada will generally accommodate a reasonable payment schedule. You may also include postdated cheques with your return. Again, reason should prevail: do not date your cheques two years from the time the payment is due.

After you file

Interest and penalties

To further encourage the prompt payment of unpaid income taxes (including quarterly instalments), the rate of interest charged on overdue taxes is 2% greater than the rate paid on overpayments. The prescribed rate of interest for a calendar quarter is based on the average yield on three-month Treasury Bills sold in the first month of the preceding quarter, plus 4% (see the table on page 81).

This rate applies to overdue income taxes, insufficient instalment payments, unpaid employee source deductions and other amounts withheld at source, unpaid Canada Pension Plan contributions and unpaid employment insurance premiums.

If you file your return late, even if it is only by one day, you will be subject to a late filing penalty equal to 5% of any unpaid tax, plus 1% for each month (to a maximum of 12 months) for which you fail to file the return after the deadline. If you fail to file on time again within a three-year period, the penalty doubles to 10% plus 2% per month of the unpaid amount to a maximum of 20 months.

If you are neglecting to make instalment payments as required, and the amounts are large enough, additional penalties apply to interest in excess of $1,000 owing on late instalments.

You may be fined $100 for each instance you fail to complete all the information required of you on your return. Even a dishonoured cheque will be expensive: Revenue Canada will add $10 to your tax bill for any NSF cheque. Of course, this is in addition to the fee your bank will charge you. In extreme situations, you could be subject to fines of $1,000 to $25,000, or up to 12 months' imprisonment, or both, if you are convicted of an offence under the Income Tax Act.

Failure to pay your taxes on time can become a rather expensive form of financing. Interest, which is also charged on penalties assessed against you but unpaid, is compounded daily. In addition, interest and penalties are not deductible for tax purposes.

Foreign property reporting requirements

New rules will require information reporting that is separate from your income tax returns. You will have to file one form if you own foreign property costing more than $100,000 (Cdn.). Another form may be required if you are a beneficiary of a non-resident trust and you received funds or property from, or were indebted to, the trust. Although the first returns are not due until April 30, 1998, reporting will be required for taxation years beginning after 1995. Refer to page 231 in Chapter 10, **Looking Ahead**, chapter for further details about the reporting requirements.

Failure to comply with the new reporting requirements may result in the substantial penalties shown in the chart below:

	New foreign reporting information returns	
	Foreign Property Form T1135	Distributions from and Indebtedness Owed to Non-Resident Trusts Form T1142
Basic penalty	$25 per day; maximum $2,500	
Failure to file; knowingly or gross negligence	No demand served; $500 per month; maximum $12,000 Demand served but not complied with: $1,000 per month; maximum $24,000	
If more than 24 months late	5% of cost of foreign properties (reduced by any penalties determined above	
False statements of omissions	Greater of $24,000 and 5% of cost	Greater of $2,500 and 5% of FMV of distributions and 5% of unpaid principal amount of debt

Amending returns

What if you have mailed your return and then discovered an error on the return or received additional information that will change your tax liability? You should inform Revenue Canada of the changes, but do not file a corrected return; a letter explaining the situation is all that is required. If you have received a Notice of Assessment, contact your district taxation office, otherwise, contact your regional taxation centre. Always include your SIN when corresponding with Revenue Canada, to help them find your file.

Revenue Canada will generally permit you to amend your return for errors or omissions up to three years after the date of mailing shown on the Notice of Assessment – the same time limit that the government has for reassessing your return. You should note that Revenue Canada will not entertain amending a return because you had a change of heart regarding an optional deduction.

220 | Resolving problems

You will usually receive a Notice of Assessment from Revenue Canada within about eight to 12 weeks of filing your return. Your return may well be assessed exactly as you filed it. Often, however, you will find changes to your return. If you agree with the changes (correction of a calculation error, for example), you should pay any additional tax owing as soon as possible to avoid interest charges.

If you disagree with the way in which your return has been assessed, remember that you are technically bound by the Notice of Assessment unless you object to it. Should you disagree with the Notice of Assessment, you might pursue one of two courses. The simplest course is to contact your district taxation office, by phone or in person. Have your Social Insurance Number handy. In many instances, problems can be readily explained or resolved on the spot.

You may have to follow a more elaborate procedure if:

- you have postponed getting in touch with Revenue Canada;

- significant amounts of money are involved; or

- you feel the matter is quite complex.

In any of these cases, you should consider filing a Notice of Objection to your assessment. A Notice of Objection may be filed on a prescribed form (Form T400A, which you may obtain from your district taxation office). Alternatively, you may initiate the appeal process by setting out the facts and reasons for your objection in a letter to the Chief of Appeals at your local district office or taxation centre. The limit for objection for individuals and testamentary trusts is the later of one year after the balance due day for your return for the year (for example, May 1, 1999 for your 1997 return, which is due April 30, 1998) and 90 days after the mailing date indicated on your assessment.

Revenue Canada is generally under no obligation to entertain any objections you may have to your assessment if you miss the deadline.

Your return will be reviewed and if Revenue Canada agrees with your position, you will receive a revised Notice of Reassessment. If Revenue Canada disagrees, you will receive notification that the assessment stands. Although you may prepare a Notice of Objection yourself, you should consider seeking professional advice, particularly if the amount of tax at stake is significant.

If you still disagree, or if you have not heard from Revenue Canada within 90 days of filing your objection, you may appeal to the courts. However, before proceeding beyond the objection stage, you should talk to your professional advisor. Interest on any unpaid tax continues to accrue during the time your appeal is in process unless you post acceptable security while your objection is still in process. You may also pay the amount in dispute and wait for a possible refund if the matter is resolved in your favour.

If you appeal to the Tax Court of Canada and the amount in dispute is less than $12,000 of tax or $24,000 in loss determination, an informal appeal procedure is available. You may represent yourself or have your lawyer, accountant or other agent represent you. The appeal process should take about six months. If the amount in dispute exceeds $12,000, general court rules apply. You can still represent yourself, but this is not advisable unless you are well versed in both the Income Tax Act and legal procedure.

Further appeals can be made to higher courts: the Federal Court of Appeal and even to the Supreme Court of Canada. The Supreme Court, however, may refuse to grant leave to hear your appeal. Your legal advisor will help you determine whether you have a case, what your chances of success are and how expensive the whole procedure is likely to be.

✔ Tax Tip 84

Even if your problem has been satisfactorily resolved by phone or in a personal visit to your district taxation office, you should note the deadline for filing a Notice of Objection. If you have not received a revised assessment or a Notice of Reassessment by a week or two before the deadline for filing an objection, consider filing a Notice of Objection in any event to protect your position, particularly if substantial amounts are involved.

Post-assessment examination

The Notice of Assessment that Revenue Canada issues is based on a limited review of your return when it is filed. Once the assessment has been issued, your return may be subject to further examination. Two main types of reviews can be carried out after your return has been assessed:

- Information slips received by Revenue Canada from your employer, from banks and other financial institutions, from the trustee of your RRSP etc., are matched with your Social Insurance Number to ensure that you have reported all of your employment and investment income.

- The various expenses, deductions and credits that you claimed may be subject to further review. You may be asked to provide receipts and other documentation to support your claims. Be sure to keep your supporting documents in case your return is selected for review.

Although any return can be selected for detailed examination, the probability increases with the magnitude of the amounts and the nature of income and expense items. In any case, recognize that if you report income from business or property, your return may be selected for a full audit. If you are going to be audited, you will generally be asked to gather all the information that you used to prepare your return and to meet with a Revenue Canada representative. You may bring your professional advisor with you; it is recommended that you do so if your return was prepared by your advisor. The auditor will go through your return with you, examine your supporting documentation and ask questions. As long as you are able to substantiate all of the items on your return, you should not have any problems.

If the auditor proposes any changes to your return and you disagree, you will have to go through the appeal process, beginning with the filing of a Notice of Objection, as described above.

Fairness Package for taxpayers

The Fairness Package is legislation designed to improve the fairness of the tax system for all Canadians. The Fairness Package contains measures aimed at taxpayers who, because of personal misfortune or circumstances beyond their control, are unable to meet filing or payment deadlines or comply with certain rules. Interest or penalties may be waived or cancelled when they result from factors that are beyond your control, for example, when illness prevents you from filing a tax return by the April 30 deadline. Of course, you are expected to have made reasonable efforts to comply with the law, to minimize delays in filing a return and to remedy the situation as soon as possible.

In certain circumstances, individuals and testamentary trusts may file for refunds for any taxation year after 1984 without regard to the normal three-year limitation. Refunds may be allowed if an individual or a testamentary trust files a return for the first time or requests a reassessment. In particular, you may be able to obtain a refund or a reduction in taxes owing if:

- your taxes have been overpaid because of the amount of tax withheld at source by your employer;

- you have neglected to claim refundable tax credits; or

- you previously filed your return and then discovered that a deduction to which you were entitled had been missed.

Of course, you will have to provide information or documentation to support your return or request. For example:

- official receipts or certified "true" copies of receipts (such as tuition fees, RRSP contributions or charitable donation receipts);

- copies of information slips (T4s, T5s etc.);

- details or calculations of specific expenses or deductions being claimed; or

- proof of payment.

If it is impossible to obtain proper documentation, you should submit full details and a written explanation for consideration.

You may not, however, request an increase in deductions such as capital cost allowance, to generate a refund.

The Income Tax Act contains more than 120 elections that let taxpayers select from specified options how the tax laws will apply to their financial affairs for income tax purposes. The fairness legislation gives the minister discretionary power to allow you to apply to make a late or amended "election" or to revoke an original election for taxation years back to 1985. This discretion is not intended to permit retroactive tax planning. The elections initially eligible for this treatment are set out in an Income Tax Regulation; others will be added as they are identified.

Books and records

You should keep your tax records for at least four years (approximately the period during which Revenue Canada can reassess your return), and preferably longer. If you operate a business, you must keep your tax and business records for at least six years, and even then you may still have to seek permission from Revenue Canada to destroy them.

Voluntary disclosure

Consider making a voluntary disclosure if your circumstances are such that you never filed an income tax return, failed to file for a number of years or filed a return that was incorrect or incomplete. Revenue Canada encourages individuals to come forward and voluntarily file or correct their returns. Although you will have to pay the tax owed, plus interest, no prosecution will be undertaken and you will not be charged penalties, which could be significant. Of course, the relief from the application of penalty charges is available only if you initiate the disclosure, i.e., before Revenue Canada identifies you for audit or enforcement action.

Directors' tax risks

You should not accept an appointment as a director of a corporation lightly. In addition to the obligations and responsibilities that you take on as a director, you may find that you are financially at risk. As a director, you face two kinds of tax risks. First, you may be liable for income tax on your director's fees even though the corporation with-holds tax from the payments you receive. If the corporation cannot satisfy the tax liability in respect of your income, you may be liable. In effect you will be taxed twice. If you have any doubt about the financial security of the corporation, be sure to satisfy yourself that the corporation is handling the withheld taxes properly.

Potentially more onerous than double taxation on your director's fees is your possible liability for corporate income taxes, Canada Pension Plan payments and Employment Insurance contributions.

Directors of corporations may be jointly and severally liable, together with their corporation, for amounts the corporation has failed to withhold and remit to the Receiver General, as well as for any related interest and penalties. Directors' liability also extends to amounts required to be withheld and remitted under the Canada Pension Plan and the Employment Insurance Act.

Over the past few years, Revenue Canada has actively prosecuted corporate directors for failure of the corporation to remit payroll deductions. The cases do not reveal any clear-cut threshold of activity for a director to satisfy the due diligence requirements. Revenue

Canada has basically taken the position that directors may be absolved of personal liability if they are found to have exercised the degree of care, diligence and skill to prevent the failure that a reasonably prudent person would have exercised in comparable circumstances. To protect yourself, you must ensure that the system of withholding and remitting source deductions is well established and functioning properly. Ignorance of the law does not appear to be a defence.

✔ Tax Tip 85

No action can be initiated against a former director more than two years after he or she ceases to be a director. Accordingly, if you are currently a director, consider resigning if the corporation of which you are a director is in serious trouble. As an added precaution, also consider registering your resignation with the appropriate corporate registry.

Some recent cases on directors' liability are outlined on page 14.

⚜ Québec

If you have to deal with Revenue Québec, you should be aware of the following:

Before you file

Tax instalments are required when the difference between Québec tax payable (net of the reduction) and Québec tax deducted at source exceeds $1,200 for the current year and either of the two preceding years.

After you file

Interest on refunds starts the 46th day after the later of:

- April 30; and

- the date you file your return.

Furthermore, as set out in the table on page 81, the interest rate paid on refunds is significantly lower (4.75% lower for the fourth quarter of 1997) than the interest rate charged on amounts due.

• Interest on deficient instalments

If you have neglected to make your Québec instalment payments, an additional interest of 10% per year is applied only if instalments are less than 90% of the required instalments. This interest is added to the normal interest rate on receivables that Revenue Québec charges.

• Resolving problems

Québec follows the same rules as other jurisdictions for resolving problems, except that in Québec:

- It is possible to file a Notice of Objection by mailing a single copy of a letter to the person in charge of such notices (the "directeur des oppositions").

- If you receive notification that the income tax assessment stands after you have filed your Notice of Objection or if you have not heard from Revenue Québec within 90 days of filing your Notice of Objection, you may appeal to the courts.

You can appeal successively to:

- the Québec Court (civil division);

- the Québec Court of Appeal; and

- the Supreme Court of Canada.

An individual can also bring his or her case before the Small Claims Court of the Québec Court. Doing so waives the right to any remedy before any other court.

An individual can also go to the complaints office of Revenue Québec. The brochure entitled *A New Mechanism for Resolving Tax Problems: The Bureau des Plaintes of Revenue Québec* (INF-138) explains how an individual can submit a complaint in writing.

Directors' liability

Corporate directors' liability with respect to unremitted source deductions also includes the health services tax.

Penalty for repeated omission to declare income

Taxpayers who have failed to report income in a year and in any of the preceding three taxation years may be subject to a penalty equal to 10% of the undeclared income. This penalty does not apply when the penalty for false statements or omissions was applied.

New administrative rules

Québec legislation has been modified over the last few years to incorporate several measures dealing with administrative issues, some as a counterpart to the federal Fairness Package rules.

10 Looking Ahead

10 Looking Ahead

What's new?

- Individuals with foreign property will have to comply with new foreign reporting requirements.

- RESP contribution limits to be increased and some RESP investor concerns to be alleviated (proposed).

- The definition of preferred beneficiary to be broadened (proposed).

- The Seniors Benefit will replace the current system of OAS/GIS benefits in 2001 (proposed).

Your personal tax strategy should include looking into the future. You need to consider your own tax affairs and concerns, as well as anticipated changes in the tax system. This chapter briefly reviews both aspects of looking ahead.

Your own tax affairs

Tax planning for a particular year is not something that you should delay thinking about until December of that year. With the exception of your RRSP contribution, which you can make within the first 60 days of the next year, all is pretty much said and done by December 31. The earlier in the year that you start your tax planning, the more opportunities you will have to act on some of the ideas in this book and to minimize your tax liability. Although you may not need a great deal of time to put some of these suggestions into place, others will require lead time. Keeping your records organized should allow you to identify opportunities and to minimize the risk of making costly mistakes (such as underpaying your instalments – if you have to pay instalments).

The rest of 1997 and into 1998

•Foreign reporting requirements

If you own foreign property, or are a beneficiary of a non-resident trust, you may have to comply with new foreign reporting rules. Although the deadline for filing the new forms prescribed under the new provisions has been extended to April 30, 1998, you will be required to report for taxation years after 1995. The forms will have to be filed separately from your annual income tax returns. Penalties for failure to comply with the new rules may be significant (refer to page 219 of Chapter 9, **Filing Returns and Paying Your Taxes**, for details about penalties that may be imposed).

Individuals will not be required to file any foreign reporting information for the year in which they first become residents of Canada.

• Foreign property

You will have to file form T1135, *Information Return Relating to Foreign Property*, if you owned or had an interest in foreign property with a total cost amount of more than $100,000 in Canadian dollars. For each type of foreign property, you will have to report income received and gains or losses realized. Using foreign-denominated funds to acquire property, or converting funds from one currency to another, can create capital gains or losses. Accordingly, transactions of this nature will also have to be reported.

Foreign property includes:

- funds held outside Canada (including a foreign bank account), a security held outside Canada and a share of a Canadian company deposited with a foreign broker;

- tangible property located outside Canada, including real estate and equipment;

- shares in non-resident corporations;

- interests in non-resident trusts, including foreign mutual fund trusts;

- intangible property located outside Canada, such as a right to royalties; and

- debts (such as notes, bonds or debentures) owed or issued by a non-resident.

Foreign property does not, however, include:

- property held in your RRSP, RRIF or RPP;

- property you use or hold exclusively in the course of carrying on your active business; or

- personal-use property (such as a vacation home).

• Beneficiaries of non-resident trusts

If you received funds or property from, or became indebted to, a non-resident trust in which you have or will have absolute or conditional rights as a beneficiary, either directly or indirectly, you will have to complete and file form T1142, *Information Return in Respect of Distributions From and Indebtedness Owed to a Non-Resident Trust.*

• Registered Education Savings Plan contributions

Registered Education Savings Plans (RESPs) permit individuals to make contributions that are held in trust to generate income to finance post-secondary education costs of trust beneficiaries. Although contributions to an RESP are not tax deductible to the payor, income generated by the contributions is tax sheltered until paid out to named beneficiaries. The income is included in the beneficiaries' incomes at that time. Typically, the tax credit for tuition fees and the education credit will reduce or eliminate tax on the income so included.

Rising costs of tuition bring increasing pressures to accumulate

savings for post-secondary education. The 1997 federal budget proposes to increase the limit on annual RESP contributions to $4,000
from $2,000 per beneficiary.

If a contributor's named beneficiary under an RESP does not
pursue post-secondary education, the income from the RESP must
go either to another eligible student or to an educational institution.
RESP income is not available to the contributor unless he or she is
a named beneficiary of the plan and is enrolled in post-secondary
education.

To alleviate some investor concerns about the potential forfei-
ture of income accumulated in the RESP, the budget proposes to
allow contributors to receive RESP income directly under certain
conditions:

- If all intended beneficiaries are not pursuing higher education by
  age 21, and the plan has been running for at least 10 years, a contributor resident in Canada will generally be permitted to withdraw
  the income from the plan.

- If you are in a position to claim RRSP deductions, you will be
  permitted to transfer RESP income to an RRSP under which you
  (or your spouse) are the annuitant, without penalty.

- To the extent that RESP income is not fully offset by RRSP
  deductions, a charge of 20% will apply to the excess amount, in
  addition to the regular taxes that will be payable. (The charge is
  intended to ensure that RESPs are not used for tax-deferral
  purposes unrelated to education or retirement savings.)

- The budget further proposes to limit to $40,000 the total amount
  of RESP income that you may transfer to an RRSP during your
  lifetime.

- Although the principal from a plan may be returned to another
  individual tax free, income that is not an educational assistance
  payment will be considered income of the subscriber (contributor)
  for tax purposes.

Finally, RESP beneficiaries are not eligible to receive educational assistance payment from the plan if they are taking distance education courses, such as correspondence courses. The budget proposes to allow full-time students enrolled in qualifying educational programs at eligible institutions to qualify for educational assistance payments under an RESP.

The measures pertaining to annual limits and distance education are effective for the 1997 taxation year. Those dealing with the return of RESP income to the contributor will apply after 1997.

• Eliminating CNIL problems

If you are planning to take advantage of the enhanced lifetime capital gains exemption this year (page 112), ensure that your ability to access the exemption is not reduced or delayed because you have a Cumulative Net Investment Loss. Carefully review your investment income and expenses to ensure that your CNIL account is accurate. In particular, make sure you have not missed any investment income. You still have time to restructure borrowings or the ownership of some investments and eliminate your CNIL (see pages 116 and 133).

✔ Tax Tip 86

If you have CNILs and also are the controlling shareholder of a corporation, consider paying yourself a sufficient dividend to cure your CNIL problem.

• Reviewing your instalment payments

Review your tax position prior to making the third and final instalments for the year to ensure that you have not underpaid. If you find that your tax liability will be larger than expected, you should consider increasing your payments, unless you have chosen to make your instalments based on Revenue Canada's instalment requirements (see page 214).

● **Spousal RRSPs**

Making a contribution to a spousal RRSP based on your own contribution entitlement is still one of the most effective ways of income splitting.

● **Salary/dividend mix**

If you are a controlling shareholder of a private company, you are likely in a position to decide what type of compensation you will receive. In choosing between salary and dividends, you should ensure that you are receiving at least enough salary to permit you to make maximum contributions to your RRSP (see page 42).

✔ **Tax Tip 87**

Your RRSP contribution limits in 1997 and 1998 will be based on 1996 and 1997 earned income respectively. To make the maximum contribution of $13,500 in each of these years, you need $75,000 of annual earned income.

● **Pension income credit**

If you are age 65 or over and are not taking advantage of the pension income credit, consider arranging to receive eligible pension income. One possibility is to convert a portion of your RRSP to a retirement income stream that will provide you with at least $1,000 of eligible pension income (see page 149).

● **"Junior" tax returns**

When you are in the midst of preparing to file your income tax returns, consider encouraging your children who are over age 18 (or younger, if they have sufficient income) to file their own income tax returns. University students often fail to file tax returns, since the credit for tuition fees offsets tax that would be payable on any income earned (or the tuition fee credit may have been transferred to you as a supporting person). The child is foregoing credits to which he or she may be entitled by not filing a return. Further, the financial benefits are not the only reason that young adults should be filing their own returns. Many young adults probably have their own credit cards, yet know little about the procedures and consequences involved in filing an income tax return. This would be an excellent opportunity to begin to shift the burden of responsibility to these young adults for their own financial affairs.

✔ Tax Tip 88

Young adults age 19 or over may claim their own GST credit (even if they have no income), as well as any provincial credits that may be available and that can be claimed only by filing an income tax return.

• Home Buyers' Plan

The Home Buyers' Plan allows individuals who are first-time home buyers to use existing funds in their RRSPs to purchase a home.

You may not participate in the continuing version of the Home Buyers' Plan if you or your spouse withdrew funds under the original Home Buyers' Plan that was scheduled to expire on March 2, 1994. If you applied to participate before that date and you actually received the funds prior to April 1994, you are subject to the rules under the original plan.

You are considered to be a first-time home buyer if neither you nor your spouse, during your marriage, owned a home and lived in it as your principal place of residence at any time in the period beginning on January 1 of the fourth calendar year before the withdrawal and ending on the 31st day before the withdrawal from your RRSP. Further, you may participate in the Home Buyers' Plan only once.

A qualifying home must be located in Canada and cannot have been previously owned by you or your spouse. You must intend to occupy it as your principal place of residence no later than one year after its acquisition. Both new and existing homes are eligible and all types of structures are included in the definition: a detached house, a semi-detached house, a townhouse, a condominium, a mobile home, an apartment in a duplex, triplex, fourplex or apartment building and even a share in a cooperative housing corporation.

You may withdraw up to $20,000 from your RRSP (up to $40,000 per couple) free of tax. You may acquire a qualifying home either on your own or jointly with one or more other persons. A husband and wife may each withdraw $20,000 from their own RRSPs as long as they own the home jointly. If you contributed $20,000 to your own plan and $20,000 to your spouse's plan, you may each withdraw $20,000 to jointly acquire a home. If you did not contribute to your own plan, but contributed $40,000 to a spousal plan, your spouse can withdraw no more than $20,000, even if you are acquiring the property jointly.

You must repay your RRSP the funds withdrawn for this purpose in at least 15 annual equal instalments. If you withdraw funds from your RRSP after March 1, 1994, the 15-year repayment period will begin in the second calendar year following the year in which the withdrawal is made. In addition, you must purchase a qualifying home before October 1 of the calendar year following the year of withdrawal. For example, if you made a Home Buyers' Plan withdrawal of $15,000 on April 15, 1997, you have until October 1, 1998 to acquire a qualifying home and your first annual repayment of $1,000 will be due by the end of 1999. You may elect to have a repayment made in the first 60 days of a year treated as having been made in the preceding year. Of course, if you repay more than the minimum amount in a particular year, in the following year your payment would be based on the amount left to be repaid, divided by the number of years left in the 15-year repayment period. If you fail to meet the repayment schedule or fall short of a payment in a particular year, the unrepaid amount will be added to your income and, accordingly, will be subject to tax at your marginal tax rate.

To request a withdrawal from your RRSP under the Home Buyers' Plan, you must complete a prescribed form (T1036). The

238

form details the location of the qualifying home and confirms that you intend to use that home as your principal place of residence no later than one year after its acquisition. Prior to receiving funds from your RRSP, you must have entered into an agreement in writing for the acquisition or construction of the qualifying home.

If you withdraw funds in accordance with the Home Buyers' Plan but the purchase doesn't go through for some reason, you won't be penalized with an income inclusion, provided that you return the funds to your RRSP by the end of the following year.

You will not be able to claim a tax deduction for contributions to your RRSP that are withdrawn within 90 days under the Home Buyers' Plan. For purposes of this rule, contributions to your RRSP within the 90-day period will not be considered to be withdrawn except to the extent that the RRSP balance after the withdrawals is less than the amount of such contributions. Of course, your RRSP room in that period will not be lost; you will be able to carry it forward for use in future years (see page 42).

• Withholding tax on pension income paid to non-residents

Generally, tax of 25% must be withheld on pension payments to non-residents of Canada. Residents of countries that have treaties with Canada, however, normally enjoy reduced rates of withholding tax.

Non-residents may elect to file Canadian tax returns, allowing them to pay tax on the pension income at ordinary graduated rates, rather than at the flat withholding rate. Since only Canadian source income must be reported for this purpose, individuals with other sources of income pay less tax on their pension income than they would if they were residents of Canada.

Effective for 1997, the extent to which an individual can obtain relief from the withholding tax rate is limited. This is accomplished by determining the ordinary tax rate that would apply to the greater of Canadian source or worldwide income. The measure applies to all elections to reduce the tax withheld on a variety of Canadian source income, including OAS, CPP, RRSPs, RRIFs and alimony.

• Underground economy initiatives

In an effort to ensure that all residents of Canada pay their fair share of taxes, more resources have been committed to Revenue Canada's audit program for unincorporated businesses and self-employed individuals. The thrust of the measures is to increase audit coverage for these groups and to bring it more in line with the continued growth in this sector. Eight hundred additional auditors will be devoted to this initiative in 1998-99 when it will be fully in place.

The longer term: proposed Seniors Benefit

The federal government intends to make significant changes to the public pension system. The highlights of the proposed changes are as follows:

- The Seniors Benefit will replace the existing OAS/GIS (Guaranteed Income Supplement) benefits in 2001.

- The new benefit will be tax free and will incorporate the current age and pension income tax credits.

- Benefits will be paid monthly; in the case of couples, separate and equal cheques will be sent to each spouse.

- GIS recipients will receive an additional $120 per year.

- The Spouse's Allowance Program will remain in place. Payments will increase by $120 per year.

- Payments will be based on the combined income of spouses, as is the case now with the GIS.

- Benefit levels, as well as the threshold at which they begin to be reduced, will be fully indexed to inflation.

- Seniors will have to apply only once for the benefit when they turn age 65. Benefit levels for succeeding years will be automatically recalculated based on the previous year's tax return.

The OAS/GIS benefits that seniors receive today will be fully protected. If you were 60 or over on December 31, 1995, you and your spouse, no matter what age, will be guaranteed no less than your current level of pension payments. You will also have a choice between moving to the new system or maintaining your current monthly payments, whichever is more advantageous to you.

The choice between the two systems will need to be made only when the Seniors Benefit is about to be introduced in 2001. In the months preceding implementation, you will receive information based on your own situation.

The longer term: estate planning

Two common misconceptions are associated with the term estate planning: the first is that it is something to be worried about some-time in the future when you are "older"; the second is that signifi-cant amounts of money must be involved. The fact is that while you may not have a formal estate plan in mind at the tender age of 21, everyone over the age of majority should give some thought to the consequences of their death, particularly if there are any dependants. You should, however, be wary of carrying out plans for the transfer of your wealth until your own position is secure and you are confi-dent of the ability of your intended beneficiaries to deal with the implications.

An estate plan can be as simple or as elaborate as you wish. Your circumstances and financial situation will, of course, affect the com-plexity of your estate plan. The size of your estate should not be an issue either: we are all concerned with ensuring that we will be able to maintain our lifestyles after retirement, that our dependants will be taken care of in the event of our death and that our assets will be distributed on our death according to our wishes.

Estate planning is not something that you do once and for all. Rather, it should be a continuing process of evaluating your personal and business circumstances and directing the manner in which your assets are preserved and ultimately distributed.

To remain effective, your estate plan should be reviewed periodically and revised to accommodate changes in your financial and personal life or in legislation, including taxation.

• Insurance

Choosing the appropriate insurance program may satisfy a variety of objectives. The most important one is to provide your spouse and children with a replacement for the income that is lost on your death and to provide them with the funds necessary to cover the payment of income taxes and other debts and expenses arising on death. Some forms of life insurance policies are looked on as investments as well as providing protection. An exempt life insurance policy provides an opportunity to accommodate investment on a favourable tax basis. As with other investments, tax consequences should not be the primary concern in evaluating the opportunity and rates of return should be carefully considered. However, the low rate of tax applicable to exempt policy earnings and the possibility of receiving the benefit of the policy free of tax (during life as well as on death) may make this a worthwhile option in some circumstances. Your professional advisors can tell you what types of whole life insurance policies are exempt.

In business situations, insurance may be used to provide funding for the eventual purchase of assets or shares in connection with a buy-out of shareholders, partners or partners' heirs.

Insurance proceeds that are payable as a result of the death of the insured are not taxable in the hands of the beneficiary.

• Up-to-date wills

Dying intestate (without a will) can defeat almost all the estate planning arrangements you have worked hard to put into place. Provincial laws dictate how your assets are to be divided if you do not have a will.

✔ **Tax Tip 89**

> Both you and your spouse should have a will. This is probably one of the most critical elements of your estate planning program.

Your will should be reviewed at least every five years by your lawyer and also by your professional tax advisor if your affairs have become at all complex. Your lawyer will suggest any necessary changes. It should also be reassessed in light of changes in the law, particularly family law. In some provinces, the law virtually dictates how family assets are to be divided even if you have drafted a comprehensive will. It should certainly be reviewed if your personal or financial circumstances have changed. For example, your will is invalid if you subsequently become divorced. Your will should be reviewed if you get married, if you adopt a child, if one of your beneficiaries dies and even if you make a large tax-free transfer to your RRSP.

• Charitable donations

Charitable gifts may be made during your lifetime or through your will. You may achieve your objectives in various ways: a bequest of cash to your favourite charity is by no means your only option.

A bequest made in a will is treated as though the gift were made immediately before death. Accordingly, a tax credit for a testamentary donation will be available on your final tax return. As discussed on page 189, the 1997 federal budget proposes changes to the tax treatment of charitable donations. Donations claimed in any one year cannot exceed 75% (previously 50%) of net income. Donations in the year of death, as well as excess donations in the year of death that are carried back and used in the preceding year, are eligible up to 100% of net income.

In addition to gifts of cash, you may specify that donations be made of other types of property that you may own. Examples include gifts in kind, gifts of life insurance, gifts of cultural property and gifts to the Crown.

Gifts in kind involve property, including shares, bonds, real estate and artwork. Although a cash gift simply results in a tax credit, a gift in kind has a further effect on your tax return. When you make a gift of property, you are normally deemed to have disposed of the property at its fair market value and to have made a gift of an equal amount. Your tax credit will be based on the fair market value of the property and will be treated the same way as if it were a gift of cash. You must also recognize any capital gain or income on the deemed disposition, i.e., as if the property had been sold.

In addition to the changes to the tax treatment of gifts in kind proposed in the 1997 federal budget and discussed on page 189, some special rules allow further planning flexibility. If the property that you are gifting has appreciated in value, you may elect an amount that falls between the fair market value and the adjusted cost base of the property to be the deemed proceeds of disposition and the amount of your gift. In this way, you can control the amount of the capital gain or income that must be realized on your return, as well as the amount of the gift. This may be particularly important if the gift would otherwise exceed the proposed 75% of net income limitation or if you have capital losses against which capital gains on the deemed disposition would be offset.

Gifts to the Crown include gifts to the federal or provincial governments as well as to certain government agencies. Universities and hospitals in some provinces have established foundations that also qualify as Crown agencies. Under the 1997 federal budget proposals, gifts to the Crown are now subject to the 75% net income limitation.

Gifts of cultural property are not subject to the 75% limitation. Such donations must, however, be made to institutions or public authorities designated as such under the Cultural Property Export and Import Act. Further, the property must be an object that the Canadian Cultural Property Export Review Board has determined meets certain criteria.

You may also consider donating a whole life insurance policy to your favourite charity. To accomplish this, you would transfer the policy to the charity and have the charity become the registered beneficiary. The cash surrender value of the policy will be the amount of your donation for tax purposes. Accumulated dividends and interest will increase the value; any policy loan outstanding will decrease it. If the value of the policy exceeds the cost of it to you, you must recognize the excess as though you cashed it in. Further, if you continue to pay premiums on the policy, the payments will be considered to be additional charitable donations eligible for the tax credit.

You have many ways to ensure that your wishes are carried out. You may begin a system of planned giving today, or you may decide that your will is the vehicle through which you will distribute your assets. In any event, consider discussing your objectives and concerns with your professional advisor, particularly if significant assets are concerned and where provincial family law may have a significant effect on your estate plan.

• Estate freezing

In many ways, estate freezing is an extension of income splitting. The idea behind this type of planning is to transfer any future growth in the value of an asset (and any tax liability on future appreciation) to your heirs. Ideally, however, you would retain control over the asset during your lifetime. In an estate freeze, the value of an asset to you is frozen for tax purposes. In so doing, an immediate tax liability could result because you may have to recognize a capital gain when ownership of the asset is transferred. To the extent that you have not exhausted it, however, the capital gain could be eligible for the enhanced $400,000 capital gains exemption. Even if the exemption is not available, other deferral methods are.

Estate freezes are often executed using a corporation, rather than through a direct sale or transfer to an intended beneficiary. Tax can be deferred, minimized or even eliminated. Ownership of the shares in the corporation should be structured so as to ensure that growth in the value of assets accrues to your heirs, while you retain control over the corporation, and accordingly over the assets, during your lifetime. Generally, personal assets can be transferred into a corporation with no immediate tax consequences, because the corporation is considered to acquire the assets at your cost.

Estate freezing is complex. You should discuss any ideas or concerns you might have with your professional tax advisor.

• Family trusts

A trust is an arrangement that offers enormous flexibility in structuring your affairs and controlling the use of your property. A trust is treated as a separate person for income tax purposes; indeed a trust is taxed much like an individual (personal tax credits, however, are not available to a trust).

A testamentary trust, basically a trust created under your will, is taxed at the same rates as those that apply to individuals. On the other hand, an *inter vivos* trust (one that you set up today) is taxed at the top rate of tax for individuals.

Family trusts, which may be either *inter vivos* or testamentary trusts, are used for a variety of purposes: for example, to achieve income splitting (although the attribution rules limit the opportunities); to provide for the maintenance and education of infants; to provide maintenance and care for a child with a disability; to centralize and preserve control of business interests; to provide financial independence for children who have reached the age of majority, while at the same time controlling the time at which the child will obtain control over the property in question; or to provide for the children of a former marriage. These are but a few of the many other reasons for establishing a family trust.

Trust assets are generally made subject to capital gains tax by being deemed to be disposed of every 21 years. Trusts are currently permitted to file an election to defer that deemed disposition until the death of the last "exempt beneficiary" under the trust. The election will be eliminated effective January 1, 1999. Trusts that have filed the election will be subject to a deemed disposition of trust assets at fair market value on January 1, 1999.

Undistributed income earned by a trust is normally taxed at the trust level. An exception to this general rule is made only in the case of a preferred beneficiary. A preferred beneficiary is an individual who is a certain close beneficiary of the trust and who qualifies for the disability tax credit. Under the current rules, the preferred beneficiary election allows the income earned by a trust to be taxed as if it had been paid out to a preferred beneficiary. Although the funds remain in the trust, the election allows the income to be taxed in the preferred beneficiary's hands, typically at a lower tax rate than the trust would pay.

The 1997 federal budget proposes to broaden the definition of preferred beneficiary to include disabled adults (18 years of age or older) who are dependent on others by reason of a mental or physical infirmity. The measure will apply to individuals for whom an infirm dependent credit can be claimed (see page 185 in Chapter 8, **Calculating Your Taxes**). The proposal is effective for trust taxation years that end after 1996.

✔ Tax Tip 90

If you have a family trust in respect of which an election to defer the 21-year deemed disposition has been made, you should discuss the ramifications of the potential deemed disposition of trust assets after 1998 with your professional advisor. They could be significant.

• Offshore protection trusts

Offshore protection trusts are becoming increasingly popular vehicles for affluent individuals who might be exposed to personal liability in a potential lawsuit. If your situation is such that you might become at risk, you might look to transferring assets offshore to jurisdictions like the Bahamas, the Channel Islands, the Cayman Islands or other such exotic havens, to protect your assets from the claims of creditors in Canada.

The idea is that if assets are held in a jurisdiction where a Canadian judgment is not recognized (or even where the domestic judgment *is* enforceable), the cost and difficulty associated with taking action in a foreign court would discourage a creditor from pursuing the matter.

When you are setting up the trust, there must be no claims or potential claims in the offing. You must be solvent, and must have no intent to defraud any of your creditors at the time of setting up your protective offshore trust.

For an offshore protection trust arrangement to make sense, an individual should have at least $500,000 of liquid and easily movable assets available for transfer. Of course, fees are associated with setting up the trust, as are annual administration costs.

A final caveat: use of an offshore trust may help you protect your assets, but it won't help you escape Revenue Canada. Canadian residents are taxable on their worldwide income. Accordingly, any income that is earned on assets in the offshore trust will still be taxable in your hands.

• Taxes on death

There are no federal or provincial death taxes *per se* in Canada. Generally, however, you are deemed to have disposed of all of your capital property immediately prior to death for proceeds equal to the fair market value of the assets at that time. Any capital gains that have accrued to the date of death would be included and taxed in your final income tax return, with one major exception: unless you elect otherwise, all assets passing to your spouse or a spousal trust are transferred at cost, with the spouse or spousal trust inheriting your cost base. Accordingly, no immediate income tax consequences result. Assets passing to anyone else, including a trust, are subject to the deemed disposition rules.

✔ Tax Tip 91

To the extent that it has not been exhausted, the enhanced $400,000 capital gains exemption may shelter any capital gains arising on qualified small business corporation shares or qualified farm property as a result of the deemed disposition rules. In addition, the AMT provisions are not applicable in the year of death.

The executors of your estate will be responsible for payment of any taxes owing on your final income tax return and for taxes payable on income earned on your assets before they are distributed to your beneficiaries.

✔ Tax Tip 92

In addition to a final return of income, the executor of an estate may choose to file up to three additional separate returns in respect of certain types of income that have been earned but unrealized at the date of death. Full personal tax credits may be claimed for each of the separate returns, which could result in substantial tax savings.

Changes to the tax system

Changes to the tax system result from changes in federal and provincial legislation and regulations, new interpretations resulting from court decisions and administrative changes by Revenue Canada. Changes to federal legislation can be made through federal budgets, as well as technical amendment bills. Technical amendment bills tend to be somewhat predictable.

Court decisions are less predictable. Important new interpretations are usually reported in the popular press. Revenue Canada can change its interpretation at any time through press releases, interpretation bulletins and information circulars.

This book reflects changes in income tax to June 30, 1997 and includes tax laws that have been passed up to that date, as well as changes proposed in the 1997 federal budget. Provincial governments generally present their budgets in late winter or spring. Of course, governments can deviate from this pattern and may bring down budgets at any time. When *Personal Tax Strategy* was written, all the provinces and territories had brought down their 1997–98 budgets. Personal income tax changes introduced in those budgets are reflected in this book.

Income taxes for the provinces and territories (other than Québec, which collects its own tax) are currently calculated as a percentage of federal rates; the federal government collects income taxes on their behalf. Someday the provinces and territories might move towards establishing provincial tax regimes independent of federal rates and to collect those taxes themselves. This could lead to a more complex array of income taxes across Canada. Still, for most individuals, the most visible change would likely be the requirement to file separate federal and provincial/territorial income tax returns.

Technical amendments can be extremely important for a few taxpayers, and insignificant to others. Some technical amendments have broad application. Your professional advisor can help you determine whether this year's technical amendments affect you.

⚜ Québec

Reform of the personal tax system

The 1997 Québec budget announced a major tax reform for individuals, effective January 1, 1998. According to the government, the effect of the tax reform will decrease total individual taxes by 15% for households with incomes of less than $50,000 and by 3% for households earning above $50,000. At the time of writing, the measures intended to implement the reform of the personal tax system in Québec had not been enacted into law.

The main elements of the individual tax reform are:

- a reduction in the number of tax brackets from five to three;

- the elimination of the 5% and 10% surtaxes and the 2% income tax reduction;

- an increase from 20% to 23% in the non-refundable tax credit rate;

- the enhancement of refundable tax credits for low-income households;

- an increase in the level of household income above which certain tax credits are reduced to $26,000;

- the introduction of an optional simplified tax system; and

- optional filing by spouses of a joint or combined income tax return.

For 1998, if a taxpayer decides to file his or her income tax return under the new simplified tax system, various tax credits and deductions will be replaced by a single $2,350 deduction per taxpayer, while other credits are maintained. This corresponds to a non-refundable tax credit of $541 per individual, converted at a rate of 23%. This amount will be transferable between spouses if they each choose simplified reporting. In addition, any refund of tax due to one spouse may be offset against tax owing by the other under both the simplified and the general tax systems.

A taxpayer who chooses the simplified tax system will still be entitled to the non-refundable personal tax credits (such as basic, dependent children, person living alone, the age credit), to the deduction or credit related to retirement (such as contributions to RRSPs or an RPP) and to the tax credit for charitable donations. Only spouses who have decided to file under the simplified tax system will be able to file a joint income tax return.

When 1998 income tax forms are mailed to taxpayers, Revenu Québec will indicate whether, based on the return filed the previous year, it would be to the taxpayer's advantage to use the simplified system. If a taxpayer decides to choose the general system, Revenu Québec will also process his or her income tax return using the simplified system to determine whether it would have been advantageous to the taxpayer to have used it. If so, the tax difference will be given to the taxpayer.

These appendices are designed to give you specific tax information in a convenient format – information that you can use to help form your personal tax strategy. In addition, the appendices provide a picture of how Canada's tax system works, including how rates and amounts of tax vary with level of income, type of income and jurisdiction.

The charts and tables in these appendices have been designed to reveal the underlying structure and patterns in the tax system – offering something more than a collection of numbers.

Reading the Charts

The charts on pages 255, 267, 271 and 273 show a range of taxable income, starting at zero on the bottom, and ending above $100,000. (No additional tax brackets exist beyond that level, so you can imagine the charts continuing off the top of the page.) Taxable income is drawn to a consistent scale throughout. Taxable income is your income from all sources, less certain deductions (see page 181).

The jurisdictions are in ascending order (from left to right), according to top marginal rate. For 1997, the Northwest Territories, with the long-standing lowest top marginal rate (44.37%), appears first. British Columbia again has the highest top marginal rate (54.17%), so it appears last. This arrangement, with taxable income drawn to scale and provinces listed in order of top marginal rate, is used in most of the appendices to *Personal Tax Strategy*.

To find your marginal tax rate on page 255, or other data on pages 267, 271 or 273, simply look for the jurisdiction in which you reside. (Rates for non-residents are also given.) Move down the chart to the box that corresponds to your taxable income.

This appendix will help you:
- determine your 1997 marginal tax rate; and
- compare tax rates in Canada.

Appendix 1
Combined marginal rates

What Are Combined Marginal Rates?

Your **combined marginal rate** (or just "marginal rate" for short) is probably the single most important tax number for you to know. It is the percentage of any additional taxable income that you will pay as income tax. If your marginal rate is 52%, then 52% of the last dollar you earn, or of any additional income you earn, will go to pay income taxes.

Your marginal rate also measures the value of any tax deduction. At a 52% marginal rate, a $100 deduction from taxable income reduces your tax bill by $52.

Combined marginal rates are made up of several components. The main ones are federal marginal rates (**Appendix 4**) and provincial marginal rates (**Appendix 5**), including federal and provincial surtaxes and provincial flat taxes. In this appendix, marginal rates take into account any provincial tax reductions and the Northwest Territories' Cost of Living Tax Credit, which behaves like a negative tax rate.

The combined marginal rates shown in this appendix apply to most income, such as **salaries** and **interest**. They don't apply to **capital gains** or **Canadian dividends**, the rates for which are listed in **Appendix 2** and explained in **Appendix 3**.

The rates shown here include the **provincial tax reductions** that Alberta, Manitoba, Nova Scotia, Ontario, Saskatchewan and Québec have. Except for Québec, the reductions normally affect only taxpayers in the lowest income brackets. Reductions are discussed in **Appendix 5**.

Top marginal rates are in bold type at the top of the shaded portion of the table. (Top marginal rates are also shown in **Appendices 2 and 3**.)

As explained in **Appendix 5**, except for Québec, provincial income taxes before surtaxes are simply a proportion of basic federal tax. Each jurisdiction sets its own proportion. This proportion (or factor) is shown on the facing page, at the top of the chart, above the name of each jurisdiction.

For help reading this chart, see *Reading the Charts* on page 252.

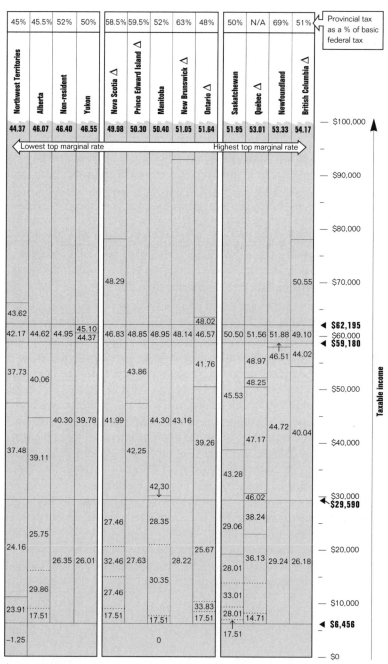

45%	45.5%	52%	50%	58.5%	59.5%	52%	63%	48%	50%	N/A	69%	51%	Provincial tax as a % of basic federal tax
Northwest Territories	Alberta	Non-resident	Yukon	Nova Scotia △	Prince Edward Island △	Manitoba	New Brunswick △	Ontario △	Saskatchewan	Québec △	Newfoundland	British Columbia △	
44.37	46.07	46.40	46.55	49.98	50.30	50.40	51.05	51.64	51.95	53.01	53.33	54.17	

Lowest top marginal rate →   Highest top marginal rate →

Values along chart (selected labels):

- 48.29 (Nova Scotia, ~$70,000); 50.55 (British Columbia, ~$70,000)
- 43.62; 48.02
- 42.17 44.62 44.95 45.10 / 44.37 | 46.83 48.85 48.95 48.14 46.57 | 50.50 51.56 51.88 49.10
- 48.97 46.51 44.02
- 37.73; 40.06; 43.86; 41.76; 48.25; 45.53
- 40.30 39.78 41.99 44.30 43.16 44.72 40.04
- 37.48 39.11 42.25 39.26 47.17 43.28
- 42.30 46.02
- 27.46 28.35 38.24 29.06
- 25.75; 24.16; 25.67
- 26.35 26.01 32.46 27.63 28.22 28.01 36.13 29.24 26.18
- 30.35
- 29.86 27.46 33.01
- 23.91 17.51 17.51 17.51 33.83 17.51 28.01 14.71
- −1.25 | 0 | 17.51

Taxable income scale: $0 – $100,000 ($62,195 ◄, $59,180 ◄, $29,590 ◄, $6,456 ◄)

△ 1997 rates differ from 1996 rates in Nova Scotia, Prince Edward Island, New Brunswick, Ontario, Québec, and British Columbia.

Appendix 2
How much tax?

This appendix will help you:
- estimate your 1997 income tax;
- compare taxes across Canada; and
- see how tax varies with income.

The big question is always: How much tax? This appendix helps you answer that question. A word of caution, though: the results depend on various assumptions, which might not fit your own situation.

Assumptions

The big Tax Look-Up Table shows the total income tax payable by a person whose only tax credit is the basic non-refundable personal credit and who has no income from Canadian dividends. Amounts shown include federal and provincial surtaxes, provincial flat taxes, provincial tax reductions and the Northwest Territories' Cost of Living Tax Credit (see Appendices 1, 4 and 5).

The table should be read with care. If you have tax credits other than the basic personal credit, or if your income includes Canadian dividends, your tax will be lower than the amount shown.

Effective rates

An effective rate of tax (total tax as a percentage of taxable income) is also given in the table. Effective rates are average tax rates that apply to total income, unlike marginal rates, which apply to incremental income only (see Appendix 1).

The row immediately below the names of the jurisdictions at the extreme right repeats the top marginal rates that appear in Appendices 1 and 3. As taxable income gets larger, the effective rate approaches the marginal rate, so this column also represents the effective rate for an infinite taxable income. (Of course, if you had an infinitely large income, you wouldn't care much about any tax rate less than 100%.)

You can estimate your income tax liability in several ways. For example:
- multiply your taxable income by an effective rate interpolated from those in the table on page 257;
- interpolate the amount of tax from those in the table on page 257; or
- use the 1997 Tax calculation tables on pages 258–61. (This method gives the most precise results.)

TAXABLE INCOME	Northwest Territories	Alberta	Non-resident	Yukon	Nova Scotia	PEI
Top Marginal rates	44.4%	46.1%	46.4%	46.5%	50.0%	50.3%
$1,000,000	$434,000 43.4%	$451,100 45.1%	$454,500 45.5%	$455,600 45.6%	$488,600 48.9%	$492,300 49.2%
$500,000	$212,100 42.4%	$220,700 44.1%	$222,500 44.5%	$222,900 44.6%	$238,700 47.7%	$240,800 48.2%
$250,000	$101,200 40.5%	$105,600 42.2%	$106,500 42.6%	$106,600 42.6%	$113,800 45.5%	$115,000 46.0%
$150,000	$56,800 37.9%	$59,500 39.7%	$60,100 40.1%	$60,000 40.0%	$63,800 42.5%	$64,700 43.1%
$100,000	$34,600 34.6%	$36,500 36.5%	$36,900 36.9%	$36,700 36.7%	$38,800 38.8%	$39,600 39.6%
$75,000	$23,500 31.3%	$24,900 33.2%	$25,300 33.7%	$25,100 33.5%	$26,400 35.2%	$27,000 36.0%
$50,000	$13,100 26.2%	$14,000 28.0%	$14,300 28.6%	$14,100 28.2%	$14,900 29.8%	$15,000 30.0%
$40,000	$9,400 23.5%	$10,100 25.3%	$10,300 25.8%	$10,200 25.5%	$10,700 26.8%	$10,800 27.0%
$25,000	$4,390 17.6%	$4,810 19.2%	$4,890 19.6%	$4,820 19.3%	$5,090 20.4%	$5,120 20.5%
$10,000	$770 7.7%	$680 6.8%	$930 9.3%	$920 9.2%	$670 6.7%	$980 9.8%

TAXABLE INCOME	Manitoba	New Brunswick	Ontario	Saskatchewan	Québec	Newfoundland	British Columbia
Top marginal rates	50.4%	51.1%	51.6%	51.9%	53.0%	53.3%	54.2%
$1,000,000	$493,900 49.4%	$499,100 49.9%	$503,400 50.3%	$508,600 50.9%	$520,800 52.1%	$521,700 52.2%	$527,000 52.7%
$500,000	$241,900 48.4%	$243,800 48.8%	$245,200 49.0%	$248,900 49.8%	$255,700 51.1%	$255,100 51.0%	$256,200 51.2%
$250,000	$115,900 46.4%	$116,200 46.5%	$116,100 46.4%	$119,000 47.6%	$123,200 49.3%	$121,700 48.7%	$120,700 48.3%
$150,000	$65,500 43.7%	$65,100 43.4%	$64,500 43.0%	$67,100 44.7%	$70,200 46.8%	$68,400 45.6%	$66,600 44.4%
$100,000	$40,300 40.3%	$39,300 39.6%	$38,600 38.6%	$41,100 41.1%	$43,700 43.7%	$41,700 41.7%	$39,500 39.5%
$75,000	$27,700 36.9%	$27,100 36.1%	$25,700 34.3%	$28,100 37.5%	$30,400 40.6%	$28,400 37.9%	$26,000 34.7%
$50,000	$15,700 31.4%	$15,300 30.6%	$14,000 28.0%	$15,800 31.6%	$17,600 35.2%	$15,900 31.8%	$14,200 28.4%
$40,000	$11,300 28.3%	$11,000 27.5%	$10,000 25.0%	$11,200 28.0%	$12,900 32.2%	$11,400 28.5%	$10,200 25.5%
$25,000	$5,390 21.6%	$5,230 20.9%	$4,760 19.0%	$5,380 21.5%	$6,230 24.9%	$5,420 21.7%	$4,850 19.4%
$10,000	$900 9.0%	$1,000 10.0%	$850 8.5%	$920 9.2%	$840 8.4%	$1,040 10.4%	$930 9.3%

Tax is rounded to the nearest $10 in the bottom two rows, and to the nearest $100 in the others. Effective rates are rounded to the nearest tenth of a percent.

Because Québec has a different system of calculating provincial tax, comparisons must be made with care. Allowable deductions in Québec will generally yield a lower taxable income than residents elsewhere in Canada would have, given the same total income.

1997 Tax calculation tables (alphabetical, by jurisdiction)

To use these tables, find the appropriate jurisdiction. In the column "Bracket," locate the largest number that is still smaller than (or equal to) your taxable income. The amount beside it ("$Tax") is the amount of tax you would pay if your taxable income were exactly equal to the bracket. If your income is higher, multiply the excess by the marginal rate in the next column ("+ % of excess").

For example, if your taxable income is $50,000 and you reside in Alberta, your bracket is $44,050 and your tax would be $11,643 + 40.06% of $5,950 (i.e., of $50,000 – $44,050). That works out to $14,027. The same amount can be read from the table on page 257 for $50,000 of taxable income in Alberta, except that there it is rounded to $14,000.

The columns for capital gains and Canadian dividends are marginal rates for those types of income. The assumption is that most of your income is salary (or interest or foreign dividends) and that you are looking up the tax rates for additional income in the form of capital gains or dividends. The tables may not apply if a substantial part of your income is from capital gains or Canadian dividends.

The tables also identify the source of the brackets (federal, provincial surtax, provincial tax reduction, etc.).

Alberta

Source of Bracket	Bracket	$Tax	+ % of excess	Capital gains	Canadian dividends
Federal surtax	$62,193	$19,048	46.07%	34.55%	31.40%
Federal	$59,180	$17,704	44.62%	33.47%	30.42%
Provincial surtax	$44,050	$11,643	40.06%	30.04%	24.71%
Federal	$29,590	$5,988	39.11%	29.33%	24.14%
Tax reduction	$16,507	$2,620	25.75%	19.31%	7.43%
Tax reduction	$9,545	$541	29.86%	22.40%	8.79%
Federal	$6,456	$0	17.51%	13.13%	4.72%
	$0	$0	0.00%		

British Columbia △

Source of Bracket	Bracket	$Tax	+ % of excess	Capital gains	Canadian dividends
Provincial surtax	$78,218	$27,672	54.17%	40.63%	36.58%
Federal surtax	$62,193	$19,572	50.55%	37.91%	34.13%
Federal	$59,180	$18,093	49.10%	36.82%	33.15%
Provincial surtax	$54,434	$16,004	44.02%	33.01%	26.81%
Federal	$29,590	$6,056	40.04%	30.03%	24.38%
Federal	$6,456	$0	26.18%	19.64%	7.06%
	$0	$0	0.00%		

Manitoba

Source of Bracket	Bracket	$Tax	+ % of excess	Capital gains	Canadian dividends
Federal surtax	$62,193	$21,263	50.40%	37.80%	36.33%
Federal	$59,180	$19,788	48.95%	36.71%	35.35%
Flat tax	$30,000	$6,861	44.30%	33.23%	29.54%
Federal	$29,590	$6,688	42.30%	31.73%	27.04%
Tax reduction	$21,500	$4,394	28.35%	21.26%	9.60%
Tax reduction	$7,794	$234	30.35%	22.76%	12.10%
Federal	$6,456	$0	17.51%	13.13%	4.72%
	$0	$0	0.00%		

△ Some or all rates are different from 1996 rates.

New Brunswick △

Source of Bracket	Bracket	$Tax	+ % of excess	Capital gains	Canadian dividends
Provincial surtax	$92,981	$36,018	51.05%	38.29%	34.47%
Federal surtax	$62,193	$20,750	49.59%	37.19%	33.49%
Federal	$59,180	$19,299	48.14%	36.11%	32.51%
Federal	$29,590	$6,528	43.16%	32.37%	26.28%
Federal	$6,456	$0	28.22%	21.17%	7.61%
	$0	$0		0.00%	

Newfoundland

Source of Bracket	Bracket	$Tax	+ % of excess	Capital gains	Canadian dividends
Federal surtax	$62,193	$21,573	53.33%	40.00%	36.01%
Federal	$59,180	$20,009	51.88%	38.91%	35.03%
Provincial surtax	$58,500	$19,693	46.51%	34.89%	28.33%
Federal	$29,590	$6,764	44.72%	33.54%	27.23%
Federal	$6,456	$0	29.24%	21.93%	7.88%
	$0	$0		0.00%	

Non-resident

Source of Bracket	Bracket	$Tax	+ % of excess	Capital gains	Canadian dividends
Federal surtax	$62,193	$19,375	46.40%	34.80%	31.33%
Federal	$59,180	$18,021	44.95%	33.71%	30.35%
Federal	$29,590	$6,096	40.30%	30.23%	24.54%
Federal	$6,456	$0	26.35%	19.76%	7.10%
	$0	$0		0.00%	

Northwest Territories

Source of Bracket	Bracket	$Tax	+ % of excess	Capital gains	Canadian dividends
Provincial special	$66,000	$19,544	44.37%	33.28%	29.96%
Federal surtax	$62,193	$17,884	43.62%	32.72%	29.03%
Federal	$59,180	$16,613	42.17%	31.63%	28.05%
Provincial special	$48,000	$12,395	37.73%	28.30%	22.50%
Federal	$29,590	$5,495	37.48%	28.11%	22.18%
Provincial special	$12,000	$1,245	24.16%	18.12%	5.53%
Federal	$6,456	($81)	23.91%	17.93%	5.22%
	$0	$0	-1.25%	-0.94%	-1.56%

△ Some or all rates are different from 1996 rates.

260

Nova Scotia △

Source of Bracket	Bracket	$Tax	+ % of excess	Capital gains	Canadian dividends
Provincial surtax	$78,035	$27,837	49.98%	37.49%	33.75%
Federal surtax	$62,193	$20,188	48.29%	36.21%	32.61%
Federal	$59,180	$18,776	46.83%	35.13%	31.63%
Federal	$29,590	$6,351	41.99%	31.49%	25.57%
Tax reduction	$21,000	$3,993	27.46%	20.59%	7.40%
Tax reduction	$15,000	$2,046	32.46%	24.34%	13.65%
Tax reduction	$9,473	$528	27.46%	20.59%	7.40%
Federal	$6,456	$0	17.51%	13.13%	4.72%
	$0	$0	0.00%		

Ontario △

Source of Bracket	Bracket	$Tax	+ % of excess	Capital gains	Canadian dividends
Provincial surtax	$63,486	$19,785	51.64%	38.73%	34.87%
Federal surtax	$62,193	$19,164	48.02%	36.02%	32.43%
Federal	$59,180	$17,761	46.57%	34.93%	31.45%
Provincial surtax	$50,962	$14,329	41.76%	31.32%	25.43%
Federal	$29,590	$5,938	39.26%	29.45%	23.91%
Tax reduction	$10,721	$1,095	25.67%	19.25%	6.92%
Tax reduction	$8,588	$373	33.83%	25.37%	9.12%
Federal	$6,456	$0	17.51%	13.13%	4.72%
	$0	$0	0.00%		

Prince Edward Island △

Source of Bracket	Bracket	$Tax	+ % of excess	Capital gains	Canadian dividends
Federal surtax	$62,193	$20,536	50.30%	37.73%	33.97%
Federal	$59,180	$19,064	48.85%	36.64%	32.99%
Provincial surtax	$48,077	$14,202	43.80%	32.85%	26.67%
Federal	$29,590	$6,391	42.25%	31.69%	25.73%
Federal	$6,456	$0	27.63%	20.72%	7.45%
	$0	$0	0.00%		

△ Some or all rates are different from 1996 rates.

Québec Δ

Source of Bracket	Bracket	$Tax	+ % of excess	Capital gains	Canadian dividends
Federal surtax	$62,193	$23,627	53.01%	39.76%	38.78%
Federal	$59,180	$22,073	51.56%	38.67%	37.81%
Provincial surtax & tax reduction	$52,625	$18,863	48.97%	36.73%	34.56%
Provincial special	$50,000	$17,597	48.25%	36.19%	33.99%
Provincial surtax	$31,000	$8,634	47.17%	35.38%	32.65%
Federal	$29,590	$7,985	46.02%	34.52%	31.77%
Provincial special	$23,000	$5,465	38.24%	28.68%	22.03%
Provincial special	$14,000	$2,208	36.19%	27.14%	19.48%
Tax reduction	$8,348	$278	34.14%	25.61%	16.92%
Federal	$6,456	$0	14.71%	11.03%	3.96%
	$0	$0	0.00%		

Saskatchewan

Source of Bracket	Bracket	$Tax	+ % of excess	Capital gains	Canadian dividends
Federal surtax	$62,193	$21,492	51.95%	38.96%	36.51%
Federal	$59,180	$19,971	50.50%	37.87%	35.54%
Provincial surtax	$39,202	$10,875	45.53%	34.15%	29.33%
Federal	$29,590	$6,715	43.28%	32.46%	27.77%
Provincial surtax	$19,512	$3,786	29.06%	21.80%	9.99%
Tax reduction	$14,000	$2,242	28.01%	21.01%	9.51%
Tax reduction	$10,000	$922	33.01%	24.76%	15.76%
Tax reduction	$7,131	$118	28.01%	21.01%	9.51%
Federal	$6,456	$0	17.51%	13.13%	4.72%
	$0	$0	0.00%		

Yukon

Source of Bracket	Bracket	$Tax	+ % of excess	Capital gains	Canadian dividends
Federal surtax	$62,193	$19,138	46.55%	34.91%	31.43%
Provincial surtax	$60,469	$18,360	45.10%	33.82%	30.45%
Federal	$59,180	$17,788	44.37%	33.28%	29.96%
Federal	$29,590	$6,017	39.78%	29.84%	24.23%
Federal	$6,456	$0	26.01%	19.51%	7.01%
	$0	$0	0.00%		

Δ Some or all rates are different from 1996 rates.

Appendix 3 Investment income: special rates

How Investments Are Taxed

Investment income is taxed in different ways.

The first set of bar charts in this appendix (**Graphs A, B and C**) show marginal rates for the three types of investment income at three levels of taxable income: $100,000 – or any level at the top marginal rate, $50,000 and $25,000. (These amounts are assumed to be salary. The marginal rates are for *additional* income.)

Interest and foreign dividends are taxed the same way as most other income (such as salary). For more details about the rates that apply to interest and foreign dividends, refer to **Appendices 1 and 2**.

Canadian dividends are subject to a gross-up and a tax credit, which together reduce tax (see page 102).

Capital gains also get favourable tax treatment: only three-quarters of a capital gain is included in taxable income and taxed. That portion is taxed at the same rate as interest, so for most purposes the effect is tax at three-quarters the rate that applies to interest. The lifetime capital gains exemption was eliminated for gains realized or accrued after February 22, 1994. Capital gains arising on dispositions of qualifying small business corporation (QSBC) shares and certain farming properties may be entitled to an exemption of $400,000 (see page 114).

Comparing Tax Rates

Graphs A, B and C show the variation in top marginal rates for different types of investment income. In all jurisdictions, the top marginal rate for capital gains is, in effect, three-quarters of the rate for interest income. (See **Graph A**.) For most jurisdictions, the top marginal rate for Canadian dividends works out to approximately 67.5% of the rate for interest income. However, as **Graph A** reveals, the advantage of Canadian dividends over capital gains is noticeably smaller in Québec and Manitoba. Québec's dividend tax credit is less generous than the provincial portion in other provinces. Manitoba has a large flat tax (up to 4%) that has a side-effect of reducing the differential between Canadian dividends and capital gains. Saskatchewan's 2% flat tax has a smaller effect, and Alberta's smaller 0.5% flat tax reduces the advantage of Canadian dividends only slightly.

Graphs B and C show how things change at lower income levels. All marginal rates decline. Québec takes over from British Columbia as the province with the highest marginal rates – dramatically so at the $25,000 level. However, in any particular jurisdiction, Canadian dividends always have the lowest marginal rate.

Comparing After-Tax Investment Returns

Graphs D, E and F on page 265, along with the accompanying tables, show how the different tax treatments of investments can affect investment decisions. The left halves of **Graphs D, E and F** answer a realistic question: **What before–tax return must I get to end up with the same after–tax result?** A $100 interest amount is included as a benchmark.

For example, suppose your taxable income is in the top bracket (say $100,000) and you earn $100 interest on a $2,000 investment (a 5% before-tax return). In Ontario you would pay tax at a 51.64% marginal rate. You keep $48.36, an after-tax return of about 2.42%. To earn the identical after-tax return from the same $2,000 capital, you would need a Canadian dividend of only $74.25 (which works out to 3.71%, much less than the 5%). If, instead, you had a capital gain of $78.93 on an asset you had bought for $2,000 a year earlier, (a 3.95% before-tax gain), you would also have a 2.42% return after tax. You would again retain the $48.36 after tax – the same as from the $100 of interest or the $74.25 Canadian dividend.

Another useful way to look at the tax implications of different types of investments is to consider how much you have to earn before tax to end up with the same amount after tax. This is particularly helpful if you are living largely off your investments, or plan to. The right-hand half of **Graphs D, E and F** indicate how much you have to earn if you expect to keep $100 after paying your income taxes.

As the graphs show, these results vary by province, as well as by the taxpayer's bracket.

264

$100,000 Taxable income

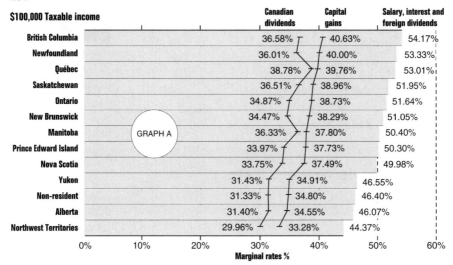

	Canadian dividends	Capital gains	Salary, interest and foreign dividends
British Columbia	36.58%	40.63%	54.17%
Newfoundland	36.01%	40.00%	53.33%
Québec	38.78%	39.76%	53.01%
Saskatchewan	36.51%	38.96%	51.95%
Ontario	34.87%	38.73%	51.64%
New Brunswick	34.47%	38.29%	51.05%
Manitoba	36.33%	37.80%	50.40%
Prince Edward Island	33.97%	37.73%	50.30%
Nova Scotia	33.75%	37.49%	49.98%
Yukon	31.43%	34.91%	46.55%
Non-resident	31.33%	34.80%	46.40%
Alberta	31.40%	34.55%	46.07%
Northwest Territories	29.96%	33.28%	44.37%

GRAPH A — Marginal rates %

$50,000 Taxable income

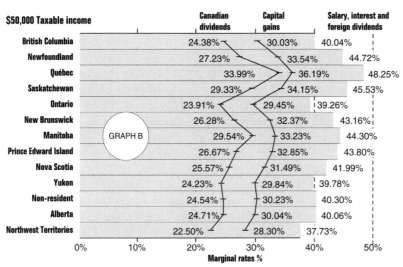

	Canadian dividends	Capital gains	Salary, interest and foreign dividends
British Columbia	24.38%	30.03%	40.04%
Newfoundland	27.23%	33.54%	44.72%
Québec	33.99%	36.19%	48.25%
Saskatchewan	29.33%	34.15%	45.53%
Ontario	23.91%	29.45%	39.26%
New Brunswick	26.28%	32.37%	43.16%
Manitoba	29.54%	33.23%	44.30%
Prince Edward Island	26.67%	32.85%	43.80%
Nova Scotia	25.57%	31.49%	41.99%
Yukon	24.23%	29.84%	39.78%
Non-resident	24.54%	30.23%	40.30%
Alberta	24.71%	30.04%	40.06%
Northwest Territories	22.50%	28.30%	37.73%

GRAPH B — Marginal rates %

$25,000 Taxable income

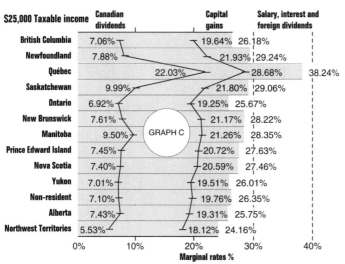

	Canadian dividends	Capital gains	Salary, interest and foreign dividends
British Columbia	7.06%	19.64%	26.18%
Newfoundland	7.88%	21.93%	29.24%
Québec	22.03%	28.68%	38.24%
Saskatchewan	9.99%	21.80%	29.06%
Ontario	6.92%	19.25%	25.67%
New Brunswick	7.61%	21.17%	28.22%
Manitoba	9.50%	21.26%	28.35%
Prince Edward Island	7.45%	20.72%	27.63%
Nova Scotia	7.40%	20.59%	27.46%
Yukon	7.01%	19.51%	26.01%
Non-resident	7.10%	19.76%	26.35%
Alberta	7.43%	19.31%	25.75%
Northwest Territories	5.53%	18.12%	24.16%

GRAPH C — Marginal rates %

Taxable income at top marginal rates

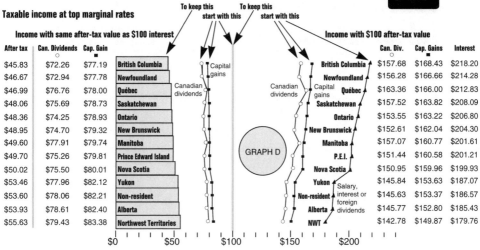

Income with same after-tax value as $100 interest — To keep this start with this — To keep this start with this — **Income with $100 after-tax value**

After tax	Can. Dividends	Cap. Gain	Region		Region	Can. Div.	Cap. Gains	Interest
$45.83	$72.26	$77.19	British Columbia		British Columbia	$157.68	$168.43	$218.20
$46.67	$72.94	$77.78	Newfoundland		Newfoundland	$156.28	$166.66	$214.28
$46.99	$76.76	$78.00	Québec		Québec	$163.36	$166.00	$212.83
$48.06	$75.69	$78.73	Saskatchewan		Saskatchewan	$157.52	$163.82	$208.09
$48.36	$74.25	$78.93	Ontario		Ontario	$153.55	$163.22	$206.80
$48.95	$74.70	$79.32	New Brunswick		New Brunswick	$152.61	$162.04	$204.30
$49.60	$77.91	$79.74	Manitoba		Manitoba	$157.07	$160.77	$201.61
$49.70	$75.26	$79.81	Prince Edward Island		P.E.I.	$151.44	$160.58	$201.21
$50.02	$75.50	$80.01	Nova Scotia		Nova Scotia	$150.95	$159.96	$199.93
$53.46	$77.96	$82.12	Yukon		Yukon	$145.84	$153.63	$187.07
$53.60	$78.06	$82.21	Non-resident		Non-resident	$145.63	$153.37	$186.57
$53.93	$78.61	$82.40	Alberta		Alberta	$145.77	$152.80	$185.43
$55.63	$79.43	$83.38	Northwest Territories		NWT	$142.78	$149.87	$179.76

GRAPH D

$50,000 taxable income

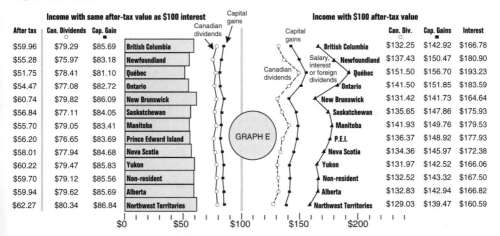

Income with same after-tax value as $100 interest — **Income with $100 after-tax value**

After tax	Can. Dividends	Cap. Gain	Region		Region	Can. Div.	Cap. Gains	Interest
$59.96	$79.29	$85.69	British Columbia		British Columbia	$132.25	$142.92	$166.78
$55.28	$75.97	$83.18	Newfoundland		Newfoundland	$137.43	$150.47	$180.90
$51.75	$78.41	$81.10	Québec		Québec	$151.50	$156.70	$193.23
$54.47	$77.08	$82.72	Ontario		Ontario	$141.50	$151.85	$183.59
$60.74	$79.82	$86.09	New Brunswick		New Brunswick	$131.42	$141.73	$164.64
$56.84	$77.11	$84.05	Saskatchewan		Saskatchewan	$135.65	$147.86	$175.93
$55.70	$79.05	$83.41	Manitoba		Manitoba	$141.93	$149.76	$179.53
$56.20	$76.65	$83.69	Prince Edward Island		P.E.I.	$136.37	$148.92	$177.93
$58.01	$77.94	$84.68	Nova Scotia		Nova Scotia	$134.36	$145.97	$172.38
$60.22	$79.47	$85.83	Yukon		Yukon	$131.97	$142.52	$166.06
$59.70	$79.12	$85.56	Non-resident		Non-resident	$132.52	$143.32	$167.50
$59.94	$79.62	$85.69	Alberta		Alberta	$132.83	$142.94	$166.82
$62.27	$80.34	$86.84	Northwest Territories		Northwest Territories	$129.03	$139.47	$160.59

GRAPH E

$25,000 taxable income

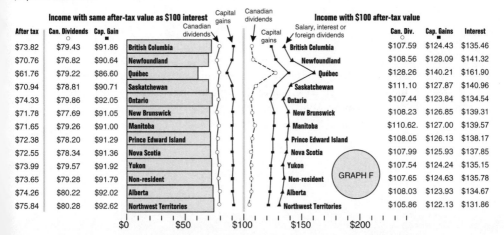

Income with same after-tax value as $100 interest — **Income with $100 after-tax value**

After tax	Can. Dividends	Cap. Gain	Region		Region	Can. Div.	Cap. Gains	Interest
$73.82	$79.43	$91.86	British Columbia		British Columbia	$107.59	$124.43	$135.46
$70.76	$76.82	$90.64	Newfoundland		Newfoundland	$108.56	$128.09	$141.32
$61.76	$79.22	$86.60	Québec		Québec	$128.26	$140.21	$161.90
$70.94	$78.81	$90.71	Saskatchewan		Saskatchewan	$111.10	$127.87	$140.96
$74.33	$79.86	$92.05	Ontario		Ontario	$107.44	$123.84	$134.54
$71.78	$77.69	$91.05	New Brunswick		New Brunswick	$108.23	$126.85	$139.31
$71.65	$79.26	$91.00	Manitoba		Manitoba	$110.62.	$127.00	$139.57
$72.38	$78.20	$91.29	Prince Edward Island		Prince Edward Island	$108.05	$126.13	$138.17
$72.55	$78.34	$91.36	Nova Scotia		Nova Scotia	$107.99	$125.93	$137.85
$73.99	$79.57	$91.92	Yukon		Yukon	$107.54	$124.24	$135.15
$73.65	$79.28	$91.79	Non-resident		Non-resident	$107.65	$124.63	$135.78
$74.26	$80.22	$92.02	Alberta		Alberta	$108.03	$123.93	$134.67
$75.84	$80.28	$92.62	Northwest Territories		Northwest Territories	$105.86	$122.13	$131.86

GRAPH F

Appendix 4
Federal marginal
rates: tax and surtax

This appendix will help you:
• find the federal 1997 marginal rate that applies to you;
• see how the federal surtax affects you; and
• understand how federal rates apply to Québec residents.

Federal marginal rates are a key element in Canada's personal income tax rate structure. Not only the federal portion of your taxes depends on federal marginal rates. Provincial and territorial income taxes are also based on federal rates (see **Appendix 5**). Québec is the only exception.

Components of Federal Rates

Your federal marginal tax rate is the percentage of the last (or next) dollar you earn that is paid as federal income tax. To find out your federal marginal rate, read the entry in the chart that corresponds to your **taxable income**.

The left portion of the chart shows the three basic federal marginal rates of 17% (on taxable income up to $29,590), 26% (on taxable income between $29,590 and $59,180) and 29% (on taxable income above $59,180). However, as the chart shows, these three rates turn into a set of five rates.

The basic personal credit ($1,098) eliminates tax on the first $6,456 of taxable income for all taxpayers, creating the 0% marginal rate (because $1,098 is 17% of $6,456). This credit is indexed, increasing annually when inflation exceeds a threshold. Low inflation has kept the basic credit the same for 1997 as it has been from 1992 on. Any other non-refundable credits to which you may be entitled increase the amount of income on which the marginal tax rate is zero.

The general **federal surtax** rate is 3% of basic federal tax. That adds, for example, 0.51% to the 17% bottom marginal rate (17% x 3% = 0.51%). When your basic federal tax reaches $12,500, an additional "high-earner" surtax of 5% of basic federal tax in excess of $12,500 applies. This occurs at a taxable income of $62,195, assuming you have only the basic personal credit. So, at a taxable income above $62,195, the total federal surtax is 8%. That adds 2.32% to your marginal tax rate (29% × 8% = 2.32%). Any other non-refundable credits you may be able to claim will increase the taxable income you can have before the higher "high-earner" federal surtax affects you. On account of the two levels of federal surtax, the 29% marginal rate turns into two rates: 29.87% and 31.32%.

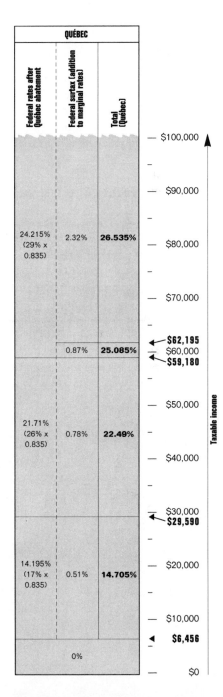

EXCEPT QUÉBEC				
Before basic personal credit and federal surtax	After basic personal credit	Federal surtax rates	Federal surtax (addition to marginal rates)	Total (except Québec)
29%		x 8% (3% + 5% "high-earner" surtax)	2.32%	**31.32%**
			0.87%	**29.87%**
26%			0.78%	**26.78%**
		x 3%		
17%			0.51%	**17.51%**
	0%		0%	

QUÉBEC		
Federal rates after Québec abatement	Federal surtax (addition to marginal rates)	Total (Québec)
24.215% (29% x 0.835)	2.32%	**26.535%**
	0.87%	**25.085%**
21.71% (26% x 0.835)	0.78%	**22.49%**
14.195% (17% x 0.835)	0.51%	**14.705%**
	0%	

Taxable income

— $100,000
— $90,000
— $80,000
— $70,000
←**$62,195**
— $60,000
←**$59,180**
— $50,000
— $40,000
←**$29,590**
— $30,000
— $20,000
— $10,000
◄ **$6,456**
— $0

⚜ Québec

For Québec residents, the **Québec abatement** reduces basic federal tax by 16.5%. This, in effect, reduces federal marginal rates to 83.5% of their original levels. For example, the top federal rate of 29% becomes 24.215% (29% × (100% − 16.5%). The federal surtax, however, is the same for Québec residents as it is for residents of other jurisdictions.

Other Factors Affecting Tax Rates

The federal marginal rates shown in this Appendix are central to the calculation of your tax bill. However, **the income tax you pay cannot be determined directly from federal marginal rates**. Your taxes will be substantially affected by:

- provincial taxes and surtaxes (discussed in **Appendices 4 and 5**), which add roughly half as much again to your tax bill.
- non-refundable tax credits to which you may be entitled (see page 182), which may reduce or even eliminate your income tax liability; and
- the types of income you have, because capital gains and some dividend income are taxed differently (see Appendix 3).

Appendix 5
Provincial marginal
rates: tax and surtax

This appendix will help you:
- see how provincial income taxes are calculated; and
- understand provincial surtaxes and flat taxes.

Provincial marginal rates (before surtaxes) are simply a proportion of pre-surtax federal marginal rates, except for Québec. **Québec sets its own rates and brackets.** The Personal Tax Flowchart (page 183) explains how Québec's approach differs.

Provincial Tax Rates

For jurisdictions other than Québec, the proportion (or factor) is shown beside each jurisdiction's name in the chart on the facing page. The factors range from 45% in the Northwest Territories to 69% in Newfoundland. (Rates for the territories and non-residents are referred to as "provincial rates" in this book.) The body of the chart shows Québec's rates and the rates elsewhere (the factor multiplied by the federal marginal rates from Appendix 4).

Provincial Surtaxes

All jurisdictions other than the Northwest Territories impose surtaxes or flat taxes, or both. Non-residents of Canada and residents of the Northwest Territories face no surtaxes other than the federal ones and no flat taxes.

The chart on page 273 shows the effect of provincial surtaxes on marginal rates for all jurisdictions and levels of taxable income. The table on page 274 shows the rates and brackets from which these results are derived.

Surtaxes are calculated as a percentage of provincial (or territorial) tax above a stated amount (e.g., 8% of provincial tax in excess of $13,500 in New Brunswick). Except for Québec, this results in provincial surtaxes being a percentage of federal tax (e.g., 8% x 63% x 29% = 1.4616% in New Brunswick). As a consequence, the amount that a provincial surtax adds to marginal rates increases whenever taxable income reaches a higher federal bracket.

Flat taxes are based on taxable income or net income, and are therefore independent of federal brackets.

In Québec, provincial tax is not a percentage of federal tax, so federal brackets affect neither the amount that the provincial surtax adds to marginal rates nor the thresholds at which particular rates take effect. However, provincial brackets have the equivalent result.

Provincial marginal rates
(percent)

A5

Province	~$15,000 bracket	~$40,000 bracket	~$80,000 bracket
Northwest Territories	7.65**	11.7**	13.05**
Alberta	7.44*	11.83	13.2
Non-resident	8.84	13.52	15.08
Yukon	8.5	13	14.5
Nova Scotia	9.945	15.21	16.965
Prince Edward Island	10.115	15.47	17.255
Manitoba	8.84	13.52	15.08
New Brunswick	10.71	16.38	18.27
Ontario	8.16	12.48	13.92
Saskatchewan	8.5	13	14.5
Québec	19 / 21	23	24
Newfoundland	11.73	17.94	20.01
British Columbia	8.67	13.26	14.79

Taxable income scale: $0 – $100,000

$59,180

$29,590

0%

** These results do not reflect the Northwest Territories' Cost of Living Tax Credit, which reduces tax payable and creates additional brackets.

Some provinces have surtaxes with more than one threshold (expressed as an amount of provincial tax). Each threshold creates a new surtax bracket.

Provincial surtaxes and flat taxes are notable for their variety in structure and level. At the top tax bracket, British Columbia's surtax adds more than 8.06% to marginal rates, while the Yukon's adds less than 0.73%. Saskatchewan's surtax affects taxable incomes as low as $19,512, while New Brunswick's affects only taxable incomes above $92,981. Flat taxes (in Alberta, Manitoba and Saskatchewan) affect even low-income taxpayers. Québec's new 0.3% additional surtax (described on page 206) applies to both provincial tax and the pre-existing surtax.

Appendices 1 and 2 combine provincial income taxes, surtaxes and flat taxes with the federal tax and the federal surtaxes set out in **Appendix 4**.

Alberta, Manitoba, Nova Scotia, Ontario, Saskatchewan and Québec have **tax reductions** that, in effect, create additional marginal rates for those with relatively low taxable incomes. The reductions eliminate provincial income tax (but not federal income tax) for taxable incomes immediately above $6,456. However, taxpayers with slightly larger taxable incomes face a higher than normal marginal tax rate. That, in effect, undoes the benefit of the provincial tax reduction. The result is that taxpayers can ignore the reductions if their taxable incomes are above a certain level (roughly $53,000 in Québec, and ranging from $10,000 to $22,000 for the other provinces that have the reductions).

Provincial surtaxes and flat taxes can affect marginal rates as much as the variation in the provincial factors that are used to calculate provincial tax. For example, at 69%, Newfoundland's factor is the highest in the country, while Saskatchewan's is among the lowest, just 50%. That difference gives Newfoundland a top combined marginal rate, before provincial surtaxes, that is 5.51% higher than Saskatchewan's. But at top rates, Saskatchewan's surtax and flat tax together add 6.125% to its marginal rates, yielding a top marginal rate just 1.38% less than that of Newfoundland.

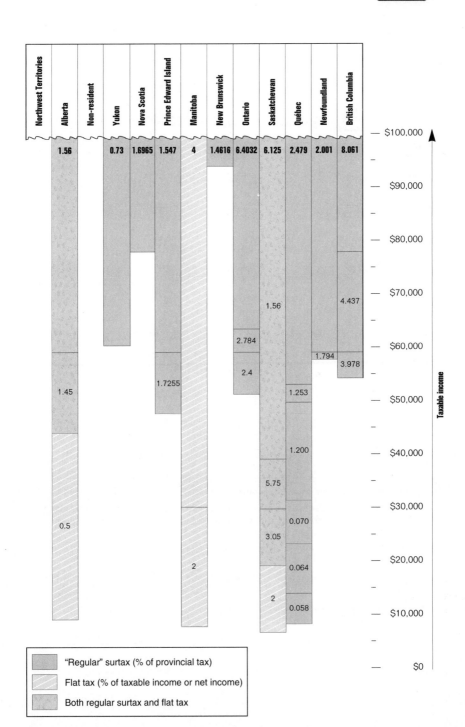

"Regular" surtax (% of provincial tax)

Flat tax (% of taxable income or net income)

Both regular surtax and flat tax

	"Regular" surtax				Flat tax	
	Rates (% of Provincial tax)	Thresholds Provincial Tax	Thresholds Taxable Income	Resulting addition to marginal rate	Rates	Thresholds (taxable or net income)
British Columbia	30% 54.5%	$5,300 $8,745	$54,434 $78,218	3.98% to 4.4% 8.06%	n/a	
Newfoundland	10%	$7,900	$58,500	1.79% to 2%		
Québec	0.3%* 5% + 0.3%* 10% + 0.3%*	0 $5,000 $10,000	$8,348 $31,000 $52,625	0.058% to 0.070% 1.20% to 1.253% 2.479%		
Saskatchewan	10% 25%	$1,500 $4,000	$19,512 $39,202	1.05% to 1.5% 3.75% to 4.125%	2%	$7,040**
Ontario	20% 46%	$4,555 $6,180	$50,962 $63,482	2.5 to 2.78% 6.4%	n/a	
New Brunswick	8%	$13,500	$92,981	1.4616%		
Manitoba	n/a				2% 4%	$7,794** $30,000
Prince Edward Island	10%	$5,200	$48,077	1.547% to 1.7255%	n/a	
Nova Scotia	10%	$10,000	$78,035	1.6965%		
Yukon	5%	$6,000	$60,469	0.725%		
Non-resident	n/a					
Alberta	8%	$3,500	$44,050	0.9464% to 1.0556%	0.5%	$9,545**
Northwest Territories	n/a					

*Québec's 0.3% special surtax applies to provincial tax and to the 5% and 10% surtaxes.

**All flat taxes (i.e., in Saskatchewan, Manitoba and Alberta) would apply to the first dollar of taxable or net income, except that the tax reductions for low income earners have the effect of preventing the flat taxes from applying until taxable income reaches at least the levels shown.

Appendix 6
Credits and amounts
that reduce your taxes

This appendix will help you:
- assess the value of various credits; and
- compare Québec credits with those in other jurisdictions.

Assumptions

The tax saving shown in the table (both for Québec and elsewhere) assumes that the entire credit can be used to reduce taxes. Because these credits are non-refundable, this will not be true if total credits exceed taxes otherwise payable. In that case the value of the credit is limited to the amount of tax.

Jurisdictions other than Québec

One group of columns in the middle of the table shows **approximate results for jurisdictions other than Québec**. (Instead of showing a different result for each province, the table is based on provincial tax calculated as a representative factor of 55% of basic federal tax. Results for each jurisdiction will vary (see **Appendix 5**).

Federal credits are generally 17% of federal amounts or claims. Federal amounts are indexed annually when inflation exceeds a threshold.

⚜ Québec

Credits that apply in Québec are shown in a separate group of columns. For Québec, the federal credit is, in effect, reduced by 16.5% by the Québec abatement (see **Appendix 4**), so that in most cases the credit drops from 17% to 14.2% of the federal amounts or claims, (100% − 16.5%) x 17%.

Other differences for Québec residents include:
- the continued use of a deduction (rather than credits) for tuition and education expenses;
- the continued availability of credits for dependants under 18 years of age;
- no transferability of tuition fee deduction;
- supporting person may claim credit for student's post-secondary studies;
- the existence of credits for persons living alone and single parents; and
- the absence of the "equivalent-to-married" credit (apart from the federal portion).

This table shows: Tax credit in first line (not bold)
Corresponding saving in second line (bold)[1]

	Federal amount or claim	Credit and saving			Special characteristics
		Other than Québec	Québec Federal[2]	Québec	
Basic personal	$6,456	$1,098 **$1,735**	$917	$1,180 **$2,130**	Available to every taxpayer
Married	$5,380	$915 **$1,445**	$764	$1,180 **$1,971**	May be reduced if income of spouse or dependant exceeds certain thresholds[5]
Equivalent to married			$764	n/a **$791**	
Dependents 18 or over, if infirm	$2,353	$400 **$632**	$334	$1,180 **$1,526**	
Dependents under 18 — First		No federal deduction or credit is available. See page 199 regarding the child tax benefit		$520 **$520**	Québec only
Dependents under 18 — Each Additional				$480 **$480**	
Single parent				$260 **$260**	
Living alone				$210[4] **$210[4]**	
Child care		For federal purposes, deduction is available (but no credit)		Varies	Same limits as federal deduction (see page 36)
Dues and professional fees				20% **$20%**	No fixed limit
Disability/mental or physical impairment	$4,233	$720 **$1,137**	$601	$440[4] **$1,063**	Unused portion is transferrable (in some circumstances) to spouse, parent or grandparent, or to child supporting a disabled parent or grandparent.
Age 65 and over	$3,482[3]	$592 **$935**	$494	$440[4] **$952**	For federal purposes, age credit is reduced above certain income levels.
Education	Up to $150[6] per month	17% (up to $25.50 per month) **26.9% (up to $40 per month)**	14.2% (up to $21 per month)	$300 per semester, up to $660 **Up to $925**	Outside Québec, maximum $850 is transferable for tuition and education combined (see page 186). Tuition credit can be claimed only by the student for Québec purposes.
Tuition fees	Minimum $100 per institution	17% **26.9%**	14.2%	20% **34.7%**	
Pension income	Up to $1,000	17% (up to $170) **26.9% (up to $269)**	14.2%	20% up to $200[4] **34.7%**	
CPP/QPP and EI premiums	Up to maximum premium of the year	17% (up to $353) **26.9% (up to $558)**	14.2% (up to $298)	20% up to $420) **34.7% (up to $729)**	
Medical expenses	Over lesser of $1,614 (federal) and 3% of net income[7]	17% **26.9%**	14.2%	20% **34.7%**	Not transferrable, but one spouse may use the other's medical expenses or charitable donations (see page 187).
Charitable donations — First $200	Up to 75% of net income				
Charitable donations — Over $200		29% **45.8%**	24.2%	20% **45%**	

(See page 278 for footnotes.)

Credits and amounts that reduce your taxes

1 The combined saving is an approximate reduction in taxes. It is calculated incorporating the federal surtax at the lower rate (3% of basic federal tax). For jurisdictions other than Québec, savings in provincial tax are approximated as 55% of the federal credit (see Appendix 5). For Québec, the saving related to the federal surtax is added to the federal credit and the Québec credit to yield the combined saving.

Taxpayers whose taxable incomes exceed $62,195 pay the federal surtax at a rate of 8% of basic federal tax. Their benefit from a credit will be higher by 5% of the full federal credit (not reduced by the Québec abatement) shown in the table.

2 The Québec abatement reduces the federal credit by 16.5%.

3 Age 65 and over credit starts to reduce when income reaches $25,921 and disappears when income reaches $49,134.

4 These Québec credits are reduced when income reaches $26,000 and disappear at $33,000 (living alone), $40,667 (age) and $32,667 (pension income).

5 The reduction begins when the spouse's income exceeds $538 (outside Québec) or $0 (Québec), and when the infirm person's income exceeds $4,103. The reduction in Québec is more complex.

6 The education credit will be limited to $200 per month for 1998 and subsequent years.

7 In Quebec, only the 3% threshold applies (i.e., the $1,614 threshold has been eliminated).

Glossary of Tax Abbreviations

ABIL	Allowable business investment loss
AMT	Alternative minimum tax
AVC	Additional voluntary contributions
BIL	Business investment loss
CCA	Capital cost allowance
CCPC	Canadian-controlled private corporation
CIP	Cooperative investment plan (Québec)
CNIL	Cumulative net investment loss
CPP	Canada Pension Plan
DPSP	Deferred profit sharing plan
EI	Employment insurance
FST	Federal sales tax
GST	Goods and Services Tax
IRA	Individual retirement account (U.S.)
MURB	Multiple-unit residential building
OAS	Old age security
PA	Pension adjustment
PSPA	Past service pension adjustment
PST	Provincial sales tax
QBIC	Québec business investment company
QPP	Québec Pension Plan
QSBC	Qualifying small business corporation
QSSP	Québec stock savings plan
RPP	Registered pension plan
RRIF	Registered retirement income fund
RRSP	Registered retirement savings plan
SBC	Small business corporation
SDI	Société de développement industriel du Québec
SIN	Social Insurance Number
UCC	Undepreciated capital cost

Price Waterhouse offices across Canada

Halifax, N.S. B3J 3N4
1801 Hollis Street
Suite 900
Telephone: (902) 420 1900
Telecopier: (902) 420 1755

Québec (Québec) G1V 4W2
Tour de la Cité (Sainte-Foy)
870 - 2600, boul. Laurier
Telephone: (418) 658 5782
Telecopier: (418) 656 6640

Montréal (Québec) H3B 2G4
1250, boul. René-Lévesque ouest
Bureau 3500
Telephone: (514) 938 5600
Telecopier: (514) 938 5772

Ottawa, Ontario K2P 2K3
Barrister House
180 Elgin Street
Suite 1100
Telephone: (613) 238 8200
Telecopier: (613) 238 4798

Toronto, Ontario M5K 1G8
Toronto Dominion Centre
Royal Trust Tower
Suite 3000, Box 82
Telephone: (416) 863 1133
Telecopier: (416) 365 8215

Metro Toronto North M5H 3V7
5700 Yonge Street
Suite 1900
Telephone: (416) 218 1500
Telecopier: (416) 218 1499

Mississauga, Ontario L4Z 3M3
Mississauga Executive Centre
Suite 1100
One Robert Speck Parkway
Telephone: (905) 272 1200
Telecopier: (905) 272 3937

Hamilton, Ontario L8N 3R1
4 Hughson Street South
P.O. Box 1018
Telephone: (905) 525 9650
Telecopier: (905) 525 8200

Kitchener, Ontario N2G 4W1
Canada Trust Centre, Suite 900
55 King Street West
Telephone: (519) 579 6300
Telecopier: (519) 579 8701

London, Ontario N6B 3L1
Canada Trust Tower
275 Dundas Street, Suite 1501
Telephone: (519) 679 9160
Telecopier: (519) 679 1435

Windsor, Ontario N9A 6T3
Bank of Commerce Building
100 Ouellette Avenue
Suite 1200
Telephone: (519) 258 6052
Telecopier: (519) 258 5457

Winnipeg, Manitoba R3B 0X7
2200 One Lombard Place
Telephone: (204) 943 7321
Telecopier: (204) 943 7774

Regina, Saskatchewan S4P 4K5
1777 Victoria Avenue
Suite 900
Telephone: (306) 757 5917
Telecopier: (306) 757 7956

Saskatoon, Saskatchewan S7K 7E6
123 - 2nd Avenue South
Suite 400
Telephone: (306) 244 6164
Telecopier: (306) 653 3813

Calgary, Alberta T2P 3V7
425 - 1st Street S.W.
Suite 1200
Telephone: (403) 267 1200
Telecopier: (403) 264 4745

Calgary, Alberta T2W 4X9
(Calgary South Office)
10201 Southport Road S.W.
Suite 1000, Southland Plaza
Telephone: (403) 974 5300
Telecopier: (403) 258 1121

Edmonton, Alberta T5J 2Z1
1501 Toronto Dominion Tower
Edmonton Centre
Telephone: (403) 493 8200
Telecopier: (403) 428 8069

Kamloops, B.C. V2C 6P5
200 - 206 Seymour Street
Telephone: (604) 372 5551
Telecopier: (604) 372 1422

Vancouver, B.C. V6B 5A5
Price Waterhouse Centre
601 West Hastings Street
Suite 1400
Telephone: (604) 682 4711
Telecopier: (604) 443 2635

Surrey, B.C. V3T 5T3
Station Tower Gateway
13401 - 108th Avenue
Suite 1600
Telephone: (604) 582 3400
Telecopier: (604) 582 3401

Richmond, B.C. V6X 3J6
5611 Cooney Road
Suite 100
Telephone: (604) 231 5500
Telecopier: (604) 231 5599

Visit the Price Waterhouse website at: **www.pw.com/ca**

Index

Italicized page numbers indicate an illustration (chart, graph, table).
Bold type indicates some references that may be most useful.